# FOUR CORNERS

*Where the Holy Spirit*
*Touches Navajo Hearts*

STAN SAGER

WITH A FOREWORD BY REV. FRED W. YAZZIE

**Providence House Publishers**

PROVIDENCE PUBLISHING CORPORATION
FRANKLIN, TENNESSEE

Printed in the United States of America

11      10      09      08      07      1      2      3      4      5

Library of Congress Control Number: 2007921981

ISBN-13: 978-1-57736-381-1

*Page design by Joey McNair*

*Cover design by LeAnna Massingille*

*Cover art inspired by a rug design by Alice Mary Yazzie. Cover photo by Paul West.*

*All photos are courtesy of the Four Corners Native American Ministry.*

PROVIDENCE HOUSE PUBLISHERS
an imprint of
Providence Publishing Corporation
238 Seaboard Lane • Franklin, Tennessee 37067
www.providence-publishing.com
800-321-5692

*For Shirley, Gayle, and Ann*

# CONTENTS

# FOREWORD

*A letter to the reader from the Reverend Fred W. Yazzie,*
*the first ordained Navajo United Methodist clergy*

Dear Reader:
What an honor and a privilege it is to be asked to write
an introduction to this history of the Four Corners Native
American Ministry. It is a must-read book for anyone interested
in Christianity on the Navajo Reservation and among Native
Americans in general. It will also help inspire those who
believe that evangelism is something to let somebody else do,
because the story tells how Navajo United Methodists learned
to be evangelists.

In the pages that follow, you will read about Navajos who
genuinely committed their lives to Jesus, were changed, and
found that there was no turning back to their old ways. You will
learn of the conflict between the traditional Navajo or animistic
religion and Christianity. The clashes will be something that few,
if any, will ever have experienced, but you can learn from what
we Navajos have discovered about how Jesus comes first.

As I read the manuscript, I relived the history of early
Methodists who reached out to the Navajos, and I remembered
my own life in Navajoland. My mother gave birth to me on the
Reservation during the days when our people traveled by horse
and wagon. Those frontier days passed into history before my
own eyes when I saw the advance of the Space Age.

My grandmother was influenced by training at the Methodist
school many years ago, when it was located under the foothills of
Hogback Mountain, before the flood you'll read about later. She
took training from the dedicated ladies who served there, though
she did not become a Christian until many years later. When she
died at age ninety-nine, it warmed my heart to know that she
knew Jesus. One day, I shall see her again.

I have a request to make of the readers of this book. As you
learn about how Jesus entered the lives of Navajos, please: listen

to what they have to say, feel their emotions, and imagine their body language.

Then, think of us Navajos as people who have been created by God. You may be surprised to find that we are not all stoic. If you visit one of our United Methodist churches on the Reservation, you will meet people who speak more than the word "Ugh!" There is much expression here among the Navajo United Methodists, because there is great excitement at meeting the "God-Man," as we call Jesus in our language. He has become the Lord of our lives and is present within us, for the Holy Spirit has truly touched Navajo hearts.

As this book explains, Navajo United Methodists believe that Jesus truly was raised by God from the dead, and because He rose, we are able to overcome the traditional taboos, superstitions, and fears of death that are a part of our culture. These beliefs are culturally ingrained and traditional. Because of Jesus, we know that death has died, and that those who accept Him will live eternally.

The Four Corners Native American Ministry is the presence of United Methodism on the Reservation. It is the presence of Christ. It is my prayer that this book will help others to find for themselves that Jesus is real, well, and alive.

As you read, listen to what God is telling you through this book. Ask yourself what God's challenge is for your life. If you are not Navajo, how sensitive does this book make you to the people called Navajos?

We are a strange tribe in many ways, but that aside, this book should help you to view us more realistically. Think about whether you view us, and other racial groups, through your own eyes, or through the eyes of God, and love us as God loves all His people.

May heaven bless you as you read. May you be touched and may your heart be "strangely warmed."

*Rev. Fred W. Yazzie, "Navajo to the Navajos"*
*Navajo Reservation, Ojo Amarillo, New Mexico*

# PREFACE

For many years, New Mexico United Methodists, both Navajo and non-Navajo, listened when I provided church-related legal advice as a volunteer attorney. Here's what I learned from the Navajo United Methodists when I began to listen to them:

Navajos residing on the Reservation who accept the way of Jesus Christ as an alternative to worshipping native gods make an agonizing decision. Their choice means separation from non-Christian Navajos, including family. Often, the separation is marked with verbal, emotional, and sometimes even physical abuse. The decision involves adopting a completely new lifestyle—no more taking part in ritualistic dances patterning the ways of the old gods, no more surrendering one's self to the native drums whose rhythms summon those gods, and no more turning to the medicine man for religious ceremonial healing rites.

To the new United Methodist Christian, the trade-offs are more than worth it. The convert enjoys a new life full of associations with other Christians by participating in church meetings, Bible study, fellowship dinners, and other gatherings. Hymn singing, joyful hearts, and prayers for healing replace the fear of witches and spells, just as they substitute for powwows filled with the call of the drums and the lure of liquor and drugs. The new life is one in which a right relationship with Jesus Christ means being right with the world, as well as with family and neighbor.

Deciding to follow Christ is the choice of life over death, for in the native Navajo belief system there is no life after death. Navajo traditionalists believe that when a person exhales his or her last breath, an evil spirit, or *chindi*, is released. Therefore, to evade the evil, the living avoid death and places where death has occurred. For the individual, the blackness of death is the end because there is no soul. This is why Navajo United Methodists give up their native religious practices when they become

Christians, though they intentionally cling to nonreligious elements of their culture.

Many critics of the Four Corners Native American Ministry disagree with the practice of members giving up their native religion when they become Christians. The detractors blend symbols of the gods of the native religion into Christian practices. This results in a mixture that Ministry Navajos feel is watered-down Christianity, calling for a return to the ways of the old gods, where they cannot find the hope and joy they discovered when they accepted Jesus Christ. This disagreement marks a theological split between the Four Corners Native American Ministry and the Native American International Caucus (NAIC), the organization that funds United Methodist Native American activities.

Ministry members maintain that the NAIC's view overlooks the independence of these Christians who desire to worship God in their own way and to be faithful to the Scriptures, emphasizing the fact that the message of Jesus Christ has compelled sacrifice from believers across the centuries. They also point out that life in the remoteness of the Navajo Nation Reservation is not the same as life lived by Native Americans who lost much of their native culture when they embraced the secular values of the white man, leaving them to search in native religious practices for what they lost.

❖

This book grew out of curiosity about such things. The curiosity took root over the course of more than twenty years of attending church meetings as chancellor, or legal advisor, of the New Mexico Annual Conference of The United Methodist Church and its resident bishop. During that time I collected a head full of questions: *Are observations like those above fact or fancy? Why are volunteers coming to the high desert from all over the country to work for nothing and sleep on the ground? How can the Navajos be building churches and making disciples when the rest of United Methodism seems to be in a skid?*

There had to be a story there. Somewhere in all of this, the Spirit had to be moving. Somewhere within the Four Corners Native American Ministry, there had to be an administrative mastermind. I began to look for answers.

I kept on looking as a three-time delegate to the General Conference and while serving as a director of one of the church's general agencies. I met a lot of United Methodists, including Native Americans connected to the denomination-sponsored organization, the Native American International Caucus, in which all the Native American United Methodists participated. All, that is, except for a single tribe—the Navajos. The Navajos held themselves aloof from the NAIC, though it had financial resources available for Native American ministries.

My questions multiplied. *How had the Navajo United Methodists become, as it were, the lost tribe of United Methodism? How had the General Church let this ministry slip away from it when it was warming the hearts of Navajos in an environment so hostile to the church that those who became Christians were accused of having sold out to the white man? Why were the Navajos so independent, and how did they get that way? Is there room in The United Methodist Church for an evangelical Native American outreach?*

With these issues in mind, and since no one had written about the Navajo United Methodists except for occasional brief articles, I figured it was time for their story to be told. Then, in the course of researching and writing this book, I came upon two final questions: *Are the choices faced by a Navajo considering following Jesus Christ any different from the choices other American Christians make when it comes to their relationship to God? Though the cultural differences put the Navajo choice into a far different context, doesn't the rest of Christian America choose between the way of Jesus Christ and love of neighbor, or instead, elect to follow the drumbeat of the gods of money, position, power, and prestige?*

Those are the questions the Navajos left with me. I hope you will think about answers to those questions as you read.

# ACKNOWLEDGMENTS

Reverend Paul and Mrs. Dorcas West cooperated in the research and writing of this book in every way possible, granting interviews at the drop of a hat, answering questions, and pointing me in the right direction. Reverend Fred Yazzie, Rev. Roger Tsosie, and Dr. Brodace Elkins offered useful facts and insights. Those who provided access to files included Liz Collins, New Mexico Annual Conference archivist; personnel at the New Mexico Annual Conference offices; Bishop Max Whitfield; Vivian Farley; and the staff at New Beginnings. Shea Goodluck-Barnes provided invaluable insights.

Dr. Rene Bideaux, formerly with the General Board of Global Ministries (GBGM), spoke with great good humor when others, except for Rev. Shirley Montoya and Rev. Tweedy Sombrero (thanks to them), wouldn't. Julianne MacAchran, New Mexico Conference director of communications, and Gayle Sager Keenan, my daughter, read the manuscript and offered suggestions.

Not one of the Diné whom I asked for an interview said no. I regret only that I could not include all their stories, and that I could not have interviewed each and every Four Corners lay pastor. Maybe next time.

There are many other helpful people who contributed, but there is not enough space to mention them all. You have my heartfelt thanks. And finally, thanks to my wife, Shirley, whose patience was tested and not found wanting.

CHAPTER ONE
# Creation of the Four Corners
# Native American Ministry

*We walk by faith, not by sight.*
—2 Corinthians 5:7

It was March 25, 1977, on the Navajo Nation Reservation in northwest New Mexico. As it does most mornings on the Reservation in early spring, the wind whipped in from the southwest across the church's unpaved parking lot. It lifted sheets of sand and hurled billions of the tiny projectiles against the adjacent parsonage, scoured the cars parked in front of it, and worked the grit it carried into cracks, crevices, cups, saucers, and underwear. But nobody inside paid any attention, for the Spirit that gripped those gathered there was more powerful than the wind.

The Rev. Paul N. West hosted the meeting that morning at the Shiprock United Methodist parsonage where he and his wife, Dorcas, and their three children lived. West had come to this sandy place on the edge of a hill overlooking the highway north of town two years earlier to spread the Good News among the Navajos. He had spent that two years figuring out what worked in the United Methodist ministry to the Navajos, and what didn't. During that time he had developed a feel for the native culture and a love for the Navajo people, and he was filled with ideas whose time had come. He was ready to put those ideas into play by reaching out beyond the local Shiprock church and deep into the Reservation.

West and the Rev. Fred W. Yazzie, who was the first ordained Navajo United Methodist clergy, knew they needed the help of

1

the Albuquerque District and the Navajo Methodist Mission School at Farmington if the outreach they had in mind was to be effective. They invited Albuquerque's district superintendent, the soft-spoken Dr. Ed Hamilton, to the meeting. Dr. Tom Cloyd, former Navajo Methodist Mission School superintendent and a guy with imagination, came too. West, armed with paper, a ballpoint pen, and all those ideas, perched on the edge of a chair. Two in the circle around the cramped living room knew the Navajos as the others never could, for they were Navajos themselves: Yazzie, then honing his powerful preaching skills at the Bistahi church, and Chee D. Benallie Sr., the resolute outreach director for the Shiprock church; in all, there were two Navajos, three Anglos; four ordained United Methodist clergymen, and one lay preacher.

Before the group convened, West and Yazzie had preliminary conversations concerning the fact that the needs of the people in the three existing Navajo churches were not being met. They weren't connected, and to survive under the weight of the non-Christian society on the Reservation they needed support from other Christians or the churches would fail. Their meeting would begin by addressing that issue. The group prayed together, read from the Scriptures, then jumped into talk of how to do the Lord's business on the Reservation.

It didn't take long for those sitting there to make a decision. The three churches would dedicate themselves to mutual support. There would be no outside financial help—the Methodist Mission School, a couple of dozen miles away in Farmington, had neither the time nor the money to lend a hand. A new entity would forge ties among all the churches because they would all have to pull together to survive. Though the term was not actually used, the five men planned to develop a network of "connected" churches on the Reservation. After all, connectionalism was the heart and soul of the United Methodist way of organizing for ministry.

Once connected together to support and encourage each other, those drawn to the churches would take Jesus Christ to fellow Navajos behind native leadership. The network of little churches would expand. Since the Navajos are a matrilineal-descent society (one that traces family through the maternal side) both male and female leaders, preachers, and teachers would be trained. Enrollment in training would begin with the call. Lay pastors would also be trained in preaching from the Bible and planting new indigenous churches. In those new churches they would spread the love of Jesus Christ and the hope of eternal life.

Eternal life through Jesus Christ: that was the theme Yazzie knew would reach the hearts of the Navajos, who feared death because their native religion offered nothing beyond an earthly existence. He knew all about those native beliefs because they were what he'd been taught as a boy. As a clergyman he had seen the promise of eternal life touch the hearts of some Navajos as a result of his preaching.

The ideas flew from one person to the next and then back again. The energy grew and rose and swelled until the sounds of

*Reverend Paul West conducts a baptismal service.*

the wind and the irritation of the sand and the dust and the gritty eyes were no more than background music.

In a later interview, West described their vision: "It should be an indigenous, a wholly indigenous church, self-supporting, self-governing, and self-propagating. And [the new ministry] should be doing all three of those, at least." People from all the churches would come together, exchange ideas, communicate, and discover that they were not the only ones who were trying to keep the faith in a culture in which Christians were often ostracized by the majority. They would call this replacement for earlier United Methodist efforts that had stumbled in trying to minister to the Navajos the Four Corners Native American Ministry (4CNAM) of The United Methodist Church.

The new ministry would take the Navajos as they were—with their history of abuse at the hands of white men, with a few seeds of Christian instruction planted in a handful of Methodist Mission School graduates during the school's eighty-year existence, and with the Navajo tribe's suspicion of white missionaries with avowed good intentions. And faith would hold it together.

But faith alone would not prevail unless the new ministry could be shaped to deal with the total context in which it would reach out to people. The new ministry must recognize the dominant native religion, respect the culture and traditions, adapt to the lack of education and the poverty on the Reservation, and also nurture the deep spirituality and the warm hearts of the people, and it must touch those hearts with Jesus Christ.

So just who are these Navajo people that the Ministry aimed to reach, and how did they become what they are?

CHAPTER TWO
# The Navajos

*Let the peoples renew their strength . . .*
—Isaiah 41:1

The Navajos call themselves the *Diné*, or "the People." They live on the largest Indian reservation in the world; its 2000 census-counted population of 175,200 makes the Reservation the most populous by far. (Though the Cherokee nation tallies more tribal members, fewer of them live on a reservation.) Many of them use the term "Indian" rather than "Native American" or "American Indian" when referring to their race.

The Diné are young, with an average age of 22.5 for those living on the Reservation.[1] With over twenty-seven thousand square miles within the Navajo Nation, it is larger than the state of West Virginia, which is itself larger than nine other states. Many of the Navajos residing on the Reservation, though not all, speak their native language. Many read it, and all are proud of it. The Bible has been translated into Navajo, as has the Roman Catholic Mass, and a book full of favorite hymns. Those of the Diné who are United Methodist Christians will talk about their faith in either Navajo or English, whichever language is available to them. They do it with little prompting, proudly, not ashamed of their Lord Jesus Christ, and they do it with the aim of making a listener into a believer.

The Reservation is a vast and silent expanse of desert and mountains, containing natural resources that have not yet all been identified. Its capital is Window Rock, just inside the eastern border of central Arizona, where one who drives into the setting sun sees a sign that reads, "Window Rock, Capital of the Navajo Nation," followed in a few yards by one that reads, "Leaving New Mexico." The Reservation covers a sizeable chunk of Arizona and extends into New Mexico and Utah. To the Navajos, those state boundaries matter very little. They are citizens of the Navajo Nation and of the United States, but most important, they are members of a family and of a clan.

Two stories are told about how the Diné came to the southwestern part of what is now called the United States. One is the tale related by the anthropologists and the linguists, the other is the traditional mythological narrative of the Navajos themselves. The first comes up with specific scientific conclusions, though the path it takes in getting there has some twists and turns; the second is told in infinite and colorful variety. Since both have affected the direction, the development, and the very existence of the Four Corners Native American Ministry, both are told here, though in summaries that are far from exhaustive.

## CHAPTER THREE

# Navajos in the Southwest: "Scientific" Explanation

*And they went forth together . . .*
—Genesis 11:31

What is known about the origin of the Navajo comes from artifacts, linguistics, ruins, and Navajo traditions. From these sources anthropologists have built their conclusions about how the Diné reached their present home in the Southwest. Many of their facts have come from a study of the Navajo language.

Navajos are part of what is called the pre-Athabascan linguistic group. That means that the words they speak come from a source common to a family of languages spoken by natives found primarily in Alaska, western Canada and the southwestern United States, including the Navajos and the Apaches. The family of languages is called Athabascan, a Cree word for an area east of Lake Athabasca in northeastern Alberta, Canada, into which the Athabasca River drains. The river itself was once an important part of the itinerary for fur traders, and may have provided a portion of the route by which Native Americans traveled in their migration that ultimately led to the Southwest. The Athabascan languages are derived from a larger and more ancient group called the Nadene family of languages.

The connection between Navajo and Native American languages spoken further north on the continent comes not only from the fact that many words are shared, but also that tones convey meanings. The same word spoken with differing intonations may have different meanings, requiring a careful and attentive listener and causing confusion for a beginning student of the language. The same word often has opposite meanings in different contexts. "Up" may sometimes mean "down," and "good" is sometimes "evil."[1] It is these shades of tones and meanings that, in part, made the messages of the Navajo code talkers so incomprehensible to the Japanese in World War II, though the talkers also encoded some words to have meanings entirely different from any accepted definition.

Linguists use a method of study that involves analyzing the rate of vocabulary replacement, or changes in words that creep into the basic language roots over time, to estimate when peoples who today speak related languages split off from the group that spoke the most original form of the parent language. The study leads to the conclusion that probably the Nadene–speaking ancestors of today's Navajos arrived in Alaska from Asia around three thousand years ago. From there the people who became known as Navajos made their way in numerous slow migrations over some twenty-five hundred years to their ultimate destination in the Southwest.

Related tribes are the Mescalero, Jicarilla, and Chiricahua Apaches of today's southwestern U.S., as well as the Tlinget and Haida of the northwestern coast of Alaska and Canada, and the Hupa, Chasta-Costa, and others who live on the west coast. Probably, scholars conclude, the Navajos did not arrive in the area of their vast Reservation until somewhere between 1000 and 1300 A.D., not long before the Spanish arrived.[2] Though their stay has often been uneasy, fraught with skirmishes with Americans moving westward through their lands, battles with the neighboring Hopi, and a relocation effort in the 1860s by the U.S. government, the Navajos remain today in the same general area they found and claimed as a homeland about a millennium ago.

So what does the origin of the Navajos have to do with the path taken by the Four Corners Native American Ministry? The connection is more direct than might be expected, bearing on the very inception of the ministry.

In 1975 two young United Methodist missionaries to Malaysia, Paul West and his nurse wife, Dorcas, were looking for a new assignment while on leave from their missionary duties. West was a slight-appearing young man of average height, with hair that was not quite blond, a neatly trimmed vandyked beard, and well-muscled forearms resulting from a youth of hard work picking strawberries, tomatoes, and other crops by hand on Southern Indiana farms. He had been born in a log cabin in rural Brown County, Indiana, near a crossroads called Gnaw Bone. Early on, he decided that the life of a strawberry-picking farmer was not for him. Instead, as a result of a vivid dream of Africa experienced when he was fifteen, he heeded a call to become a missionary pastor. He pursued his dream at Asbury College and Asbury Seminary, then traveled as an evangelistic youth worker to Klang, Kuala Lumpur, and Taiping.

Dorcas West was a slim young woman with warm brown eyes and a ready smile. The Nebraska farm home of her parents had trained her to hard work, too. After a year as a Christian exchange student in Germany, she graduated as a registered nurse from Nebraska Wesleyan University and Bryan Memorial Hospital. She had spent a year in pediatrics in Chihuahua, Mexico, under the Methodist Board of Missions. The couple met in 1964, at an orientation conference for short-term missionaries held in Stony Point, New York. By the time they left Malaysia, they had three small children.

Not one to waste leave time in rest or relaxation, Paul was off attending a youth conference in Oklahoma while Dorcas and the children stayed with relatives in Indiana. At the conference, Paul was reached by Dr. Bervin Caswell, district superintendent of the Albuquerque District, who telephoned with an invitation. He explained that he was looking for a pastor with cross-cultural experience to minister to a church in Shiprock, New Mexico, on the Navajo Nation Reservation.

In a 2003 interview, Caswell explained that he had first called the General Board of Global Ministries for help in finding a missionary to serve the Navajos through that New Mexico church. He was told by the General Board that the Wests might just fit the need and where they could be reached. Caswell invited West to serve the Shiprock church in New Mexico. West would work as a missionary to the Navajos under the home missionary system of the General Board. Paul agreed to talk to Dorcas, and he promised that the two would pray about it.

Paul and Dorcas got down on their knees, and the two of them, God, and the General Board that paid the salaries of missionaries, both in foreign lands and in the U.S., jointly decided the church in Shiprock would be just the place for the young family. If they were to return to Malaysia following their leave, the Wests would have to enroll their small children in boarding schools. They knew they should keep the family together, and they knew they could do that in Shiprock. The clincher for the Wests was that they'd been serving Asians in Malaysia. How different would it be to serve Asians whose ancestors had left that continent to live in the Southwestern United States and who were now called Navajos?

Everything fell into place. Paul, Dorcas, and their children would move to Shiprock, New Mexico, where Paul would serve as a missionary to the former Asians. The General Board of Global Ministries (GBGM), Paul's employer as a missionary, would pay his salary and support through its National Division,[3] and the New Mexico Annual Conference would have a minimal financial obligation to its first and only Native American church, an outreach that was struggling financially.

But a hitch developed. En route to New Mexico from Indiana, the Wests were intercepted by a staff member of GBGM. She tracked them down in Illinois, and informed them that the deal was off. They would now have to be supported by the New Mexico Annual Conference. She then added an enigmatic comment: "The staff at the board doesn't like New Mexico."[4]

Puzzled, the Wests continued on their way, arriving in Shiprock to a warm greeting from the Navajos. After they had settled in, they met with the presiding bishop, Alsie Carleton, to tell him that they had good news and bad news. The good news was that they were present and ready to minister to the Navajos; the bad news was that the General Board had backed out. Bishop Carleton's joy at the good news masked his disappointment at the bad. Still, the Wests were there to stay.

Theirs turned out to be a relationship made in heaven, or someplace close to it. The Navajos had a spiritual and administrative leader who would stick with them for over thirty years; the Wests were still missionaries to Asians, though hundreds of generations removed from Asia; the West children and their parents were together as a family year-round; and the New Mexico Annual Conference had its newest pastor and an outreach ministry to the Navajos.

What might have been best of all, though at the time it didn't seem that way—neither the annual conference nor the Wests had to answer to an entity headquartered in a tower in New York. As for GBGM, it had saved itself a monthly salary, living expenses, and related support expenses for a missionary to the Navajos at the cost of a reputation only briefly tarnished in a single tiny annual conference.

Within two years of their arrival, the Wests, along with Reverend Yazzie and Navajo members of the church in Shiprock, launched the program that reached out from that location and further into the Reservation. It was modeled on the outline developed during the March 1977 parsonage meeting, and it built on the foundation laid by Yazzie, who had begun the spadework some ten years before.

It wasn't until years later that Paul West learned of the financial burden that his coming without the support of the General Board had placed on an annual conference with skimpy financial resources. The conference and its bishop, recognizing the need for a ministry on the Reservation, had stepped up to see that it was funded, somehow, and without a word of complaint or a question asked of the General Board that had been instrumental in the relocation of Reverend West.

CHAPTER FOUR

# Navajos in America: Mythological Explanation

*And nations shall come to your light . . .*
—Isaiah 60:3

**A**uthor's Note: Navajo United Methodists of the Four Corners Native American Ministry who find references to the old religion offensive may want to skip this chapter since it describes some of the old customs and traditional Navajo spiritual beliefs. The reason for including this information is not to offend those who have put the old ways behind them, but to help persons who have no knowledge of traditional Navajo religious beliefs and culture to understand the unique challenges that face the Four Corners Native American Ministry when it reaches out to those living in a culture with little or no knowledge of the Bible, of Jesus Christ, or of the immortality that is promised by the Savior of all peoples. The theology of the Navajos associated with the Four Corners Ministry will be discussed in later chapters.

As with all Navajo legends, the emergence myth that explains how the Navajos happen to be present on earth is told in many variations. This description is drawn from several sources.[1]

"Diné," the name given by Navajos to themselves, is a shorthand version of a term meaning "Earth People" or "Earth Surface People." In the Navajo spiritual tradition, Diné are the ordinary humans, both living and dead.

The Holy People are another class. The term "holy," according to Navajo historian and anthropologist Clyde Kluckhorn, does not refer to the possession of moral sanctity, for the deeds of the Holy People often fall short of the biblical notion of holiness. They are called "holy" in the sense that they are powerful and mysterious, belonging to the sacred and not to the profane world. The Holy People have the ability to travel on rainbows, sunbeams, or lightning, though they are not all-powerful or all-knowing. While some argue that it is inappropriate to call them gods, they are referred to as Navajo deities. They are sometimes entreated and appeased.

Myths told by the Diné say that in antiquity the Holy People emerged through a number of previous underworlds, where they had been subjected to numerous trials and tribulations. Generally, there are said to have been four underworlds, but the number can vary from three to eleven with the telling. This world is often called the fifth world. The ascent into this world was accomplished miraculously through a magic reed that led upward to a lake in northwestern New Mexico, though some claim it was near Pagosa Springs, Colorado.

The first to emerge was a cicada, followed by animals, other insects, and masked spirits like those depicted in Navajo ceremonies. Once here, the Holy People built a sweat house, and then sang the Blessing Song. Then they met in the first house, a hogan, built as specified by Talking God, who had uttered the world into being. They arranged the world in this house, first naming the four sacred mountains placed by the Holy People to mark its boundaries. The Holy People put the sun and moon into the sky, and made clouds, trees, and rain. Then evil monsters appeared and began killing the Earth People.

Meanwhile, Changing Woman, a favored figure among the Holy People, married the sun and bore twin boys. Spider Woman was one of the few Holy People who loved the Earth People. In the twins she saw the potential to do away with the monsters, so she gave the two boys magical powers, including the tools of the rainbow, feathers, and protective songs to enable them to overcome dangers on a quest to find their father, the sun god. In the search, the twins traveled on an arduous but successful journey. When they finally reached him, Father Sun gave them lightning bolts of various kinds to help them fight the monsters.

The boys returned and slew the monsters. As each one was killed, it turned to stone. Rock formations on the Reservation are the bodies of those monsters, and the Malpais lava flows of the Southwest are their blood. The soaring Shiprock monolith itself is said to be the remains of a slain monster.

Because she saved the people, the Diné made Spider Woman one of their most important and honored deities. She taught the people the art of weaving upon a loom constructed by her husband, Spider Man, with cross-poles of sky, and earth cords to support the structure, warp sticks of sun rays, and a comb of shell to clean the strands of wool. Spider Woman and her legacy of weaving are said by some to be representative of the Navajo matrilineal society.

So what does this mythological origin of the Navajos have to do with the path taken by the Four Corners Native American Ministry? In examining the responses of the Ministry to this mythology, remember that the myths carry religious significance for traditional Navajos.

When the Wests arrived on the Reservation, they found few second-generation Navajo Christians in their Shiprock church. They found a people that, while sometimes said to be the most highly evangelized people on earth, had either not heard of Jesus Christ or had rejected Him as part of the white man's religion. They were a people with their own culture, and few Anglos, even within shouting distance of the Reservation, understood it or even tried. Instead, the Navajos were viewed as primitive, pagan, backward, and lacking in intelligence.

Under Reverend West, and particularly with the guidance of Reverend Yazzie, who was then serving the Bistahi church, the Ministry began to reach out to the Navajos. The Ministry dedicated itself to developing native leadership and avoiding imposing Anglo-American cultural values upon a people not accustomed to the practices of the "white" society. As a missionary trained to minister to persons of a different culture, and having experience in foreign missions, West knew he and the Ministry must respect that culture, guard against paternalistic approaches, and observe proven principles of effective cross-cultural communications.

The Reservation Navajos who had not accepted Jesus Christ lived in a culture whose mythology permeated all aspects of life. If they were to accept Jesus Christ, it would not be on the terms dictated to them by a cleric, but on terms dictated by Jesus Christ himself as they came to know Him. But some of the mythology and the deep-rooted religion which it described would still influence these new Christians.

Dr. Sheila Moon, a Jungian psychologist, spent years studying the Navajos and their mythology, which she likened to culturally tinted dreams. The myths can be used for understanding the people to whom they are important, she said, for they contain "whispered messages." The phrase "whispered messages" appropriately describes the lingering influence of myths on Navajos who become Christians.

Moon observed that Navajos have historically faced hardships "by turning to the ways of singing, chanting, performing the ancient rituals, telling the ancient tales told to them by parents, grandparents, elders or the group to which they belong. . . . Navajo social structure and Navajo ritual are barely separable."[2] The whispered messages of the myths give directions to the followers of the old ways for living, believing, and facing life issues. Those directions are not easily set aside by the Navajo who accepts Jesus Christ.

These whispered myth-messages tell the traditional Diné that the world is a very dangerous place, and that its inhabitants can be untrustworthy or evil. Although some of the beings and powers, such as Changing Woman and Spider Woman, were helpful, the sun and the moon demanded sacrifices, Coyote is a trickster who is almost consistently evil, and other beings inflict sickness and threats to health and prosperity. They, therefore, must be avoided or warded off.

The sings, chants, and ceremonies still practiced today carry whispered messages of fear of the ghosts of departed Surface

People. That fear is manifested, among other ways, in ritualistic handling of dead bodies and of the structures in which they died. A hogan in which a person died is not used again, but is destroyed, often by fire. Ghosts are believed to be the bad or evil part of a person that is left behind when the person's good essence has left the body. Ghosts are believed to appear after dark as humans, coyotes, owls, mice, or strong winds.

Witchcraft also poses a threat and a danger to the traditional Navajo. Like ghosts, witch-like Skinwalkers appear mainly at night, but are evil men and women who wear animal skins, notably of a coyote or a wolf. They may cast spells, administer poison, or even shoot small objects, such as a bit of bone, into a person. These result in fainting, seizures, or pain.

None of this is hypothetical or to be laughed off by the traditional Navajo. The fears are real and life-shaping, often leading people to seek out and pay medicine men or women to set things right. The medicine man is not an entertainer who spins yarns; he is believed to be a healer who understands human nature and the mythological history of the Surface People, having the power to fix what went wrong. Healing rituals employ the mythological history, and the right to practice those healing rituals as religious ceremonies has been protected by the Congress since 1978, when it adopted the American Indian Religious Freedom Act.[3]

The cure lies not in treating the symptoms of the illness or disability, but in getting at the cause. The supernatural beings who caused the experienced illness must be appeased through rituals, which may include the sweat house, sand-paintings, and ceremonies variously referred to as chants, dances, or sings. The cure for a victim of witchcraft, if the witchcraft has not gone too far, is through ceremonials. A successful cure, some believe, will result in the death of the Skinwalker, though the death may not be immediate. Disease and accidental injury may be brought about by the Holy People or by violations of taboos. Any deviation from what is natural, safe, good, or harmonious may be considered illness, and the aim of a curing ceremony for the affliction is to restore relationships to the normal.

Paul G. Zolbrod suggests in his translation of Navajo emergence myths, *Diné bahane`: The Navajo Creation Story*, that the creation story gives Navajos an ethnic identity. In the process, it defines "meaningful relationships" within the community and between the community and the cosmos. Zolbrod likens trying to understand the Navajo without this background as trying to study Christianity without opening the Bible.[4]

Shea Goodluck-Barnes is a Navajo social worker at a United Methodist program for Navajo victims of domestic violence in Farmington, New Mexico, called New Beginnings. An international lecturer and visionary, she says about understanding the Navajo: "Understand our spirituality and everything falls into place."

Whispered messages of these beliefs are rooted in the traditional Navajo. The thoughtful missionary respects the reality that those messages are programmed into new converts, and understands that a conversion does not instantly delete those beliefs. Some of the messages linger after the acceptance of Jesus Christ. And that is why the mythological/religious history culturally ingrained into the Navajos has not been overlooked by the Four Corners Native American Ministry.

There are still other factors that have affected the Navajo view of the world, and that the Ministry has recognized in plotting its course.

CHAPTER FIVE

# Other Influences on the Navajos

*My sighing is not hidden from thee.*
—Psalm 38:9

The Navajo view of the world has been influenced by four principal traumatic episodes: 1) the coming of the Spanish Conquistadores, 2) the arrival of the Americans and the resulting banishment of the Navajos to the Bosque Redondo near Fort Sumner, New Mexico, 3) the federal government's Livestock Reduction Act of the 1930s, and 4) the relocation of Navajos in an attempt to integrate them into the predominant white culture in the 1950s.

Shea Goodluck-Barnes described the first disruption of the Navajo worldview as the coming of the white man. Their advent, she said, shaped a view that is incompatible with Manifest Destiny, the notion that the United States was the chosen nation and predestined to push the frontier ever westward.

> When the first white men, the Conquistadores and their padres, came walking into our land (only the leaders rode horses) . . . whether they accepted those who already lived here was based on how well the natives would change, and how well they would accept the Spaniards' god. If they contested the god, they were automatically conquered . . . And we soon learned how fatal it would be to contest their god.

Later, a new wave of Americans came to the Southwest. "By that time the word had gotten around that you don't oppose the invaders. I guess when you have as great a loss as that [imposed by the Spanish] you become careful and subdued." Goodluck-Barnes is skeptical of the Southwestern histories written by white Americans: "Whose interests does it satisfy? Whose behavior does it justify? Does it rationalize? We Navajos have never written down our part. It's only by word of mouth. It's only what you can *see* of the end result of yesteryear."

Despite the fact that few traces of the early years of the Navajos remain to be seen, there is no doubt that the Navajos who first arrived in the Southwest were nomadic. Many families still move from one location to another, depending on the condition of land for the grazing of their sheep or cattle. Early homes were hogans so flimsy that the residents had no regrets at leaving them behind when they moved on, though today's hogans are generally more substantial. Possessions were few, and a Navajo family could pick up and move with an hour or so of notice. Mobility is thought to be the source of the Navajo love of jewelry as a form of transportable wealth.[1]

Though they borrowed heavily from their neighbors, the Pueblos, learning agriculture from them, most Navajos were hunters and raiders. The Navajos were independent, instead of organized into a tribe, nation, or communal body. Families or groups of families stuck together as the larger, loosely connected group moved about. Their nomadic existence resulted in strong family and clan loyalties.

As more and more Spaniards moved into their ancestral area, Navajo raiders retaliated by growing more aggressive. Spaniards were seizing their livestock at will and justifying the thievery with the argument that no Navajo ever had a horse, sheep, or goat that he hadn't first stolen from them. Retaliation escalated into a cycle. To the Navajos, it was only fair that they should have their chance to take back from the Spaniards.

The Spanish presence in the Southwest brought both benefits and burdens. Even though the Spaniards were abusive and always felt free to grab whatever land took their fancy, most of the time they left the natives alone. The Navajo ability

*And always the sheep. Near Round Rock, Arizona.*

to appropriate horses, sheep, and goat herds—though at the risk of losing their lives—added to their mobility. The livestock could be ridden, driven, or led from one place to another. A result was that farming practices the Navajos had learned from Pueblo neighbors became less attractive. Periodic droughts may also have led to raids on the Spanish. Crop failures may have made it necessary for those who farmed and whose fields had turned to dust to seek food in the stored grains and flocks of the intruders.[2]

The missionary friars who had settled among the Pueblos and the Hopis and built their churches did not have an effective ministry with the Navajos. The Pueblos and the Hopis lived in permanent communities, so the padres could pick a spot to build a church and be sure that their converts would stick around for more than a few Sundays. The Navajos, though, lived in small groups and moved too often for the Franciscans to keep up. If the friars built a church, it would be left behind. For this reason, the nomadic Navajos were rarely evangelized. Since their arrival in North America, the Navajos have retained their nomadic lifestyle and the effect of that way of life on family, possessions, and self-reliance. They have also kept their independence, and many have had difficulty shaking their distrust of the white man.

✧

The second major traumatic event for Navajos took place when the residence of the Navajos in the area of the present Reservation was interrupted by United States troops during the Civil War. The bluecoats uprooted over five thousand Navajos and herded them off to the Bosque Redondo, on the Pecos River in the vicinity of Fort Sumner, New Mexico. The government's purpose was to break the Navajos of their habit of pillaging their white neighbors and passers-by whenever the fancy struck them. The Spanish had largely ignored the looting, but the Americans lost their patience when settlers trekking west through the area were raided by the Navajos. The settlers persuaded the government to stop the tactics of the Navajos. The solution the Americans came up with was to make all the Navajos become farmers and force them to move to the Bosque Redondo.

It was in July 1863, when Colonel Christopher "Kit" Carson of the First New Mexico Volunteers reported to his superior officer the initial results of his operations against Navajos in New Mexico. He wrote that his command had moved west from Los Lunas, New Mexico, to Fort Defiance, in present Arizona. En route, Carson's troops and the Ute Indian spies he had hired slaughtered many Navajo men and captured a large number of women and children, as well as livestock.

Colonel Carson planned to give the women and children to the Utes, "for their own use and benefit, and as there is no other way to sufficiently recompense these [Ute] Indians for their invaluable services [as spies for the troops]." Carson justified himself by assuming that the Utes would sell the women and children to Mexican families, who would give them a better life as "servants" than they would find at the Bosque Redondo.

The colonel's commanding officer vetoed the plan. Instead, he ordered that the captured women and children be sent to Santa Fe as prisoners, for undisclosed purposes. He did approve of paying small amounts for seized horses, cattle, goats, and sheep since he needed meat for the troops. But it was the soldiers and the Utes who received the bounties paid for the livestock, while the Navajo owners were left with no animals and no money in their pockets for their loss. The troops also confiscated harvested corn and wheat and fed the grain to the cavalry's horses and cattle. They torched the remaining fields of unharvested wheat, corn, beans, and pumpkins.[3]

Carson's expedition failed to round up all the Navajos, though some five thousand were sent to the Bosque Redondo. Three hundred or so survivors holed up in Canyon de Chelly, and though Carson's sweep through the canyon netted handfuls of the elusive Navajos, some escaped. The devastation that remained left bare subsistence for those who managed to slip away, most of whom had their families driven off by Carson's troops.[4]

One result of the forced relocation on the Pecos was that the government demanded its prisoners organize into a tribe. The federal authorities were frustrated by the fact that the independent Navajos had no leader to step up and represent the whole imprisoned body, no one for the bureaucrats to deal with or with whom to make a treaty. As likely as not, though, the federal government would have been the first to mock the terms of any paper signed. For the first time, the Navajos formed a tribal entity that satisfied the dictates of their white captors, though the concept of a tribe meant little to the Navajos.

The matters that had caused the government intervention were intended to be settled at Fort Sumner by the Treaty of 1868, made between General William T. Sherman and the "chiefs and head men" of the Navajo Nation. The signed document guaranteed the boundaries of the Reservation, schools for the children, 160-acre farms for any head of a family willing to commence farming, and a ten-dollar-per month allowance for clothing and manufactured goods. In turn, the Navajos agreed not to oppose railroad construction through the Reservation, not to attack wagon trains, not to capture women or children from settlements, and never to kill, scalp, or otherwise harm white men. The Navajos would return to the Reservation.

It might have been feelings of guilt that caused the treaty authors to include the provision that the U.S. would give to the Navajos the sum of $150,000 to be used for removing the tribe from the Bosque Redondo, and to buy sheep, goats, beef cattle, and corn. Any remaining balance was to be invested for maintaining the Navajos pending their removal from the Bosque Redondo.

The area the forcibly relocated Navajos were expected to inhabit when they returned to the Reservation was smaller than they'd occupied before Carson and his men rounded them up, slaughtering those who tried to stay behind. It was only after years of negotiations with the federal bureaucracy, Congress, and the Santa Fe Railroad (which had been granted land through the Reservation) that the lands were extended to their present boundaries. Much of the accretion came about because of a Franciscan priest.

Research done by Father Cormac Antram, OFM, who has spent his adult life as a priest on the Reservation, credits Father Anselm Weber, an early Franciscan missionary among the Navajos, with enlarging the Reservation by some 1.5 million acres. Weber intervened with the federal government during the period from 1907 through 1918. The added lands were little farms, watering places, homes, and grazing lands. According to Antram, Weber wrote that if he had not come to the aid of the Navajo farmers, "These places would have fallen into the hands of the white and Mexican stockmen. At the same time, my activities greatly increased the Navajos' opinion of us Catholic priests."[5]

But warm feelings toward a Franciscan priest were not enough to override negative attitudes toward the white man in general—not when the government continued to blunder in handling these first citizens of America.

The third major upset of the Navajo way of life is still remembered by older members of the Four Corners Native American Ministry board of directors. By the 1930s, the Reservation was so overgrazed by swelling herds of cattle and flocks of sheep that the livestock could barely find enough grass to keep them alive. The federal government, apparently not having learned from its experience in brutal tinkering with the lifestyle of the Navajos by trying to make them into farmers at the Bosque Redondo some seventy years earlier, imposed the Livestock Reduction Act on the Navajos, with the aim of promoting the growth of more grass on the grazing lands.

But herding their cattle and sheep was one of the most necessary elements of Navajo culture and livelihood. It was a rare family whose children were not trained as shepherds. The program to reduce the number of livestock did immeasurable damage to the Navajo economy, though the Bureau of Indian Affairs (BIA) had hoped to make a policy that would assure the health of that economy by protecting grazing land for the future. The program impoverished many Navajos, putting them in desperate straits and making them destitute. Some starved, and it became necessary for many to change their lifestyles in order to survive.

Today, more than seventy-five years after the program was put in place, memories of the decimation of the herds and flocks still stir up frustration and hard feelings among the Diné.

The fourth federal intervention that devastated the Navajo way of life took place in the 1950s, when the U.S. federal government tried to assimilate the Navajo people into off-reservation culture through a relocation program. The idea was to shuffle Navajo families off the Reservation by providing cheap housing and low-paying jobs, with the hope that they would mainstream into the white society. The Navajos who left their homes to buy into the inducements were rooted out of their cultural place. Away from family who remained on the Reservation, many Navajos felt out of balance, and they fell into alcoholism and other negative lifestyles. With their connection to family and clan interrupted, the exiles longed for the freedom of the Reservation; family and clan left behind longed for the return of those who had been relocated. The program was termed by Navajo Nation President Thomas E. Atcitty as "a total failure."[6]

Goodluck-Barnes points out a central aspect of the Navajo worldview that has been ignored by too many missionaries and by government officials eager to impose change:

> [A]nything that relates to our [Navajo] way of life is not compartmentalized, like a compartment for the spiritual. It emphasizes humility in your place. And that is the way to inner peace and connection with your spirituality.

She says that spirituality, to a Navajo,

> takes, I believe, really walking and daily appealing to maintaining your sense of balance. Religion is a European concept. So [for the Navajo] there's a balance between the physical and spiritual life . . . what we [Navajos] refer to as "harmony" . . . There's no concept of religion in our way.

She has concluded that disruption of the traditional way of life of Navajos, by removing them from family, clan, and Reservation, has caused spiritual upheavals unimaginable to the white do-gooders.

Though the Four Corners Native American Ministry has endeavored to bind itself into Navajo values, including sensitivity to past injustices imposed by the white man, it has put Christian values first. Likewise, the Ministry has worked to overcome distrust of the white man, especially as shown in suspicion of the motives of white Christian missionaries.

Ultimately, the routes followed by the Methodist Mission School and the Ministry, in terms of addressing the native culture and religion, diverged. The result was that the school became a secular institution while the Ministry remained an evangelical Christian outreach. Nevertheless, the Ministry owes a debt of gratitude to the mission school and to those who got it started and made it work. They laid the foundation on which the Ministry was to build, and for that reason it will be useful to take a look into the Ministry's heritage.

## CHAPTER SIX

# Genesis of Methodists Working with Navajos

*The Lord has sent his angel . . .*
—Acts 12:11

---

The flood was not of the magnitude of the one that floated Noah's ark to the mountains of Ararat, but for the dry and dusty Four Corners area of the Southwest it was frightening, deadly, and unlike anything previously experienced. There was water enough to wash away the Methodist Mission School, yet while the power of the torrent swept away hopes and dreams for the ministry to the Navajos, the receding waters left hope and vision—if not a rainbow.

It was on October 5, 1911, that the waters rose, twenty years to the month after Methodists had pitched their first tent on the edge of the Reservation. In those two decades, the dreams of a pair of gutsy young women who had signed up as missionaries for the Missionary Society of the Methodist Episcopal Church (North) had gelled into reality. In October 1891, Mrs. Mary Louise Eldridge and Miss Mary E. Raymond gathered up their skirts and jumped from the wagon they'd ridden in from Lawrence, Kansas, to the rocky banks of the San Juan River. They landed at Hogback, New Mexico, on the eastern boundary of the Navajo Nation Reservation, twenty miles or so west of the town of Farmington, in a land they feared was populated mainly by rattlesnakes.

Mary Raymond, after a sickly childhood in Iowa, had taught in that state and in Nebraska before taking a faculty position at the Haskell Indian Institute located in Lawrence, Kansas. She left there for the Pine Ridge Sioux Reservation in South Dakota, where she met another whirlwind, a widow named Mary Louise Eldridge. She had worked at Haskell, serving as a nurse, though not during the same time that Raymond had taught there.

The pair, finding they shared a love of adventure, decided to sign up as a team with the Missionary Society for the Navajo mission field. The society charged them with starting the first permanent Protestant mission work for the Navajos. The assignment took them to the locality called Hogback, named after a nearby spiny ridge of the same name, in the northwest corner of the Territory of New Mexico. The area was known as the Four Corners.[1]

But the handful of local Navajos that herded a few sheep and scratched out a living in the neighborhood were certain that offers of friendship and kindness by the women were only a ruse; that the two missionaries, white people who could not be trusted, were there to steal their children. A few of them watched from a distance and were reassured as the women and workers they hired constructed a small adobe building that seemed too small for a school. The adobe structure was soon followed by two small additions, and suspicions grew that just maybe this really was to be a school that would pluck off Navajo children.

Winter sicknesses eventually struck, and the power of the medicine men proved useless. The Navajos soon learned that the women had medicine that would cure the sick. During the first winter of the missionary team's stay, thirty to forty sick people appeared daily at the door of the little building, seeking help. The barriers were down, and the Navajos no longer feared that their children were fair game for Methodist women with kidnapping in mind.

So the mission grew, though not into the school the ladies had envisioned. Raymond and Eldridge had discovered that the immediate needs were medical, so that is what they offered. They also gave the native women yarn for weaving and taught the men how to irrigate and farm.

When Raymond was offered a government position as field matron to the Navajos, she accepted it. Her job provided an income she could share in the mission work, though her duties took time away from delivering the news of Jesus Christ. She soon married Thomas M. F. Whyte, who ran a trading post in the vicinity. The women continued their work, taking a wagon and driver into the Reservation on trips to scout out their neighbors. To their surprise, they found cultivated lands and fields of irrigated crops.[2]

Mary Raymond Whyte's longstanding infirmity was further weakened when she gave birth to a son. In 1894, her brother took her back to Kansas, where shortly after the death of her baby, she also died. When word got back to the mission, one Navajo told Mrs. Eldridge, "She was my friend. I came here from far away and was very cold and hungry. She made me warm, gave me food and a warm cloak."[3]

Eldridge carried on the work of meeting the physical needs of the Navajos, though she eventually took a job as matron when financing from the Missionary Society wasn't enough to support her and her mission. She then created a government-sponsored irrigation project with some success. Her effort to launch a Sunday school for the white settlers quickly failed, however, and she refocused her work on meeting needs. She found that reaching out to fill the needs of Navajos and their families, as the Navajos perceived those needs, was an effective missionary tool.

Shortly after the death of Mary Raymond Whyte, the Missionary Society sent reinforcements. The new recruit was Mary E. Tripp, a forty-six-year-old New Yorker who felt she had a spiritual calling. When she joined Eldridge, Tripp set out to make Christians. She started a Sabbath school, which met each Sunday morning. She held prayer meetings, and also took comfort to the sick.

Though the Christianizing ministry was aimed at Navajos, it drew only the families of white settlers. The Navajos watched from a distance because they could neither speak nor understand

English, and neither of the missionaries could speak Navajo. Then the ladies found a jewel—Frank Damon, the son of a Navajo mother and a Scotch-Irish father, who spoke and understood both English and Navajo. Damon went to work for the mission as a bilingual interpreter,[4] which opened the door to the Navajos, who now could hear about the white man's God in a language they understood. When they asked questions, they got answers. The interpreter was soon so caught up in the work that he was converted, becoming an advocate for Jesus Christ and a member of the team. The ladies had learned two interrelated lessons: the value of native leadership, and the value of communication in the Navajo language. The mission's work would never be the same.

It was all going so well that the Christian Reformed Church sent a missionary they had posted at Fort Defiance to learn how to minister to the Navajos. An 1898 report issued by the secretary of the Women's Home Missionary Society said, "Some of the Navajos are beginning to comprehend the truth of the gospel, and are daily praying to God, and will come alone to talk with the missionaries about living Christian lives, and how they can know what is right and pleasing to the Lord."[5]

With momentum underway, Tripp opened a day school for Navajo children in her cabin in 1896. Attendance was irregular, and Tripp figured out why: the parents moved from one place to another with their sheep, and the children's duties as shepherds took priority over attendance at day school. Approximately two years later, Tripp closed the doors on the first Methodist school serving the Reservation.[6]

In the aborted day school, though, Tripp had found a clue to the secret of success in reaching out to Navajo children. She decided what was needed was a boarding school. If the children lived in a school dormitory, they could stay in one place while their parents followed the flocks to seasonal grazing lands. Other children in the family could handle the shepherding.

Tripp found her dream location a short distance away, a place that could be developed into an industrial farm for training the children in how to make a living. With cash contributions begged from the Methodist Women's Home Missionary Society, from the Troy Annual Conference in New York, and others, Tripp bought forty acres of bottom land on the west bank of the San Juan River two miles below its confluence with the Animas. The Navajos called the area "between waters." To the postal service, it was known as Jewett.[7] The door of the first building of a boarding school was opened by January of 1899.

What started as a single-building mission soon began to look like a school campus with the construction of a two-story multi-purpose mission home. Tripp hired teachers, planted crops and fruit trees, and bought chicken and livestock. The school took on a look of permanence it had never had at Hogback. Then illness struck Mary Tripp. Having been diagnosed with cancer, she died in 1907.

By the day in 1911 that the San Juan and Animas Rivers dumped the rains they had carried from the Rockies of southern Colorado into the lands of the Jewett mission, the complex included not only the buildings Tripp had built, but an irrigated farm and orchard with corn, vegetables, pumpkins, apples, and livestock that made the school self-sufficient, a new school-house and a laundry, as well as farm out-buildings. There were thirty-one children enrolled, and every one of them had his or her own bed.

Then the waters came, and it was all gone.

One of those who survived the flood was Frank Damon. He had lost his vision a few years earlier, probably to the trachoma that afflicted so many Navajos. Nevertheless, he helped evacuate the children before returning to man the mission telephone. Only when the floodwaters took out the lines did he mount a horse and ride through belly-deep water to safety.[8]

But it was Superintendent J. M. Simmons who earned the headlines in the Farmington newspaper. After organizing the evacuation of the children in the middle of the night, Simmons returned to the mission. There, he helped Damon climb aboard a horse. Simmons mounted one himself, but was knocked off and nearly drowned. He swam a mile and a half, aided by cotton-wood branches and a bobbing trunk full of bedding. Just as he was about to sink for the last time, he spotted a raft torn from its moorings upstream. Climbing aboard, Simmons found an ear of corn, an egg, half a dozen apples and an onion, all lodged in a bucket. Simmons peeled off his wet clothes and built a fire right there on the raft, with matches he dried out on the deck. He cooked the egg, roasted the apples and corn, and ate dinner. Finding three pillows in the trunk lodged against the raft, he dried them with the heat of the fire, made a bed and took a nap. Thirty hours after he had been swept away from the mission, his craft came to shore, where a Japanese man found him.[9]

All those hours in the river and on the raft left Superintendent Simmons with a bellyful of the Jewett site. By the time he'd cleaned the sand from his ears, all that remained of the little school was a collection of children with no place to go, two horses, two cows, and the mission dog. Rather than rebuild from scratch on the shifting sands along the San Juan, he made a decision: the mission had to be moved—and this time to a rock of a location.

Simmons, however, did not stick around long enough to see the move to completion. He resigned, and was followed in the superintendency by a local couple, Mr. and Mrs. Gus Bero of Farmington. The Beros set out to forge ties with the community and to rebuild the school out of reach of the floods. Another era in the history of the Methodist work with the Navajos was underway.

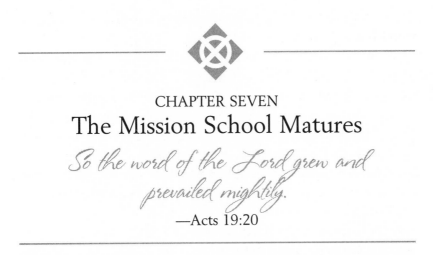

CHAPTER SEVEN

# The Mission School Matures

*So the word of the Lord grew and prevailed mightily.*

—Acts 19:20

The new location was on high ground above the dry bed of the La Plata River, a couple of miles west of downtown Farmington. Aided by contributions from around the country, the new school soon took shape. This time, the issues faced by the staff, aside from the rebuilding, were different than those faced by the three founding Marys—Eldridge, Raymond Whyte, and Tripp. The focus was not just on keeping the doors open, but on building up capacity and enrollment. The work was still stressed by tight finances; some of the budget deficits were made up by selling surplus fruits and vegetables as the mission school farm, garden, and orchard began to produce.

As the years passed, the school grew in effectiveness and respect. With the influence of Christian teachers, students and sometimes their parents were turning away from the old religious ways and embracing Jesus Christ. Many were placed in jobs. When the school geared up for World War I, a Red Cross chapter opened on the campus, boys marched off to the army, and Superintendent Milton M. Thorne (who had followed the Beros) left to work in the war effort.[1]

Experience in Indian work was number one on the list of qualifications for the superintendent when the Women's Missionary Society hired a government Indian worker and former farmer, James Odle, in 1918. Nevertheless, Odle would not have been hired had he not also been a dedicated Christian. Enrollment grew to fifty-three by the 1924–25 school year.

During the Odle tenure, one of the school staff members wrote a nine-page paper, in which she described the people to whom an outreach of the school was being directed, and the native religion that challenged the faculty by competing for the young minds and hearts. "Navajo Indian Field Work" was written by a person who identified herself only as "L. D. W." The writer was probably Lena Wilcox of Farmington, since that name is the only one in Malehorn's listing of school personnel that matches the initials.

The author of the paper told of life as she found it on the Reservation in the early 1920s, though she used terminology that today seems to carry a lack of cultural sensitivity. Wilcox wrote:

> We see only a few sheep skins or blankets thrown on the floor to serve as beds and a fire built on the ground in the middle of the room if it is winter—in the summer the fire is built and the cooking is done outside the hogan. There are a few tin or iron dishes, spoons, etc. and that is all.

Wilcox was surprised to find no schools, no churches, no hospital, or doctors.

> Yet, [she wrote], the family ties are very strong and there is a firm loyalty to relatives. They live little better than savages and the children look more like little wild animals than like human beings . . . When a few of the children are sent to government or Mission schools they have never eaten from a table or slept in a bed and do not know what a knife, fork or spoon are for. And this remember is the United States of America and not the heart of Africa.

Wilcox also described the native religious practices of the Navajos of her time:

> This strange wild people have a religion as strange and wild as the people themselves. They are extremely religious in

their pagan way and believe in a variety of spirits that dwell in various forms of nature and in one Great Spirit, greater than all the others, who lives in the sun.

Wilcox had acquired a knowledge of the religion that was more than superficial. She found, "There are also many evil spirits—the Chindee [*sic*]—which cause all of the suffering and ill luck in the world. The Navajo is very superstitious, as are all primitive people, and has a charm for almost every thing. His religious life finds expression in the form of 'sings' or 'dances' which are the ceremonies of the Navajo tribe."

Her investigation did not overlook the shaman, or medicine man:

> the high priest of the Navajo. . . . [T]he only way to ward off the threatened evil is to have a sing and pay a fee to the Medicine Man [and] feed all the visiting Navajos for as long as the sing lasts. Often . . . a sing costs a family every sheep and goat that they possess.

Wilcox found that the Navajos she visited wanted nothing to do with the white man's religion. "He says it is all right for the white man but says it is not practical for the Navajos." One explanation given to her for the attitude was that the religion was written on paper, "and Navajos cannot read it any how. Navajos must have something in the heart."[2]

Superintendent James Odle, while working in the culture Wilcox described, stated the school's purpose: "to . . . develop young people who can introduce Jesus Christ to their people and let His Spirit work in them."[3] At that time, however, there were no Methodist churches on the Reservation to which the students could return, and it would be nearly half a century until the school got serious about starting any.

In 1929 the Women's Missionary Society sent C. C. Brooks to replace Odle as supervisor. He was assisted by his wife, identified only as "Mrs. C. C. Brooks." The pair pushed for the expansion of the school, though cost-cutting in reaction to reduced giving in the midst of the Great Depression sliced enrollment from over a hundred in one year to seventy-seven the next.

The first high school class graduated in 1939, a year after the school received full accreditation as a high school. At the celebration, Superintendent Brooks restated the reasons for the school's existence:

> First, to bring him (the Navajo) to a vital knowledge of Jesus Christ as his personal Saviour. Second, to give him the best possible training for the life he will live after he leaves us. Third, to provide trained Christian leadership for the Navajo.

Also in 1939, a government commission reported on the school, saying:

> Certainly the results of this school in the training of young Navajos for service to their people is one of the most impressive missionary achievements on the Navajo Nation Reservation.[4]

Some of the mission school graduates went on to college. The first Navajo graduate to earn a degree, Stella Tsosie, graduated from Colorado State College of Education, Greeley, in 1947. (She later married Herman Lee, and in 1977 was elected chair of the board of directors of the newly formed Four Corners Native American Ministry.) The names of former students began to pop up in listings of tribal leaders, indicative of the quality of the training the school was providing. The impressions left by the mission school on its faculty and students were lasting, and a teacher decided it was time to record how the institution had been founded and how its influence had grown.

In 1948, Pauline Malehorn (Mrs. W. H.) undertook the task of writing a history of the school. She taught English and was the school librarian as well as its historian and curator of antiquities. Malehorn recruited some of the members of the typing class to sit down at their Underwoods and bang out copies of her manuscript. One of her conscripts was high school junior Frank Hanagarne, who volunteered because he wanted an association with the book written by his English teacher.

Young Hanagarne, after leading the school's basketball team to state-wide notice earned by a second-place finish in the state boys' basketball tournament, finished his mission school days and went on to MacPherson College in Kansas, a Church of the Brethren institution. He graduated in 1953 with majors in math and chemistry, only to be drafted into the army. He found that it was easy for him to adapt to basic training, explaining in a 2003 interview that it was the discipline at the school that made army life easy.

> Everything [at the school] was one, two, three, four, and so on. There was no flexibility in your life. It was: go to bed, wake up. . . . And there were a lot of people that could not adjust to military life. But my feeling on it was, *Hey, I've been doing this all my life, and I'm getting paid for it now* [laughter].

The thing that Hanagarne missed most at the mission school were the love of his parents. "The things we were not provided were the love and care you would get from a parent. There was not that relationship. I'm not saying it was harsh, but that the love of a teacher versus that of a parent—there was no relationship capability there." Hanagarne recalls profiting from the religious training he received. "From a religious standpoint, I would say, yes, I gained definitely a great deal from it. Didn't know it at the time. It was a definite plus."

Former student Ruth Westbrook grew up at the school from 1943 to 1954, living there in a girls' dorm for nine months each year. During an interview in 2003, she remembered the spiritual seed that was planted in her while she was a student, though she, too, missed the love of her family.

> So I look back now and I call them missionaries. . . . those that worked there. We saw them read their Bibles. They had their Bibles. . . . I saw how they had their devotions every morning in their own places where they lived in the dorms. Everything was spiritual.

Westbrook said she uses the term "missionaries" in a good sense:

> Well, this was a missionary country. This was like a Third
> World area. . . . most of the parents traveled in [horse-
> pulled] wagons . . . to visit their children. There were a lot
> of kids that their families came to visit them maybe once
> or twice during the school year, when it was warm. . . . I
> thank God for these people that planted the seed in me.

Three years after Superintendent C. C. Brooks retired in 1943, the school's vision expanded. It branched out of its comfortable campus just outside well-watered Farmington— with its three rivers, orchards, green pastures, and vegetable gardens—to a location that was about as unlikely a spot as could be chosen for growing anything at all, including a school. It was called Bistahi.

CHAPTER EIGHT

# The Bistahi and Shiprock Ventures

*A door was opened for me in the Lord . . .*

—2 Corinthians 2:12

In 1946 the school was encouraged by the National Division and the Women's Division to set up an outpost in the community of Bistahi, New Mexico.[1] They built a branch of the school there, and equipped it with a small number of faculty for teaching. It provided a location for elementary-age Navajo children to be boarded during the school term, just as children were boarded and taught on the main campus near Farmington.

To call Bistahi a "community" exaggerates the meaning of the word, for there were (and still are) fewer than a handful of residents in a five-mile radius. The attraction to the location was that just outside the border of the Reservation, the National Division acquired from a private owner twenty acres, subject to certain reversionary provisions. A sturdy concrete block and adobe two-story dormitory, classrooms, and other facilities were constructed to teach the children of families whose scattered hogans blended into the landscape of the surrounding area.

Bistahi is an inhospitable location. It is a remote place, some thirty-five miles south of Farmington and a mile or so east of New Mexico State Highway 371. It lies about a mile inside the Bisti Badlands, a portion of which is designated as the Bisti Wilderness on maps.

Vegetation around the school was as rare as a rainy day, limited to parched tumbleweeds and occasional wisps of grama grass struggling to survive on the flat areas of the terrain. Nothing at all grew on the stubby hills. Their striated layers of black, gray, and grubby white, each carved by eroded fissures like wrinkles left by time on the face of the landscape, gave new meaning to the term "barren." Even so, parents took their children to live and be taught at the school from opening day.

The Bistahi outpost functioned as a school only until 1958, when a fire destroyed the dormitory. Although the buildings that remained were no longer used for school purposes, the location did not cease to exist as a station for Methodists. It was utilized as a preaching point and community center. In the fall of the year of the fire, a young couple arrived at Bistahi. David and Goldie Tutt soon put the remaining two-room school building to use by establishing a preaching point in one room and a social hall in the other.

Hope for a resurrection of sorts came with a one-thousand-dollar donation from the Troy, New York Annual Conference—though far more would have been required to rebuild the dormitory. Tutt was a resourceful individual, however, and he invested the money in sheet metal, metal framing, bolts, and other parts for a Quonset-type building. With the help of a handful of volunteers, a large structure with a concrete floor soon towered over the former school site. The ends of the building were filled in as high as a man could reach with adobe bricks salvaged from the burned dormitory. Where the adobe left off, fiberglass was added until it was entirely enclosed. This structure functioned as a community center and gymnasium.

Another building housed a laundry with several washing machines. The "wash-a-teria," it was called. The operation turned out to be an instant success for Navajos with no other place to launder their clothes or take a shower. But the water was hard as nails, in short supply, and completely unsuited for drinking. For a time, determined staff members hauled in usable water, but the burden soon became too great and the operation ended.

Reverend Larry Kent preached at the makeshift preaching point for a short time. David Tutt delivered sermons as a young pastor, both before and after he was ordained. A lay volunteer from Kansas, Fred Christianson, came with a call to preach, and worked at Bistahi for a few years. He married a Navajo woman, and they later moved back to Kansas. Others who filled in with preaching during the years following the fire were Roger Deal, a Navajo who lived northwest of Bistahi, and Navajo Clarence Tsosie. From time to time, Benjamin Hogue also drove out from Farmington.

During Tutt's tenure at the edge of the Bisti Wilderness, he learned Navajo. Using Bible texts, he was able to preach in that language. Tutt's facility in learning the language inspired him to begin a translation of the New Testament into Navajo. With the help of Faye Edgerton and Faith Hill, and three Navajos, Fannie Scott, Emily Johnson, and Roger Deal, Tutt was able to finish the project and move on to the Old Testament. When it, too, was completed, some twenty-one years after he first wrote down the Navajo words for Matthew 1:1, the entire hand-written translation was published by the American Bible Society and offered for sale at a heavily subsidized price. It was all there, from the opening words of Genesis 1, "In the beginning . . .," or *"Hodeeydáádáá Diyin God yótááh híniláii índa nahaszaan aytilaa,"* to the last words of Revelation.

Through it all, the little mission outpost hung on, not exactly thriving, but not dying, either. Although work at Bistahi was the first effort of the mission school to reach out beyond its campus, it had not established a church there, though one would be placed at Bistahi in later years. And Bistahi was just outside the Reservation border. The honor of calling itself the first Methodist church planted on the Reservation went to the church in Shiprock. It resulted from the mission school's decision to hire a designated missionary to the Navajo Nation Reservation.

The push to add a designated missionary started with Mrs. Brooks, wife of Superintendent C. C. Brooks, though the staff position would not be filled until some ten years after Brooks left. A few years before Dr. and Mrs. Brooks stepped aside, Mrs. Brooks had written, "Now we need a missionary, speaking

Navajo, to keep in touch with our children and their homes. It is impossible now with our present force."[2]

Maybe her son, Robert, was paying attention when she put that thought into words. Robert Brooks, a 1941 mission school graduate, signed on in the mid-1950s as the first designated missionary from the school to the Navajos. He brought with him his bride, Blanche. His charge was to keep mission school graduates living on the Reservation in touch with Jesus Christ and The Methodist Church. By the time of his appointment, young Brooks had the necessary qualifications. He was an ordained Methodist clergyman; he'd grown up with Navajos and understood them; he had strong ties to the school from his attendance there from first grade through high school. As it turned out, virtually his entire early life was spent with the Navajos.

Blanche Brooks told of one of her late husband's ventures onto the Reservation in a 2003 interview:

> When my husband and I were missionaries at the Methodist Mission School in Farmington, Bob would visit former mission students who had gone back to the Reservation. He found that they were drifting away because there was no spiritual food for them on the Reservation. There were no Methodist churches they could attend.

The young Brooks kept his eyes open for opportunities for placing a church on the Reservation, and one day he spotted a possibility.

> Robert was driving through Shiprock and he noticed that a bank . . . was putting up a new building at a place where there had been nothing. Robert had an idea. He thought that if that bank could build there where there was nothing else, so could the church. So he contacted the superintendent of the Albuquerque District, R. L. Willingham, who was very helpful. He appointed Bob to start a new church.

The first Methodist church on the Navajo Nation Reservation was called First Methodist Church of Shiprock. Its members were both Navajos and Anglos, many of whom worked in government schools, hospitals, and in private industry, including the coal-fired energy-generating plants that were springing up in the area. For a time after the congregation was formed on October 8, 1957, the worshippers met in a private home.

In a few months, the group outgrew the living room of the residence and moved the Sunday services into a school. From there, they marked time in the hallway of a second public school in Shiprock while waiting for Navajo tribal authorities to decide whether or not to lease tribal land to a Methodist church in the face of policies that prevented the sale of any Reservation real estate.

The school hallway location did not slow down the growth and prosperity of the new church. Brooks took in thirty-three new members on a Sunday in March 1962, fifteen of them on profession of faith. On the same Sunday, the building fund topped two-thirds of its goal for commencing with construction.

It took five years for the Navajo tribal government to act on the request for land. With a lease for two acres finally in hand, the church hired a contractor, and the dirt and sand began to fly. A sanctuary, classrooms, and parsonage were completed in 1963. The cost was ninety thousand dollars, and in thirteen years it was free and clear of debt.

Three years after the church moved into its brand new sanctuary, one of the Navajo Mission School graduates, Rev. Fred W. Yazzie, finished his studies at Asbury Theological Seminary in Wilmore, Kentucky. When he returned to the Reservation and to the mission school that had started him on his quest to serve Jesus Christ, he was an ordained minister. Once back home, Yazzie, the first Navajo to be ordained as a Methodist clergy person, served for a time as chaplain at the mission school, then began an outreach ministry designed to take the Word to the Navajos. His first base was the preaching point in Bistahi, and he later replaced Henry Begay as preacher to the Navajo services at Shiprock. All the while, Yazzie was preparing the soil in which the Four Corners Native American Ministry he was to help organize would take root.

## CHAPTER NINE

# The First Navajo United Methodist Pastor

*And the gospel must first be preached to all nations.*

—Mark 13:10

Though he had grown up speaking English, Rev. Fred W. Yazzie knew that to be effective on the Reservation he had to preach in Navajo. The biggest boost to increasing his vocabulary came from his congregation. They were eager to chime in with a missing word whenever he stumbled in the middle of a sermon, trying to explain a Christian concept in a language with which he was wrestling. In time, Yazzie became a powerful speaker, both in English and in Navajo.

For him, as it is with many converting Navajos, the decision to become a Christian had been met with family resistance. In a 2003 interview, Yazzie described the reaction of his father, who was the son of a medicine man. "When I was fifteen years old . . . I went to the Methodist Mission School. I was converted there. I was so thrilled. I went home, and I told my mom and dad that I became a Christian. I was so happy."

But the decision the young man had made so joyfully did not please his parents:

> And oh, wow, did I ever offend my mom and my dad! And my dad just looked at me so mean, and he said, "What! What have you done? You are a Navajo. And your Navajo religion is over here. What have you been doing? Have you been using peyote?"

> Now, Dad was of the animistic way. And at that time
> peyote was really not so popular, but he thought I had been
> using peyote to become a Christian, and that's not so . . .
> My dad was upset with me for years and years . . . [but] just
> before he died he was converted to Christianity.

After graduating from the Methodist Mission School, the young Yazzie took a degree from Taylor University, an evangelical, interdenominational liberal arts college in Upland, Indiana. He then moved on to Asbury Theological Seminary in Wilmore, Kentucky. Asbury is a strongly Wesleyan, Methodist-related seminary, though it is not supported as part of the United Methodist system of seminaries. The school is

*Rev. Fred W. Yazzie
counsels a church member.*

known for producing some of the most theologically conservative United Methodist clergy and theologians, trained "to spread scriptural holiness throughout the world."[1]

Yazzie returned to Four Corners as a persuasive advocate for spreading the name of Jesus Christ across the Reservation. He knew from his own observations that the old ways continually tempt the new Christian Navajos residing on the Reservation to return to their traditional religion. To counter that temptation, Yazzie preached that Jesus must always be first for the Christian. He taught his beliefs not only to the congregations to which he ministered, but in later training sessions for those Christian Navajos who were called to preach. From the first days of his ministry, Yazzie planted seeds that would grow to shape the Ministry's direction.

◈

In 1996, the New Mexico Annual Conference adopted in the form of a resolution a paper Yazzie had drafted prior to the birth of the Ministry. It presented the beliefs he and the other Four

Corners Ministry Navajos hold against mixing traditional Navajo religious practices with Christian worship and experience.

The traditional Navajo blessing, "Walk in beauty," represents a state of harmony with creation, Yazzie explained. The Navajo word for "beauty," can be used "to describe the Navajo's Christian experience, but only as long as it is not treated as an end in itself." It should be used to illustrate walking in the "beauty of Christ" or "the beauty of God." A copy of the resolution was sent by the offices of the annual conference to the Native American International Caucus as an explanation of the Navajos' theological stance.

Yazzie discussed the traditional, or animistic, way which his father had followed, as the spiritual belief system held by many traditional Navajos:

> The other religion that we have is called the animistic religion. You can read about believing in spirits in Romans, chapter 1. It says the rock has a spirit, a tree has a spirit, a moth has a spirit. And so that is a big religion which the Navajos call more traditional, a religion that came with the Navajos, and we still have a large number of people who believe in the animistic religion. You might hear them say, "I am of the traditional religion," meaning animism.

Yazzie's theology excludes the incorporation into Christian worship of the old ways, as represented by feathers, drums, smoke, a rainbow, or other symbols of spirits seen by the traditional Navajos in inanimate objects:

> The [United Methodist] Navajos have their way of worship. They don't want to get into cultural things. These are Navajos who have sold out to Christ. They don't want to change their ways [of worshipping Christ]. They came from the animistic religion, or some of them have come from the peyote religion, and they don't want to go back. When they find Christ is the answer—and the only answer—then they become very evangelical, they want to be Christian.

He has often found that the general church has not understood the beliefs held by the 4CNAM Navajos:

Sometimes . . . a program comes through the conference or through New York or through the Board of Discipleship in Nashville . . . that might speak to the Native American . . . [and] other Native Americans can latch onto that. But our Navajos are strictly biblical. They want the Bible. They want to be fed from the Bible, with Navajo language being used, and they believe in their way of worshiping God that's not diluted with something else.

Before he had served for long as an ordained minister on the Reservation, Yazzie discovered that he had another sort of calling, too. It also predates the formation of the Four Corners Native American Ministry, and is his personal ministry to his people, though it has also been embraced by the Ministry. This uniquely Fred Yazzie way of evangelizing was one he happened on almost by accident—or by some divine plan. How he discovered this calling, and how he has used it to reach others, is best told by the one who began it and keeps it going, Yazzie himself.

One of the ways it has happened to me over the years is hospital visitation . . . In the traditional Navajo religion, the animistic religion, I grew up with a lot of fears and super-stitions and taboos about death: Don't look at death, don't touch death, don't talk about your own death, don't talk about somebody else's death. So death is a subject that Navajos don't really get into, even today. And so I felt the Lord really led me into this ministry throughout the years.

At the start I didn't realize I was doing it. Then, later on, some doctors approached me and said, "Fred, when you come here to the hospital and you pray for these people, they are healed. And they are going home. What do you tell them?"

But really, what I do is just talk about Jesus . . . The old folks don't know Jesus by the word "Jesus" . . . *Doodatsaahii* is the name, "He who doesn't die." So Jesus to them was "He who doesn't die." He died but he came back to life. So in that sense, the old folks know him that way.

One time a family asked me to see an old, old lady in San Juan Regional Hospital, and they couldn't get through to her with the name Jesus. . . . So, when I went back and started using the name Doodatsaahii, she understood . . . I could see her face change. She opened up her eyes and looked at me, and then began to nod . . . [she] knew who I was talking about when I talked about Jesus.

So that's what I do. I present Jesus, then I don't pressure them. And then later I present more. And later they tell me they want to believe more, they want to know how they can invite Jesus into their hearts. And they do this before they die. Many Navajos find Jesus before they die. And they will say they found Jesus, they were born again, they were made children of God.

That latches on to their families, and families begin to say, "You know, you contact Rev. Fred Yazzie, and he'll go there, and he'll talk about Jesus."

And so, throughout the years, by word of mouth . . . "Have you tried Rev. Yazzie? Has he gone up there to see you?" . . . then they begin to know what salvation is—what being born [again] in Jesus means. . . . And so that's the way of salvation coming into the lives of these people. And that's my method.

The theology shaped by Yazzie was to become a stumbling block to the integration of the Navajo Methodists into the theologically more liberal mainstream of The United Methodist Church's plan for reaching Native Americans through the Native American International Caucus. But then, Navajos had always been independent, and to them a brand of beliefs that did not fit into the mainstream was just fine, as long as Jesus Christ and the Bible were at the center. So the work grew in outreach and effectiveness as Yazzie was bringing Navajos to Jesus.

But there was an invisible but effective brake on starting any more new congregations. It grew from a long-held belief that Methodists could not start churches on the Reservation, and it held back further expansion of the work of the United Methodists among the Navajos until the belief was challenged by a feisty Methodist bishop who sent a delegation to a conference in Ganado, Arizona, in the early 1970s. The group returned to the New Mexico Annual Conference on fire for a mission to the Diné. In Ganado, they had found that the constraints on new Methodist church starts on the Reservation were either all hokum, or the times had changed so much that to leave an antiquated rule in place would kill evangelism by the Methodists and other mainline Protestant denominations on the Reservation, denying many Navajos access to the Good News of Jesus Christ.

The crumbling of the barricade was to be a giant step forward for Methodist work on the Reservation through the New Mexico Annual Conference. It stimulated the annual conference into a search for a missionary to the Navajos.

CHAPTER TEN

# You Can't Hold Back the Wind

*The wind blows where it wills . . . so it is with everyone who is born of the Spirit.*

—John 3:8

New Mexico Annual Conference officials understood that sometime, somewhere, there had been an agreement made with other denominations that barred Methodists from placing churches on the Reservation. The restriction made the decision by Albuquerque District Superintendent R. L. Willingham and young Rev. Robert Brooks to start a Methodist church on the Reservation in Shiprock little short of revolutionary. Though the congregation was formed in October 1957, that's as far as the work on the Reservation went until the mid-1960s.

The belief was that some kind of a comity agreement had been struck among Methodists, Presbyterians, Episcopalians, and the Christian Reformed Church. The vague tradition was that Methodists and Presbyterians would educate Navajo children— Methodists were to work off of the Reservation, Presbyterians would work on it; Episcopalians would address health issues; and the Reformed Church would start and operate churches. However, no one could find any record of such a pact.

Perhaps the accord was a vestige of President Ulysses S. Grant's Peace Policy, sometimes called the "Quaker Peace Policy," for the Christianization of the American Indians. The policy originated in 1868 as a strategy for dealing with the "Indian problem." Grant had decided that if the American Indians could be converted to Christianity, and especially if they could be made into peace-loving Quakers, it would take the fight out of them and tranquility would reign.

Other denominations, unhappy at the possibility of being shut out of the Indian mission field, jumped on the bandwagon. As a result of a series of meetings sponsored by the Board of Indian Commissioners, the major denominations of the time were given the right to nominate replacements for the often-corrupt individuals then holding positions for Indian agencies. The theory was that devout Christians serving as Indian agents would end payoffs and halt the sales of arms and liquor to the Indians. Instead, they would spread the Word among their charges, who would soon become Bible-toting pacifists.

Germane to the Christianization of Navajos, Presbyterians were assigned almost all of the agencies in the Southwest. The Presbyterian allocation included responsibility for placing new churches, schools, and all other resources for converting those living on the Reservation.[1] Although this exclusive Presbyterian franchise for spreading the Word on the Reservation did not comport exactly to the terms of the comity agreement as understood by New Mexico Methodists, the conclusion can be drawn that Grant's Peace Policy probably gave rise to the "comity agreement"[2] and was the ultimate source of the perceived ban on Methodist church starts.

For years Methodists asked no questions about the ban. They just did their work educating children at the mission school in Farmington, and later at the Bistahi outpost. Graduates were sent back to the Reservation to be nurtured by churches of other denominations, if by any church at all. Thus reined in, The Methodist Church barely managed to catch the coattails of the greatest ever church-planting period on the Reservation, the twenty-seven-year stretch from 1950 to 1977. It was a time called "The 27 Unbelievable Years" by missiologists Thomas Dolaghan and David Scates in their evangelizing study, *The Navajos are Coming to Jesus*. The authors disclosed that during the "unbelievable years" on the Reservation, there were seventy-six Indigenous Pentecostal congregations planted, sixty-one

Baptist, thirty-two Assembly of God, thirty non-denominational, fifteen Nazarene, eight Wesleyan and Free Methodist, eight Christian Reformed, two Presbyterian, two Methodist, and a few dozen others, all totaling 308 brand-new congregations.[3]

At some point in the early sixties, it became obvious to Bishop W. Angie Smith that Methodists were being left in the dust when it came to preaching the Word to the Navajos. In 1964, he sent a delegation of three annual conference members to Ganado, Arizona, for an interdenominational consultation convened by Presbyterians concerning evangelical work among the Navajos. The three Methodist representatives from New Mexico were Albuquerque District Superintendent Dr. Fisher Blanton, Conference Women's Society of Christian Service Chair Lillian Imle, and the Rev. Brodace Elkins, chair of the New Mexico Conference Board of Missions.

Elkins recalled the Ganado meeting:

> All those who were there thought there was a comity agreement among the denominations, and the Presbyterians and the Methodists had the responsibility for education. . . . the Methodists did not start churches. The Reformed Church had responsibility to start local churches. . . . But at Ganado we learned there was no comity agreement.

The trio from New Mexico had their eyes opened to the possibilities raised by the nonexistence of the comity agreement when graduates of the Farmington mission school approached them during the Ganado meeting to ask why the Methodists had no churches on the Reservation. "We took this back to the annual conference," Elkins said, "and it got interested in establishing local churches." District Superintendent Blanton began to run with the idea, but he was soon transferred to Oklahoma.

The first step in escalating delivery of God's Word to the Reservation was to expand the existing work at Bistahi, though the outpost was not officially recognized as a church. Bistahi operated as a three-way collaborative effort: the mission school provided supportive services and some of the pastor's expenses, and acted as fiscal agent for the Bistahi work; the annual conference made preaching available; and the National Division contributed part of the pastor's pay.[4]

Reverend Yazzie was appointed in 1971 to work with a GBGM Women's Division project at Bistahi and to preach there. The division, through the mission school and in collaboration with the annual conference, launched a program called the United Methodist Navajo Ministry. It soon foundered as a separate entity, though some work at Bistahi continued until the National Division decided to end it and leave. In 1979, the National Division advised the Women's Division that the program that had been carried on at the property had been discontinued. It was during this time that Chee Benallie came to serve as Yazzie's replacement.[5] The Women's Division ultimately took steps to rid itself of all interests in the land. (See details in chapter 15).

By the time the New York organizations pulled out, the Four Corners Native American Ministry had been formed and was looking past Bistahi into a future filled with Navajo United Methodist churches on the Reservation. The Ministry soon found that, with the work in the hands of local indigenous people who felt a call from God to evangelize, the boundaries of the New Mexico Annual Conference could not hold back the spread of God's Word to Navajos who wanted to hear it, any more than a state line drawn on a map could hold back the wind.

## CHAPTER ELEVEN

# "I Ironed My Cotton Dress and Went Again"

*Who shall separate us from the love of Christ?*

—Romans 8:35

In 1966, with the churches at Shiprock and Bistahi up and running, a third group of Navajo Methodist worshippers, most of them graduates of the Farmington mission school, began to meet for prayer and singing in various homes in Window Rock, Arizona. They were backed by Albuquerque District Superintendent Dr. Charles Thigpen, who viewed them as an outreach of his district. As the numbers of worshipping Christians increased, they moved to the Window Rock Recreation Hall, from there to the Window Rock Motor Inn, then to the library at tribal headquarters.

Joe Washington, a Choctaw Indian, was installed as the first lay preacher for the Window Rock church. By 1969, the small-but-thriving congregation had persuaded the tribal government to let them lease a tract of land to construct permanent church facilities just off Navajo Tribal Highway 12, located on the north end of town.

During the tenure of Chee Benallie as its lay pastor, the church surged for a time in 1977, when the indomitable Henry C. Begay pitched the tent provided by Four Corners Ministry and preached nightly revivals in Window Rock. Three years later he returned, this time to pastor the church his tent ministry had helped encourage. He stayed for sixteen years, until 1996.[1] By the time Begay settled in as pastor in 1980, the

United Methodists, through the New Mexico Annual Conference, had three functioning Navajo churches.

But the Window Rock church was on the wrong side of the western boundary of the New Mexico Annual Conference and outside the bounds of the South Central Jurisdiction of the church, of which the annual conference was a part. That caused the Western Jurisdiction, in which Window Rock was located, by 1968 to begin to ask questions. For the New Mexico Annual Conference, the issue became whether its lack of authority to start churches in eastern Arizona should be allowed to trump the Navajo desire to hear the Word of God. Conference officials set to work to figure out how to legitimize the Window Rock church as a part of the New Mexico Annual Conference without offending the neighboring Southern California–Arizona Annual Conference, or the Western Jurisdiction of which it was a part.[2]

The New Mexico Annual Conference's investigation revealed that the Methodists of Arizona and the Western Jurisdiction had no activity in an area extending roughly fifty miles into Arizona from the New Mexico border, stretching from Mexico to Utah, and none was planned. The New Mexicans figured there would be no downside to the Methodists of the Southern California–Arizona Conference if the boundaries of the New Mexico Annual Conference were to be extended to include that fifty-mile strip, and the Arizona Methodists agreed.

A resolution permitting the addition of the fifty-mile strip was approved by the New Mexico Annual Conference. Word later came that the Southern California–Arizona Annual Conference had also approved it. The next step to make it official was a resolution presented to the two jurisdictional conferences. Though the South Central Jurisdiction gave its blessing in a resolution adopted on June 26, 1968, the Western Jurisdiction failed to act. Nevertheless, the two adjoining annual conferences considered that the deal had been made. Since 1968, the fifty-mile strip has been treated as part of the New Mexico Annual Conference and reported as such in all journals of the South Central Jurisdiction. The Window Rock church had been legitimized and the door to starting more churches in the area had swung open.

The first report filed by the Four Corners Native American Ministry, carried in the 1979 *Journal of the New Mexico Annual Conference of The United Methodist Church*, detailed the condition of the little church: "The Window Rock church has had a hard struggle to survive."[3] Not long after, however, the church in the Navajo capital came out of its doldrums.

In collaboration with the mission school in Farmington, the New Mexico Annual Conference started what it called the "Navajo Mobile Ministry" in 1968. Then, in 1970, the Ministry bought a truck specially built so that one side could be lowered, exposing a chancel for worship purposes. The vehicle also had rudimentary living facilities to accommodate the needs of its driver/preacher. The purchase price was paid in part by a grant from the Women's Division, with the balance raised within the Albuquerque District.

The truck began to roll over the Reservation roads, setting up wherever its annual conference–appointed driver, the Rev. Larry Kent, figured he could attract a handful of Navajos. But the effort failed; Navajos were not interested in gathering at a truck parked at a crossroads to hear an Anglo preacher exhort them in English. Another flaw in the mobile ministry plan could not be cured by switching to a Navajo-speaking driver: the truck was too fragile to navigate the never-ending rocky roads of the Reservation and too vulnerable to the sand and dust borne by the endless winds. By 1973, the vehicle was unusable, having been beaten and shaken to pieces.

The annual conference had relearned the lesson that it was critical for Navajos to preach to other Navajos in their own language if any were to listen. Kent continued to work among the Navajos, for a time preaching at Bistahi, and later serving as superintendent of the Methodist Mission School in Farmington.

*Philip Begay teaches at Window Rock United Methodist Church.*

During its brief operation, the mobile ministry had managed to establish a preaching point in the late 1960s, in Crownpoint, New Mexico. Initially, Methodists met in the town hall, then the conference acquired a mobile home and a double-wide mobile chapel with the hope that Crownpoint would soon warrant a full-time pastor.

A small congregation led by Fred Yazzie struggled there until 1969, when the Albuquerque district superintendent decided that the Crownpoint mobile home and double-wide chapel could be better utilized in Window Rock. The two structures were dragged off to the newly acquired land in the Navajo capital, and the local congregation moved into the facilities. The tiny Crownpoint congregation was so displeased at being cast out of its place of worship that the group ceased to exist with any Methodist connection.

During the few years of the mobile ministry's activities, outreach through the Shiprock church was progressing. In 1964, Rev. Robert Brooks was replaced in the Shiprock pulpit by two pastors serving in successive short-term appointments. They were followed by Rev. Maurice Haines in 1967, who stayed until 1975. Though Haines was a self-effacing, quiet individual, he was an inspired recruiter under whose leadership the church in Shiprock grew to over 230 members.

One member of the Shiprock congregation, Eleanor Clah, told of the reverend's persistence. The stately lady, in traditional Navajo dress and with sparkling black eyes, explained that when she was nine she had attended school on the Ute Reservation in Colorado, and she also took care of the family sheep. Her grandfather was a medicine man, who taught her that "the Book" was "only for the white man and not for the Navajos because we have our own religion."

Years later, Clah jumped through a window to take her children away from her abusive, alcoholic husband. With no support, she worked as a janitor:

> We were very poor. Reverend Haines came and invited me to church. I said I was too poor. He said the Lord did not care. He will take you as you are. So I went. Then I stopped [going] because I did not think I fit in. Reverend Haines [returned and] asked me to come back. So I ironed my cotton dress and went again. Then I accepted Jesus Christ, and I taught in the Sunday school.

Clah sent her children to the mission school, and she enrolled in a Bible school in Cortez, Colorado, so she could learn more about that "Book." Speaking again of her grandfather, the medicine man, Eleanor Clah said, "He was wrong. The Bible is for everybody." Clah became a leader in the church at Shiprock, and a hard-working and persuasive board member of the Four Corners Native American Ministry.

Of the Ministry, she noted, "Paul West has been a blessing. He has stayed."

Another individual who was influenced by Haines was Chee Benallie, an armed forces veteran who had served in Australia in the 1940s. When his enlistment ran out, he took a job training machinists in the aerospace industry in California. A few years later, he returned home to Shiprock. He then took up alcohol, even though he'd had a spiritual vision while in California that featured John Wesley, the Holy Spirit, and a horde of people marching four abreast into a smoking pit.

He told this story of becoming a follower of Christ:

> The minister came after me. I was drunk. . . . He said, "Come to church. Is your name Chee?" I said, "Yeah." He said, "Come to church." And I didn't know him, that Reverend Haines. I said, "No, I been drinking last night, I smell like beer." He said, "That's all right. You tell me what you think of my preaching." So he took me and dragged me here, to this church, at that time.

Benallie hoped to make it a one-time appearance. But Haines picked up Benallie and dragged him to church Sunday after Sunday, until he finally decided there was no use resisting. When Benallie gave up drinking and surrendered himself to the Lord on February 14, 1971, "He started training me to preach, and I took training. . . . When I started preaching it was real easy . . . they sent me to the church in Window Rock, in 1977."

Benallie would be one of the founders of the Four Corners Native American Ministry, and one of its most effective recruiters and church-starters.

Meanwhile, up the road, changes were brewing near Farmington.

## CHAPTER TWELVE

# The School Edges Toward Change

*Guard the truth
that has been entrusted to you . . .*

—2 Timothy 1:14

It was during the tenure of Reverend Haines at the Methodist Mission School in Farmington that attitudes that would change the shape of the school began to take root. It was a half-dozen years or so after Dr. Brodace Elkins and the rest of the contingent from New Mexico took part in the conference held in Ganado.

In 1941, mission school Superintendent Rev. C. C. Brooks had described the mission of the school: "The comprehensive purpose of mission work [at the school] is to make Christ known as the Saviour and Master of individual human lives and His truth the guide to all social relationships."[1] The school began to inch away from that position when changes in perceptions toward Native Americans swept across the land in the early seventies, right about the time that the Rev. Rodney Roberts became school superintendent.

Roberts moved from the pulpit of the First United Methodist Church in Aztec, New Mexico, to the superintendency of the school in 1970, where he remained until 1973. Rodney Roberts died in 2002, survived by his wife, Joan Roberts. She taught high school English at the mission school during her husband's tenure, and was later ordained as a United Methodist clergyperson after the couple had left the school.

The Rev. Joan Roberts remembered the period while her husband was superintendent as one during which Native American activists and the issues they focused on were just beginning to catch on with the mainstream media. The publicity reached as far as Farmington, New Mexico, where it was soaked up by students at the mission school. When questioned in 2003 about those years, she said:

> That was a time when books like *Bury My Heart at Wounded Knee* and some of the Native American activists' writings were just beginning to appear. At the same time, the parents of many of our kids were very much tradition-alists. And . . . some of our kids, especially when they got into high school, there was some conflict for them, and it was difficult for them to deal with because they wanted to move into more of an active role in their heritage, which hadn't been a part of the school before.

The attitude of the Board of Global Ministries toward the school also began to change. It wanted to edge the institution "in a more independent direction," according to Roberts. "Independent" meant more self-sufficient in funding, as she understood the board's position:

> The other problem, and it wasn't just while we were there, it had been a problem there and it still continues to be, continues to be in whatever work is there on that campus— United Methodist work—is funding for mission projects. It was very difficult to come by, and you had to fight for it. At the same time . . . if you raised money on your own, they cut off what they were sending you.

While Rodney Roberts was superintendent, the slippage at the school was barely noticeable, but in a decade it became as relentless as an avalanche. Eventually, it would lead to a far different institution than it had been. As seen by observers at the Four Corners Native American Ministry board, the issue became one of survival of anything at all that was United Methodist-connected on the campus.

But while the school was blending into the culture, the work on the Reservation through the First United Methodist Church, Shiprock, and the New Mexico Annual Conference was building momentum. That work, too, would turn into an avalanche of sorts, but it would move in a direction 180 degrees away from the direction the school took. Much of its initial momentum would come from the base of devoted Navajos recruited by the Rev. Maurice Haines.

## CHAPTER THIRTEEN

# This Place is a Mission Field

*The harvest is plentiful,*
*but the laborers are few . . .*

—Luke 10:2

Although Reverend Haines was nearing the end of his tenure at the church in Shiprock, during January of 1975 he was a key figure in putting together the Consultation on Ministries with the Navajos meeting. Twenty-seven persons appeared for the consultation, including Bishop Alsie H. Carleton, the resident bishop of the New Mexico and Northwest Texas Annual Conferences. Other representatives and officials of both those conferences attended, as did persons from various tribal entities, including the Navajo Health Authority, the Tribal Council, the Navajo Alcoholism Council, the Tribal Museum, and the Navajo Division of Education. A representative of the Board of Global Ministries in New York came, as did a BIA official and Rev. Fred Yazzie.

At the consultation, Yazzie summarized his preaching work at Bistahi, and his efforts at helping Navajos get transportation for health care and also help to read mail written in English. Next, Haines reported that the Shiprock church was under Navajo lay leadership at that time. He warned that the churches in both Shiprock and Window Rock were located in communities strongly influenced by Anglo culture. Navajos living in those areas had grown accustomed to the ways of the white man, he explained, and that would impact the type of outreach to which the local Navajo population would respond. The churches in those locations, he said, must develop and train Navajo leaders in ways far different than those who worked for churches located farther from the Reservation border. Those remote churches that serve only Navajos, Haines said, many of whom speak only Navajo and have no understanding of the dominant Anglo culture, will require indigenous leaders who know their people and speak their language.

After hearing from tribal representatives who summarized the Reservation's demographics and their significance to the population and to the church, the group discussed the status quo. It didn't take long to decide that the present pattern for Methodist work on the Reservation should be scrapped, and the sooner changes started, the better. A pilot project should be created to kick off a new style of work, one to reach out to the Navajos and help bring about self-determination, one that would serve both youth and older generations.[1]

The sparks struck by the consultation were carried back to the bishop's cabinet, which was still buzzing at the reports of the meeting at Ganado. Albuquerque District Superintendent Bervin Caswell was instructed to begin searching for a trained missionary as leader for an outreach to the Navajos. The hunt led to home missionary Paul N. West, who was attending a youth conference in Oklahoma while on leave from Malaysia. Caswell offered him the Shiprock church, and Reverend West and his family were soon on their way to New Mexico.

West, his call to serve Asians now morphed into a calling to minister to the Navajos, soon replaced Haines in the pulpit at Shiprock. It would be a learning experience for West, and when he asked the conference for orientation, he found it would be a do-it-yourself effort or nothing at all. He would have to teach himself the ropes through on-the-job training. West asked for a copy of the National Division's policy on Indian missions. Though The United Methodist Church had been involved in ministry to Native Americans for well over a hundred years, the agency told him there was no existing policy, but a manual was "in process." Then came the bad news. Though the National Division had picked West to send to New Mexico when Caswell called in search of a missionary pastor for Shiprock, the division discouraged work with Native Americans by white pastors.

West's first step was to familiarize himself with the culture and the needs of the people he was to serve. His cross-cultural communication training at Asbury Seminary would be useful, but he knew he could accomplish nothing until he earned the trust of his parishioners. Becoming acculturated to the Navajo way of thinking did not come overnight for the white pastor who had spent ten years in the mission field in Malaysia.

In a 2003 interview of both Paul and Dorcas West, he explained:

> [My wife, Dorcas, and I] used to think [the Malaysians and the Navajos] were similar, but they weren't. So then we went into culture shock. It wasn't right away. But the more we found out about the Reservation, the more we questioned how in the world this place could exist right in the United States, where people didn't have water and electricity. And the telephone system was actually worse than in Malaysia. I mean, it broke down more times and they had more problems with it.

Adjustment to a society that lacked water, electricity, and telephones was not the biggest challenge. For Dorcas West, it was the language. "The language, at the time we went [to Shiprock], was 65 percent did not speak English, so it was a much higher percent than in Malaysia. I mean, Malaysia was a British protectorate." Both Wests studied Navajo for a time, and learned the phonetics of the language reasonably well; both eventually read and sang Navajo well enough not to be embarrassed at a songfest. When Four Corners Navajos told them that learning the language would require repeating each and every word seventy-five times, and also possessing a good ear for distinguishing the two tones the language uses, the Wests understood why the learning curve was steep.

But language limitations were not going to hold Reverend West back. He thought he had figured out a way to reach the

Navajos. In West's view, "poverty was the biggest problem. And so I started attacking that." For months, beginning a year or so after his arrival, West worked to persuade the tribal government to permit use of an empty factory on the Reservation for reproducing blueprints that were being sent by West's uncle, a California businessman, to Hong Kong for hand copying. West hoped that Navajos could be hired to do the copy work, and unemployment and poverty would be alleviated, at least in one Reservation community. He soon learned the frustrations of dealing with tribal and government officials:

> And, I thought everybody would jump for this. But nobody did. Like, they don't want this. I mean, they're not helping, there's no encouragement. The BIA and the tribe have all these regulations that discourage anybody. To try to get a building or land takes you five to ten years. They have all those regulations. And then—the local people themselves. They didn't want change . . . I thought, *Boy, what am I doing here?*

The stone wall they had run into was a low point in the ministry of Paul and Dorcas West. But they held fast to their roots of faith:

> Well, you know, when you pray, sometimes you get an answer, and God talks back to you. And He said, "That's not why you're here anyway. Not to change the people. Not to change the economy, or not to change the way they are. Your job here is to share Jesus Christ and His love with these people. And that's why you're here. Now, can you do that?"

That changed the picture, West explained, and he stopped worrying about employment issues.

> And about the same time I discovered in . . . [*The Navajos are Coming to Jesus*], a [chapter] that explained the two value systems. One was the dominant society, they call it. The dominant society value system is: 1) money, 2) education, 3) a career, 4) owning your own home and land, and 5) your family. So that's the way of the dominant society.

The Wests had been in Shiprock long enough to have learned that Anglo society values did not mean much to Navajo worshippers in the Shiprock church. They had their own values, and a white Methodist preacher was not about to change them. But West was more than willing to learn from the Navajos themselves, and from others who had studied Navajo society and their love of Jesus. West's studies soon taught him the ways in which Navajo values differed:

> But Navajos are completely different [according to Dolaghan and Scates]: 1) their family, 2) their hogan, 3) their sheep, 4) their pickup [truck], and 5) their turquoise and silver jewelry. I really didn't realize I was so much of the dominant society until I saw how I was judging them on how they handled money.

West concluded that money was not even in the Navajo value system, nor was how they handle a job, except for sheep herding and jewelry making:

> So I realized I was up here judging them with Anglo standards, and once I came down here and looked straight in their eyes and said: "I understand where you're coming from," then I was changed. Family is the most important . . . is really of great value, but . . . there are some problems with family. Families always have some problems. We found that out when we started the thrift shop, we started the home for women, we started the alcohol counseling center—and all of those related to family. They all took off.

West learned a great lesson that would result in one victory after another in bringing the Word and work of Jesus Christ to the Reservation. "Any time you work with families, they're going to respond."

But West's growing understanding of the Navajos could not have moved forward into effective action without the help and support of Rev. Fred W. Yazzie. Early on, they agreed that the Reservation did not lack for opportunities for the work of the Lord through two missionary-thinking United Methodist pastors. West recalled what he and Yazzie had talked about:

> Talking to Fred Yazzie, I said, "To me, it looks like a mission
> field out here. What do you think, as a Navajo?" He said, "It
> is a mission field. . . . That's how I see it." And that's how
> we decided to get together and start the Four Corners
> Ministry for mission outreach on the Reservation.

As they talked and prayed, it was obvious to West and Yazzie
that the three churches located in Shiprock, Bistahi, and
Window Rock were in a slump. They weren't reaching out
and were not bringing in new people. Their original enthusiasm
had flagged. West had held Maurice Haines' former pulpit for
three years by this time. It had been long enough for West to
have studied the dynamics of the three Navajo congregations—
with Yazzie's help in understanding the culture, and with the
encouragement of congregational members who took West
under their wings.

To the two clergymen, there was nothing wrong that an
infusion of prayer, a plan, and the inspired energy of the right
people to do the work could not cure. A reversal of fortune for
the churches began to come together in early 1975, but the
turnaround would take time. West and Yazzie believed they had
a handle on what was wrong: they needed to raise up trained
indigenous leaders who would inspire others in the work of the
Lord, and the churches should be connected together for
support and encouragement. West and Yazzie had the patience
needed for the task. It was time to take the first step.

They decided to pull a small group together and work up
the details of a plan. They set about to do just that, and after
the March 1977 meeting at the Shiprock parsonage, Methodist
work on the Reservation would never again be the same.

But while they were beginning to wrestle with these issues,
the Holy Spirit was moving on the Reservation in ways in which
the two United Methodist clergymen could not have dreamed.

CHAPTER FOURTEEN
# Shirley John
# Begins Her Journey

*Follow me.*
—Luke 9:23

It was in the dead of winter of the year Rev. Paul West brought his family to Shiprock, in the middle of a night so black a Navajo blanket might have been thrown over the stars, that Shirley John sat on a boulder the size of a car. A few feet below her, on the flat sand of a dry streambed that made a passable road, half a dozen pickups were parked. Occasional pops and cracks from their engines as they cooled in the frigid air were the only sounds that interrupted the silence.

The site for the night's activities was a hogan planted on a plateau a short climb and a hike of a hundred yards from the stream bed. From John's view, the structure was visible only now and then, by the glow of cedar embers rising out of the smoke hole at its top. Through the haze of the liquor that filled her, she struggled to focus her eyes in the direction of the hogan, for it was her job, as the designated look-out, to stay alert and watch.

John hadn't been told by the group inside the hogan just what she was to look out for, but she knew. Though it was her first visit to the place, she understood that what was going on inside was against the law. She also knew that sometimes the feds or the tribal police would swoop in and scoop up a handful of Navajos who were practicing just such a ritual. They'd be charged with possession, and maybe distribution, of an illegal substance— peyote—a hallucinogenic drug that induced the visions so essential to the practice of the rites. In a few years, Congress would legalize the use of peyote for religious purposes, but on that starless night there was no thought of what a faraway legislative body might do; there was only the fear of getting caught.

There was little use scanning for intruders when she could see only the dim outline of her hand before her face, so Shirley John sat there on the cold rock and listened. She listened, pulled her J. C. Penney blanket tighter around her neck, and wondered why she had been picked to come out to that rocky place. Maybe it was because she was a medicine woman and the granddaughter of a medicine man and a medicine woman; maybe it was because she often led the dances—the *yei be che* and the fire dance. Whatever the reason, evidently the people thought she could be trusted, even though they knew she was a drunk—so much a drunk that she bragged that her rap sheet for alcohol-related offenses was longer than her arm, and that the lawmen had had to build jails just for her in Window Rock, and also in Chinle, Arizona, just so she could sleep off her drunken stupors in a place warmer than an alleyway.

So she stared blindly into the black shroud of the night—and then something happened. Here's how John described it during an interview:

> And there was a hand, and a human head. And it said, "Go to them. To those people. They are devils, and they are evil." And I thought to myself, *It's none of my business to argue with those people inside. What a fight there would be.* And when I turned, the hand gripped me. And then, I froze. I was so scared I couldn't move. And a voice said, "Don't go to the left, don't go to the right, but go forward." That was the message. And then the arms pushed me, threw me back and forth, and pushed me toward the door, all the way. I couldn't turn.
>
> When I came to the door, I knocked. I wasn't thinking about the person that was pushing me. I wasn't thinking when I opened the door. The minute I opened the door, there was a bunch of people inside there, looking at me. I said, "You people are not doing right. You people are just

being wicked. *Out*, every one of you should get out *now*. So *get out now*. Just *get out*." And so they did.

And this was supposed to be, to them, really sacred, and me coming in there was against their religion. But I told them that, and everybody was outta there. And I thought, *Well, what did I do? What happened?* But the people in there, they didn't complete the ceremony all the way. I'd stopped them.

Shirley John didn't know it yet, but she had just taken the first step on her way to a new life. In another two decades, the one-time medicine woman would make a plea to the board of directors of the Four Corners Native American Ministry that was formed in the living room of West's parsonage shortly after her nighttime adventure. But first, she had a journey to travel, and the Holy Spirit had to work within her for a while.

CHAPTER FIFTEEN

# What Do You Do When the Stream Runs Dry?

*Increase our faith!*

—Luke 17:5

During the two months that followed the March 1977 organizational meeting at the parsonage of the Shiprock church, the new Ministry put a board of directors in place. It was 90 percent Navajo, setting the pattern for indigenous leadership that had been identified as key to the success of the Ministry. Also in 1977, Chee D. Benallie was appointed to serve as lay pastor to the Window Rock church.

The board of the brand new Four Corners Native American Ministry went to work. The strategy it followed had been worked out by Rev. Paul West in the absence of guidance from the National Division or the annual conference. He relied on the work of Roland Allen's *Missionary Methods: St. Paul's or Ours?*,[1] and pored through other books addressing the development of an indigenous church, confirming in the process the lessons he was learning from the Navajo people.

The board embraced the principle of indigenous leadership. They were already part-way home with that portion of the plan, for when West had arrived in Shiprock, the administrative board at First United Methodist Church was exclusively Navajo, many of whom had graduated from the mission school.

By the end of 1977, the new Four Corners board had settled on a plan of ministry, embodied in a document titled "A Proposal for a New Ministry Among Native Americans." The proposal outlined a joint venture between the New Mexico Conference and the National Division of the Board of Global Ministries. The National Division was never drawn into the work, and the proposal was never published outside the board, yet it supplied a framework on which the Ministry's work would grow.

At the time the proposal was written, the work in Window Rock was all but dead, and the Bistahi outpost was still not a constituted church. The conference had inherited the Bistahi complex consisting of a house, garage, gymnasium, and a three-classroom unit, left behind by the mission school when it withdrew to Farmington. The land belonged to the National Division, and there were rumors that the real estate and improvements were going to be turned back to the original owner, leaving the conference work high and dry. In the midst of all these storm clouds, however, the new Four Corners Native American Ministry board of directors focused on "future possibilities."

The board spotted those possibilities in the facts that: population on the Reservation was growing, the tribe was

*From* Journal of the New Mexico Annual Conference. *1977 pp. 68–69.*

| 1977 APPOINTMENTS [RELATING TO THE FOUR CORNERS WORK] ALBUQUERQUE DISTRICT | |
|---|---|
| District Superintendent | Edward E. Hamilton |
| Shiprock | Paul N. West |
| Window Rock | (Chee Benallie)* |
| SPECIAL APPOINTMENTS FOUR CORNERS NATIVE AMERICAN TEAM | |
| Ministry | Fred W. Yazzie |

*( ) denotes local pastor*

about to open ten thousand acres of farmland to irrigation just south of Farmington every year for the next ten years, a coal gasification plant was to open soon on the New Mexico side of the Reservation, and new towns were to be built near each of these projects. Not only would the commercial activities produce concentrations of Diné to be reached, but there were still the tens of thousands of Navajos on the Reservation who were mired in those traditional, animistic-spirit worship practices that so troubled Reverend Yazzie and the lay pastors.

The challenge of taking Jesus Christ to the new communities and also to the population in the Reservation's interior seemed overwhelming. First, the board had to figure out how to pull the existing struggling churches together, and how to provide consistent and continuous leadership support for each small group of believers. While the new communities would have higher concentrations of people, they would be more urbanized, more resistant to the "white man's religion," than those who lived further inside the Reservation. Could they be reached through churches near their homes, providing family-like gatherings, and perhaps including some preaching in English?

The possibility of using local residents as part-time pastors to shepherd small churches, perhaps even hogan chapels, located in or near small family settlements, seemed doable. Many people were living much as they had when Kit Carson attempted to round up Navajos over a century earlier—residing in scattered hogans nearly invisible in the vastness of the space. The hogans were collected together, if at all, in small family clusters of half a dozen or fewer structures, including a brush arbor used as a summer house. The families could form the nuclei of small churches or worship groups, and leaders could be developed within the little family clusters.

A team ministry concept of local, part-time volunteer pastors seemed to be the model that would fit all the demands—if they could just put it together. The board laid out the steps: working laypersons would be trained, and each would

pastor a small parish; a tent ministry would rally local popula-
tions to come to Jesus; once interest had been developed,
worship groups would be formed; the various groups of
worshippers would get together periodically and exchange
ideas, pray, eat, sing, worship, and have a good time; there would
be training at these meetings, and everyone would get to feel
part of a larger worshipping family; animistic teachings of the
medicine men would be refuted; the fear of evil spirits would be
cast out, and replaced by love; qualified church leaders would
be put in place; the affairs of the local churches would be overseen through sharing; and nonbelievers would be evangelized.

It was not a coincidence that the operation as visualized would
be a lot like the first-century evangelization of Macedonia and
Achaia and the oversight of the church in Ephesus, tracking the
advice outlined by the apostle Paul for the young Timothy. The
board had resolved to "Fight the good fight, holding on to faith and
a good conscience" (1 Timothy 1:18–19 NIV).

Now that the direction had been set, the work at Bistahi,
Window Rock, and Shiprock would no longer be the only focal
points. A tent ministry would hit the reservation roads, stopping
where the Spirit directed. It would help pioneer new churches
near the sites where the tent was pitched. Local Christians
would be inspired to get busy for their Lord.

But no sooner had the direction been set than the work at
Bistahi was threatened with extinction. When the National
Division and the Women's Division had decided they could no
longer support the work at that location, the result was that the
real estate would be forfeited to the original owner. The board
members got back down on their knees. When the praying
ended, the board voted on what to do, and then they instructed
West to follow through.

West recalled that a letter he had written on September 18,
1979, to Joel Martinez at the General Board of Global Ministries,
recorded the lengths to which the Four Corners Ministry was
willing to go in order to save the Bistahi property for serving the
Navajo people. The document recited that the Ministry board had

said, with no equivocation, "the church work at Bisti [*sic*] will be carried on."

Yazzie was appointed to serve the Bistahi congregation full time and to live on the premises. District Superintendent Ed Hamilton called a charge conference to be held in Bistahi in October. After subsequent visits to the site in August and September by Ministry director West, Hamilton concluded "that the [Bistahi] people are once again beginning to make full use of the facilities and the church attendance is strong once more."

The Bistahi people called on the two GBGM Divisions to give them independence in using the Bistahi property to develop programs and services to meet the needs of the local people. They asked the division to "put control of the property in the hands of the people the property was intended to serve." It was not to be.

Legal issues surrounding the reversion of the property to the original owners came to a boil shortly after the National Division and the mission school withdrew. Despite pleas from the Ministry, the New Mexico Annual Conference, and the National Division, legal counsel for GBGM balked, saying the Bistahi people's wishes did not matter; the property had to be returned to the original owner. The lawyers blamed their opinion on a reversionary clause in the deed that provided for its return to the original seller if it should ever cease to be used for a mission. The General Board's lawyer said occupancy by a mission organization of the annual conference would not satisfy the restriction. The real estate was lost to the church.

Nevertheless, the Four Corners board, the annual conference, and Yazzie believed the community held potential for winning Navajo converts to Jesus Christ. West went to work negotiating with the owner to whom the title had reverted. The plan was consummated by purchase of five acres, at two thousand dollars per acre, a hefty sum for desert land, especially for a ministry that was struggling for its very survival. By that time, squatters had taken over the former Bistahi outpost buildings, requiring their eviction and restoration of the improvements they had trashed. Bistahi became something of a symbol of the possibilities for the fledgling ministry, though the flush of success resulting from the rescue soon faded.

Despite the fact that the Bistahi land issue had been put to rest, the board of the Four Corners Ministry did not find that its path was now smooth. In January 1979, the money crunch was so severe that West wrote to Yazzie that no church in the Four Corners Ministry was able to support him. If the money supply didn't improve, he had five alternatives, none of which was to stay with the Four Corners Ministry. One of the options was to take sick leave, since Yazzie was ill at the time. But fortunes eventually changed, and the crisis passed. It was as West had said, "We can do anything with prayer and faith." On the Reservation, it was nothing new for the streams to dry up; but eventually, they always ran again.

Every alternative for funding was considered by the Ministry in the late 1970s and early 1980s, including seeking grants. At first, such easy money seemed appealing, but West warned that chasing after grant money could lead the Ministry into a dependency from which the stress of withdrawal would more than offset the temporary rush brought by a short-term injection of cash.

West described his longtime stand on grant money as a tempting source of support, and the pitfalls in accepting grants:

> There's been some criticisms [of the Ministry's view of grants] from those even in mission circles. I feel [these indigenous churches] need to be self-supporting, and that came out of my lessons with the boards [that] made grants. The grants are given for three years, and reduced each year. That was from . . . the General Board of Religion and Race. They would give you, like, fifteen thousand dollars the first year. Second, ten thousand, and third, five thousand. Fourth year, you're on your own.

West described why grants would be the ruination of the Ministry:

> Here you are, you get fifteen thousand dollars—you think
> you're rich. Then you get ten thousand. By the time of your
> fourth year you're poor again. That's not the answer on the
> Reservation. . . . You've got to start with nothing and
> develop it on your own. From your own resources. You
> can't depend on outside resources.

From his own experiences as a foreign missionary, West knew
that even the Board of Global Ministries did not have an inex-
haustible supply of money:

> [If] they run into hard times, they're going to cut back. I
> told the Board, "You can't depend on them, you can't
> depend on any of them." So basically, I went for grants at
> first, and we got several. But after that, I said, "This is not
> working, the people are looking to the grants, just like
> they've looked to historic mission [supporting organiza-
> tions]" and said to them, "We're a mission, you have to
> support us." I said [to the board], "No."

Most of the members of the Board paid attention to what
West was saying and swallowed the temptation to go after grants.
But a handful of people from Bistahi didn't buy in. West
recalled, "Some of the people [on the board from Bistahi], they
talked the talk: 'Well, we're a mission. We were started by the
mission school. We need help. You're to help us.' And [there was]
no help-yourself idea." Eventually, they proved West's point by
sitting idle and waiting for someone to come along and help.
"And so, twenty-five years [later], they still have ten or fifteen
people. They haven't grown. They still have the same mentality."
One of the grants that the Ministry applied for and received
early in its existence was from the General Board of Global
Ministries. The amount was fifteen thousand dollars, sent to the
annual conference treasurer in monthly payments for distribution
to the Ministry for 1978. Notification of the award was sent on
January 2, 1978, to Dr. Brodace Elkins, chair of the conference's
Board of Missions, who would soon become Albuquerque district
superintendent, with a passion for placing Navajo churches. At
the time, Elkins was also a director of the New York–based Board

of Global Ministries. With that connection, and agreeing with West's assessment of the perils in relying on grant money, Elkins was able to steer the Ministry in the direction of seeking funding from another, more reliable, source through that board.

The alternative to grant money was contributions made by individuals who had a personal interest in supporting the Navajo work. Elkins knew how to tap the source through a program of the General Board of Global Ministries called the Advance for Christ. Working with West, Elkins sought approval of the Four Corners Ministry as a recipient.

Advance for Christ is a system of giving set up in The United Methodist Church's *Book of Discipline*, the collection of legislation passed by the church's General Conference as laws addressing the polity and governance of the church. Through this program, donors may make contributions through their local churches that are earmarked for specific ministries or missions. Collections are funneled from the local church treasurers through the annual conference treasurers, transmitted to the General Board of Global Ministries, then ultimately paid to the designated ministry. The convoluted pipeline the money flows through is designed to improve accountability by providing oversight through the General Board.

The Four Corners board went for it. With the cooperation of the New Mexico Annual Conference and the Albuquerque District, the Ministry sent an application to the Board of Global Ministries. The Ministry was ultimately approved as a recipient of Advance for Christ giving. The help provided, however, would be no better than the base of donors, and it would take time for that base to be developed. One addition to the base came through help from an unexpected source—though it was a source that from time to time was a burr under the saddle of the church hierarchy that rode herd on mission outreach ministries.

The September 1979 newsletter, *Good News*, published by the Forum for Scriptural Renewal, carried a column titled "4-Corners Ministry—A Chance for You." *Good News* was, and is, an unofficial organization tied to United Methodism by virtue of its claim to be a renewal ministry within The United Methodist Church aimed at its evangelical members. The newsletter reported that the organization's board of directors had "adopted 4-Corners Native American Ministry as a home mission project [to] recommend to our evangelical constituency." At the time, according to the writer of the column, only 10 percent of the Navajos were Christian, yet "this underfinanced Ministry" aimed to bring Jesus Christ to the largest reservation in the country by developing local indigenous churches.

For the underfinancing, the newsletter blamed the National Division of the General Board of Global Ministries, while reporting that the New Mexico Conference could no longer support the Ministry either and was about to take "drastic action." Paul West was reported as saying the need of the Ministry was for "everything." West's address and phone number were listed.[2]

The column drew a reaction from the superintendent of the Methodist Mission School in Farmington. Reverend Hector M. Navas wrote to West, reminding him that the National Division had given the Ministry over $25,000, that the Women's Division had contributed over $10,000, and that both the National Division and the annual conference had listed the Ministry as an Advance Special Project. The year before, Navas continued, the Northwest Texas Conference, part of the same Episcopal Area in which New Mexico was situated, gave $37,144.40, and $25,137.44 was received from the New Mexico Annual Conference.

West did not need to be reminded; he and the Four Corners Board had worked hard to establish the credibility to earn that support. West responded by pointing out to Navas that he had not written the article. His only part, he wrote, had been to respond to a phone call from the staff writer who drafted it. West had been given no opportunity to verify the article's accuracy.

So West and the board continued efforts to boost the Ministry's credibility and to expand its base of support. They accepted contributions from every donor who cared enough to send money, whether the giver carried a *Good News* or the General Church banner. It was a matter of necessity, rather than one of choosing what side to be on in a battle between denominational factions.

Progress was slow while the Ministry took tentative steps, careful not to overload the system it was building for placing churches and winning converts. Its movement was by trial and error, but the one-step-at-time advances were just fine with the Ministry board of directors, for on the Reservation, and to the Navajo board members, time did not mean much. West and Yazzie resisted all efforts by outsiders to calculate the success or failure of the Ministry based on time. The Four Corners Native American Ministry set about to work methodically in the name of Jesus Christ, applying slow-moving Reservation time.

Their outreach had to fit the culture, so the Ministry could reach out to those buried in Navajo culture, bringing them to new light. The Ministry had to learn to reach people like—well, like Shirley John, who was still having adventures that would eventually lead her to the Four Corners Native American Ministry.

CHAPTER SIXTEEN

# The Light by the Woodpile

*A great light from heaven*
*suddenly shone about me.*

—Acts 22:6

Despite what happened to her that dark night on the Reservation, Shirley John continued in her old ways, though she sometimes paused to remember. Try as she might, she just could not reconcile what had happened with anything in any experience she'd ever had. And the medicine men she consorted with could give her no answer. So her drinking continued; she led the dances; she collected medicine woman fees for banishing spells, performing rituals, and for magical healing that helped only her pocketbook; she hung out with the guys, and she spent a lot of time in the two jails that had been built "just for her."

But she knew that all was not well with her heart. John knew she wasn't behaving like most Navajo women. She recalled: "I was wearing pants, and I had short hair. I wasn't a lady. I was acting like men. Running around with guys instead of ladies." It was then that the voice she had heard before spoke to her once again:

> A few years later . . . on a February afternoon while I was sitting in the sunshine beside a pile of wood at my aunt's house, I heard the voice again. It said, "Don't go to the left, don't go to the right, don't go back, but go forward." That day, I sensed that the light was brighter than the afternoon, seven times brighter than that day's light. There was a light, and the drunken spirit that resided within had left me.

John shook her head, cleared her eyes, stumbled inside, and babbled her story to her aunt. She sat her down, sifted through the tale, and told her niece about the apostle Paul, who had also seen a bright light in the middle of the day. Her aunt opened the Bible for her to check out the story. There, she said, she found the words of Paul's adventure on the road to Damascus: "About noon a great light from heaven suddenly shone about me. And I fell to the ground and heard a voice saying to me, 'Saul, Saul, why do you persecute me?'" (Acts 22:6–7)

John was convinced that the Holy Spirit had come upon her with a message that was just for her: He was guiding her to walk a straight path forward, a path that did not deviate either to the right or to the left. Willingly, she went with her aunt to a gospel church, where she stood up and gave testimony to what she had experienced.

But her husband was not convinced, even though Shirley John sobered up "just like that," as she put it, for the first time in years. "This is not something that is like what our parents told us," her husband said.

Thoughts of her grandfather came to Shirley John's mind. The recollections of her ancestor brought no comfort:

> We called him a, you know, a Skinwalker. And we knew that was bad. Skinwalkers go out to kill people. And even after they're dead, you go up and cut off a piece of their flesh and dry it up, and you bewitch people with that, and they *die*. That's the way it was.

Despite the pull of the family tie to witchcraft and the power it brought, Shirley John was not about to give up what she'd found:

> "This is from God," I told my husband. He said, "Yes, but we can't see Him." And I said "Yes, but I can feel His voice." And that day, I told my husband that I was already a Christian. I told him, "If you don't want to go along with me, you can go home. If you don't love me, you don't have to follow me."

So he trailed along when his wife went to church one Thursday night, and there, with Shirley John alongside, he had a conversion experience. "I wanted him to be part of this new family," Shirley John said, "so I took him there." She remembers it all as though it were yesterday, though it was nearly three decades ago that she saw the light and began witnessing for the Lord.

So Shirley John began to study the Bible, that Book from which her aunt had led her to read about the light that the apostle Paul had seen. That light, she knew, came from the same source as the light that had bathed her that February afternoon by her aunt's woodpile. And the more she read, the more she wanted to read. She soon found some verses of Scripture in Isaiah 30:20–21 that told her what had happened that dark night on the Reservation when she had been the designated lookout:

> And though the Lord give you the bread of adversity and the water of affliction, yet your Teacher will not hide himself any more, but your eyes shall see your Teacher. And your ears shall hear a word behind you, saying, "This is the way, walk in it," when you turn to the right or when you turn to the left.

For the first time, John understood that the words she had heard out there on the Reservation came from the Teacher, from her Lord Jesus Christ, and that He was telling her she was not to walk to the right or to the left, but in the way He was showing her—straight ahead.

John made some changes. She let her hair grow to the length at which "proper" Navajo ladies wear their hair, braiding it when it got long enough. She got rid of the pants she'd been wearing, and dressed like a Navajo lady, with a full, deep purple skirt that hung in graceful folds, and a long-sleeved velvet blouse that matched. Once more, John began to wear her womanly turquoise and silver jewelry, and to conduct herself like a lady. No longer did she hang out with the men. And even her face— that dark-skinned, angular face—and its black eyes were filled with light, shining with a look of hope, expectation, peace, and purpose that had not previously been there. And the law offi-cers at the jails in Chinle and Window Rock did not see her again, for she was walking the straight course, straying neither to the left nor to the right.

Then John read further in the same chapter of the Book of Isaiah. In the twenty-second verse, she found more to think about: "Then you will defile your silver-covered graven images and your gold-plated molten images. You will scatter them as unclean things; you will say to them, 'Begone!'"

Shortly after reading this, she launched into studying the New Testament, where she discovered more of the same in the Book of Acts. The nineteenth chapter told of new believers coming, "confessing and divulging their practices. And a number of those who practiced magic arts brought their books together and burned them in the sight of all . . . So the word of the Lord grew and prevailed mightily" (Acts. 19:18–20).

It did not take her long to decide that the medicine woman paraphernalia, prayer sticks, cedar shavings, pollen bag, and medicine bag had to go, because the words of Isaiah and of Saint Paul had spoken to her. She got rid of them; no more would they tempt her back into the old religion, away from the Jesus she had found in the black of the Reservation night, and again in the brightest light she would ever experience. John was convinced that it was the Lord's intention that she put away all reminders of the native religion, native gods, and native myths. In time, "Begone!" said to the native religious symbols, was to become a central focus of John's message.

But still, she had not yet heard of the Four Corners Native American Ministry or what it was doing to witness for her Lord. One thing she did know, however, was that she was being called to preach the message about what was lighting her up from inside.

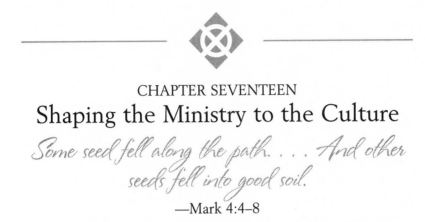

CHAPTER SEVENTEEN

# Shaping the Ministry to the Culture

*Some seed fell along the path. . . . And other seeds fell into good soil.*

—Mark 4:4–8

In striving to understand the Navajos whom Reverend West had come to New Mexico to minister to, it was not long until he came to a revelation:

> It struck me that they were very conservative . . . in their lifestyle, which would be their culture, tradition . . . Conservative [in the sense that they] don't want change. . . . They're all traditional. It's because the white people threaten them, that's for sure. When they came in conflict with the white people, I think it made them even more conservative, more withdrawn. They were hidden, and they were hidden from our society. And even the government couldn't find them all, and didn't care very much. . . . The other was that they were more on the Pentecostal side. Their expression of church. They wanted to clap their hands long before it was in our contemporary style of worship.

West was not alone in his assessment. Reverend Yazzie made a similar (though more detailed) evaluation of his people, supporting his conclusions by referring to the work of Dolaghan and Scates in *The Navajos are Coming to Jesus*. Though the book was published in 1978, Yazzie said that he believed that the categorization of Navajos for evangelism purposes made by the two missionary/anthropologist authors, based on degrees of acculturation, had not changed much in the years since its publication. Yazzie described how Navajos were (and still are) being acculturated to the dominant Anglo culture at different rates. This fact, he believed, made it necessary to tailor the way the message of the Good News of Jesus Christ is delivered, depending on the audience.

Some Navajos, Yazzie said, are "strongly vocal for the preservation of their native culture and strongly resistant to Christianity." While they may have long exposure to the Anglo culture and may have adapted to it, they have moved away from it, and many are "militant anti-Christians, some are members of the American Indian Movement, or AIM. They are not receptive at this time to the Gospel." These people are not likely to live on the Reservation, but may live near it, he said.

Many of the better-educated Navajos react differently to Jesus Christ, according to Yazzie. They may want to return to the old ways, perhaps because somehow they have become so acculturated into the white society that they have lost connection with their people, or never had any connection. Many of these people do not live or work on the Reservation. Some may be the second or third generation to be acculturated. These people may seek to connect with the old ways by rejecting parts of the white man's society they live in. They may not be open to Christianity because it represents some aspects of the white man's society from which they want to turn away. Some, however, may try a type of Christianity that tries to blend the traditional ways—including drums, smoke, and pollen—with Christian worship, in order to regain some sense of identity with their Navajo heritage.

Still another category is those Navajos who are more open to Jesus Christ. These persons will attend church services conducted in English, even though they do not understand the language well. They go because they want to understand it. They are open to Christ's message and to programs that meet their needs.

Other Navajos are mildly anti-Anglo, Yazzie had discovered, or are selective in their Anglo friends. They will go to a church where a Navajo preacher speaks the Navajo language. They know traditional Navajo culture well and are active in the traditional religion. If they are in the peyote movement, they may want to blend elements of the native religion into Christian worship, and are receptive to all religions. These people live on the Reservation, almost all in sheep camps, and they attend revivalist churches.

Yazzie and West concluded that all these factors would affect the outreach of a particular local church. The Ministry would need to develop churches whose character would depend on where each was to be located with reference to the Reservation boundaries, as well as the size of nearby towns and cities. Churches deep in the Reservation, for example, would draw people who live in sheep camps, have little education, and want to hear preaching in Navajo.

It would turn out that much of the Four Corners Ministry would be aimed at this group of Navajos, though churches in Shiprock, Window Rock, and Ojo Amarillo would draw differently acculturated worshippers. The Shiprock church did not offer services in Navajo for more than a dozen years after its opening in 1962. After West was appointed to the church, Navajo services led by Chee Benallie were begun in 1976. The Navajo services consistently drew a larger attendance than the English-language services.

Both Yazzie and West had also found that Navajo Methodists typically don't think the same way about God and how to worship him that other Indians do. The Navajos did not agree with the practice of syncretization, which is the integration or blending of native forms of religious expression—such as the beating of drums and the symbolism of smoke, the pipe, and corn pollen—into Christian worship. West and Yazzie knew that those practices were acceptable to leadership of the NAIC, though they were not deemed appropriate by those who were attracted to the Four Corners Native American Ministry.

West's first lesson in how the Four Corners Navajos felt was learned from experience. He told of the education he had undergone in Oregon in the late 1970s, early in the Ministry's existence, when he took a small group of Navajos to a meeting sponsored by the NAIC. "And I took several to Oregon—I tried to get them into the Caucus. I said, 'We need to be a part of that. They have a lot of money. It ought to be spread around. But if you don't participate, you don't gain.'"

West took Raymond Burke, Benallie, and Henry Begay to the Oregon meeting.

> They had a man from a tribe in Oregon who had lost their federal recognition as a tribe. They had sold it for two hundred thousand dollars per family. They had given up their identity as Indians. He—this young man—was trying to get it back, so this evening he played the drums. And I thought, *Boy, I like this!* I looked around and—no Navajos! *What happened to the Navajos?*

> The next morning I said to them, "What happened to you guys?" [One of them] said, "When I heard those drums, it reminded me of being back with the medicine man in the hogans and doing those ceremonies and a lot of that witchcraft, and I got out of there." So that was it—from then on, I never had success in getting the Navajos out to the Caucus.

That was not the end of Ministry contacts with the Caucus. Take, for example, the experience of Elmer Yazzie (no relation to the Rev. Fred W. Yazzie). Elmer Yazzie's father was Navajo and his mother was from Laguna Pueblo. He became a Ministry lay pastor after a religious experience saved him from alcoholism, and from taking refuge at night in a fast-food restaurant's dumpster, then foraging for breakfast in the same place where he'd bedded down.

Elmer Yazzie is an intense man whose graying hair hangs down to his shoulders in a ponytail. He seems to stare at anyone he talks to through liquid, hazel orbits that seldom blink; they probe inside for signs of weakness in the faith. Since he was called from the dumpster to life in Christ, Elmer Yazzie likes to talk about his faith, and he pulls no punches.

He shared in a 2003 interview that as a Four Corners lay preacher, he attended a United Methodist–sponsored Native

American conference, held at Claremont School of Theology in California. He arrived a few minutes late, and when he opened the meeting room door, he faced a circle of Native Americans associated with the Caucus, sitting there on the floor, passing the peace pipe, and blowing the smoke skywards. He paused, then walked to the center of the circle, where he fixed the leader of the group with that intense stare. Yazzie said, "You shouldn't be doing this. You shouldn't be calling on the great spirit, or any other spirit but God and His Son, Jesus Christ, and you can't find God in the bowl of a pipe or the tobacco inside."

But that wasn't all Elmer Yazzie had to say: "You people. You people who say you are Christians while you work the old ways into Christianity. You're more interested in being Indian than you are in being Christian. And that's un-Christian."

And Elmer Yazzie was gone.

He knew instinctively that the Ministry Navajos didn't fit the pattern of other Native Americans. He said that he and his fellow Navajos came to their faith from traditional families who practice the old ways. When they took up the Jesus Way, many were ostracized and a few experienced serious physical abuse. So,

*Rev. Paul West remarries Lay Pastor and Mrs. Guy Nez Jr. at their request. Their first wedding had been a native ceremony.*

according to Elmer Yazzie, the Four Corners Navajos got together and decided to stick to the Jesus Way because it's better. They are troubled by fence-walking Native Americans who compromise what they say is their Christian faith by incorporating into Christian practices their smoke, drums, ashes, and other symbols that call up the native deities in order to bolster their identity as Indians.[1]

Elmer Yazzie and others led the Four Corners Native American Ministry to a stand on theology while Fred Yazzie and West listened. So the Ministry seemed to settle on at least part of a theology to reach these conservative individuals who were on the Pentecostal side when it came to worship and who were reminded of witchcraft when they heard the beat of the drums.

⬩⬩⬩

But how would the volunteer lay preachers that the Ministry hoped to recruit be taught to preach? What message would they carry? Those were concerns that had to be addressed by the Ministry board and by the ordained clergy, the Reverends Yazzie and West, who formed the leadership for teaching the volunteer lay preachers of the future. The board would take up issues about what elements of the native culture called the new Christian back to the old religious ways and away from Jesus, and which elements did not, and a line would be drawn to separate the two.

Yazzie had been spreading a conservative brand of theology that fit with the conservative nature of the Navajos. It was a theology that rejected the native animism and the mythological deities and symbols that called them to mind. West was also conservative, though somewhat more open to innovation, perhaps because Yazzie had a lead on him in understanding his Navajo people. It was obvious from West's preaching to the Shiprock church that he was no theological liberal from the school that questioned the virgin birth, the resurrection of Christ, or the truth of the stories of miracles Jesus performed. His beliefs fit well with the theology of the United Methodist Navajos.

*Tent evangelism meeting.*

As Rev. Fred Yazzie explained it:

> Four Corners Native American Ministry is evangelistic in nature . . . and we are involved in evangelism and church planting. And our Navajos like this theology. It's really Wesleyan Arminian[2] theology that we present to the people. And that has something solid for them. And we don't make the presentation of Jesus to them difficult, we make it as simple as we can and present Jesus, the Savior of the World. And that's how these churches are growing.

West became very protective of the desires of the Navajos, to the point of stepping up to bear the brunt of criticism directed against the Ministry's theology from the more liberal views of most members of the NAIC and others, including visitors from the General Boards of the church. That criticism originated in persons who charged that the Ministry—and its stance against incorporating native religious symbolism into Christian worship—exemplified a form of white man's colonialism.

Elmer Yazzie became an advocate for the theology he thought was right for the Navajos. Eloquently and ceaselessly he spread it at each and every meeting of the Four Corners Native

American Ministry he attended, whether it was a lay pastor training session, a board meeting, or two or three gathered in the name of the Lord. "We don't believe in mixing the religions," was, and is, his theme. Few disagreed.

The controversy was just beginning.

But for the coordinator of the Ministry, there was little time to sit around and debate the fine points of theologies of persons who were more liberal than the Navajo United Methodists of the Ministry. The theology they had chosen for themselves was working, and West had no desire to fix something that wasn't broken. But West had a problem: his time spent on the outreach through the Ministry was limited, for he was also filling the pulpit and performing pastoral duties for the Shiprock church.

On May 7, 1980, West wrote to his congregation in the Shiprock church to tell them that the pulpit and all the duties of the pastor of the church would be taken over by the Rev. Sam Wynn, the first ordained Indian pastor of that congregation. West explained he had been giving much of his time to developing the Ministry, and he would continue doing so. With Wynn in place, he could then cover the whole Reservation, supervising the work at Shiprock, Bistahi, Window Rock, Cove, and other preaching points that did not yet have the status of churches. West would also watch over construction of the new Oljato church building and another building at Window Rock, direct eight summer teenager and adult work camps scattered throughout the Reservation, and give Begay a hand with his tent evangelism preaching. The trick would be not to let all that take time away from writing proposals for funding, visiting off-Reservation churches for money-raising, sending publicity across the country, and writing letters to the more than one thousand friends of the Four Corners Ministry. To an observer, it must have seemed that West was trying to keep a dozen balls in the air at once.

Meanwhile, in Farmington, the mission school was facing issues of a different kind. The school's response would draw the attention of many of its former students who were involved in the affairs of the Four Corners Native American Ministry.

## CHAPTER EIGHTEEN

# The Mission School Begins a Slide

*Hold fast to what is good.*
—Romans 12:9

---

The instability that had begun to surface at the mission school during the tenure of Superintendent Rodney Roberts caught the attention of graduates of the school by 1978, though it would take a full decade for the changes to reach their climax. In the meantime, the controversy over the school's apparent rejection of the spiritual values Superintendent C. C. Brooks had advocated pitted the school and its administration against the Four Corners Native American Ministry, a body that could legitimately call itself the school's spiritual descendant. Though the skirmishes fought by the school and the Ministry sometimes seemed like quibbling about petty details, there were fundamental spiritual values at issue.

In April 1978, ten persons, awkwardly identifying themselves as "the Committee of Concerned Alumni and Parents of Members of the United Methodist Church of Shiprock requesting the Assumption of the Administration of the Navajo Methodist Mission School at Farmington, New Mexico," agreed on a resolution. The document spelled out seven grievances against the school and the National Division that footed most of its bills. The grievances included charges of a broken promise to seat a new board and violation of a policy requiring indigenous leadership. The resolution ended with a call for the National Division to step aside from the administration of the school and turn it over to "an acceptable body of Navajo people," and that it keep the current funding level until other money sources could be found.

The real concern of the committee, though unexpressed, seemed to be that the spiritual dimensions of the school were changing. It was no longer focusing on educating its students in the way of Jesus Christ, but on something different, something more attuned to the old cultural ways of the Navajos. To the committee, most of whom had been exposed to the school's original mission, that was something to fight about. But it was easier to pick at details of administration than to argue broad theological principles.

Reverend Paul West sent a copy of the resolution to the school superintendent, the Rev. Hector Navas, thus beginning a series of letters about the future of the school that would stretch on for years. Spokespersons for the arguing factions were Navas, the New York National Division's man at the head of the school, and West for the Concerned Committee.

The *United Methodist Reporter*, on May 19, 1978, carried the story of the brouhaha over the school's future. In an article date-lined "Farmington, NM," the paper told of local fears caused by the "glacial pace" at which a board of directors for the school was being set up following the dissolution some thirty months before of the previous board. When another National Division–sponsored school in New Mexico was closed by a decree from the division, and when it cut funding at a third institution in the same state, apprehension among school critics grew.

The reason given by the National Division for dissolving the school's board, the paper said, was that it was "operating without (Division) approval." With the board gone, the division had installed its own superintendent, Reverend Navas, a Hispanic clergyman from Florida. The school critics remembered that at the time the division acted, no one suspected that thirty months later, the school would still be directed by a "one-man show."

West's reported gripe about the Navas administration was that the National Division's pick was "dictatorial." Navas liked running the school with no board to bother him, West told the writer. It was "just one more instance of the Navajos being told what to do without having any say-so." The final blow to the Concerned Committee members, as West related it, was the Navas decision to end mandatory attendance at weekly chapel, gutting religious education on the United Methodist campus.

One of West's backers was Dr. Taylor McKenzie, a graduate of the school. As the Reservation's first trained Navajo medical doctor, McKenzie was a man of influence among his people, and his support gave credence to the challenges directed at Navas. As a concerned alumnus, McKenzie said he didn't have much faith in "interim" boards like the one Navas had finally gotten around to proposing, because they never have much authority and are generally "hesitant to act."

Sharon Mielke, who authored the *Reporter* article, wrote that the month before the appearance of the article, the National Division had approved a new plan for the interim board, drafted "almost verbatim" by Navas. The temporary board was to have eighteen persons, ten of them Navajos. For the Concerned Committee, eighteen was too many, and the Navajo representation was too dilute. McKenzie figured that a twelve-member board would be more efficient. A National Division executive, Dr. Negail Riley, then muddied the water by saying that while the National Division would continue to support the school, it and other institutions were being urged to find other sources of support.[1]

The Concerned Committee continued its letter writing and resolution drafting, and the National Division countered, but the flurry of paper generated only frustrations as the division plodded along on its course of naming board members and calling the shots from New York. Though West's repeated predictions of the coming end of the school were prophetic, the letter writing settled little.

Meanwhile, the position of Superintendent Navas on the issues of mission school governance got a temporary boost when the *New World Outlook*, a publication of the General

Board of Global Ministries, published an article about the school in its November 1978 issue. It was titled "Among Navajos—A Symbol of Excellence,"and the writer was Ellen Clark. Even in the face of this support, Superintendent Navas admitted to a series of setbacks: the school had been put on academic probation by the New Mexico Department of Education, a dormitory had been condemned, and the whole campus was run down. All that, he said, was why the National Division had disbanded the school's board and had brought him in to set things straight. He claimed he'd addressed all the problems the school had experienced, and that the last year it had graduated twenty-eight students, the largest graduating class in its history. Finally, Navas claimed he had given the school a "new lease on life," by negotiating with the Navajo Nation's federally financed Navajo Academy, which was aching to move from Ganado, Arizona, to the campus at Farmington.

The possibility of some kind of alliance between the mission school and the secular academy struck new fears for the character of the school in the hearts of the reenergized Concerned Committee. As West put it, laying the real issue on the table, "We'd like to see the school more conservative and more directly Christ-centered." At the same time, Navas felt that instead of foretelling the end to the mission school, the move of the Navajo Academy to the campus represented "an opportunity for evangelism."[2]

The academy had been created in 1976 by a resolution of the Tribal Council. In the summer of 1978, the dream of Navas and the nightmare of the Concerned Committee came true: the academy moved to the Farmington campus. At the time of the relocation, the academy had 15 students, one teacher, and a headmaster; there were then 175 students at the mission school.

By the end of the 1979–80 school year, the student bodies had been combined, the facilities had been leased by the academy under a deal made with Navas, the academic program had been put under the academy's control, and the academy headmaster was running the academic show while the mission had responsibility for "support services."[3]

Little about the arrangements had been made known to the New York National Division, which was sending money to operate what it believed was still the United Methodist Mission School, as shown by later correspondence. In New York, responsibility to find out what was going on in New Mexico fell upon Lula Garrett, who was an assistant general secretary.

Navajos of the Four Corners Native American Ministry were watching from their distant observation point in Shiprock, though they had neither the reach nor the power to cut what they perceived as losses. All they could do was pester West to find out what those who were pulling the school's strings were up to, and why they seemed to be letting the institution that had led so many of them to Jesus Christ escape from the United Methodist corral.

CHAPTER NINETEEN
# The Making of a Preacher

*A bishop [church leader] . . .*
*must be above reproach . . .*

—1 Timothy 3:2

Concerns about the mission school could not be allowed to divert attention from the needs of churches already in place. The church at Window Rock was standing still or slipping backwards due to a lack of effective leadership. The congregation had little rapport with leaders who were out of tune with the clans and families in the church. New pastoral leadership was needed; but where would it come from? Reverend West hoped a solution would be found by assigning Chee Benallie to the Window Rock charge, since he seemed to be ready to handle a church and was eager for an assignment.

After Reverend Haines led him to find the Holy Spirit, Benallie had worked for his Lord where he was called. It was West, however, who tabbed him as having potential for leadership, and gave in to Benallie's pleas to make him into a preacher. So West asked him to handle the church at Window Rock when it faltered. The church began a turnaround under Benallie's leadership, but soon slipped back into decline. Benallie was replaced in Window Rock by tent evangelist Henry Begay, who brought numbers of his extended family, as well as others, into the church. Benallie was sent to the church in Bistahi, where he preached while continuing to serve the Shiprock church as its outreach director in charge of recruiting Christians.

Part of the training that West had arranged for Benallie took place at Perkins School of Theology in Dallas, Texas, where he pursued a summer course of study program extending over five years. His experiences at the Dallas school proved instructive for the Ministry.

Though Benallie's limited, high school education made it all but impossible for him to pursue formal seminary training, the course of study program was open because its educational prerequisites were not as high—though there was nothing easy about the work. Benallie struggled, straining to understand concepts never dreamed of during his time in a government high school on the Reservation. His studies were further hampered by language difficulties.

Not all of the struggle was on Benallie's part. The faculty who presented the classes he took worked almost exclusively with students from lifelong Christian backgrounds. The instructors knew little or nothing of Navajo culture, and had no previous exposure to a way of life in which book learning carried little or no priority. Also, their focus was on presenting theological study rather than on training pastoral leaders and preachers for small groups.

In Benallie, they were confronted by a proud Navajo man whose great-grandfather was Navajo war and political chief Manuelito. Their student had only a high school education, and the faculty had not the faintest idea of how to present theological concepts to a man like Benallie, who had grown up in fear of native deities, spirits, and witches. They understood, too, that what they were teaching to Benallie would ultimately be passed on to tiny groups of Navajos who had never heard of the Word of God, feared spirits that surround the dead, were convinced that the trickster Coyote could spread evil and death, and were under the domination of a white culture that made no move to understand them. Benallie would be reaching out to people who spoke only Navajo. To have appeal, his message had to be honest. It had to be direct; ambiguities and doubts would only confuse new Christians whose families still called them back to the old ways of the Navajo. That was not the way of a seminary that encouraged independent thinking.

Benallie was able to finish the studies when his professors recognized that the standards they applied to the work of their other students did not fit this man from the Reservation. They had to evaluate his work based on what they found in his heart rather than what he was able to commit to paper. He had worked harder, come further, and accomplished more than his classmates, though it was not always obvious because he had begun so far behind. When he left with a certificate in hand, Benallie credited the Holy Spirit with seeing him through the program.

His experience would be a lesson to the Four Corners Native American Ministry in recruiting more lay preachers, deciding how and where to train them, and searching for persons who might be successful in pursuing the ordained ministry or in becoming accomplished lay preachers.

Though Benallie's ventures into local church preaching at Window Rock and Bistahi were marked with frequent setbacks, he had other talents that could be used in the Lord's work. While serving as the Shiprock outreach director he was to be responsible for one of the great recruiting coups for the Four Corners United Methodists, helping to build up the Ministry for years to come.

There were other persons stepping up to be lay preachers, and there were groups who were meeting in homes—groups that would eventually grow into small churches. And, as always, the Ministry was open to new ways to connect with the people on the Reservation, for ways to build the momentum that would inspire its members to make disciples.

CHAPTER TWENTY
# Building Momentum

*These very works which I am doing,*
*bear me witness that the Father has sent me.*

—John 5:36

The year 1980 was the busiest yet in the Ministry's short history. The report it submitted to the annual conference session in Glorieta, New Mexico, read like a wrap-up summary for a successful episode of *Mission Impossible*.

"This ethnic ministry has been in existence for two years," the report read. It boasted that the Shiprock church was one of "the few Indian churches to become self-sufficient." The Ministry had opened a "Home for Battered Women and Abused Children," the first of its kind on any Indian Reservation in the country. Chee Benallie had established a preaching point in Wheatfield, a new permanent structure was going up at Window Rock, Sam Wynn had come in as a Native American missionary under appointment from North Carolina, Bistahi had been accepted as a conference church, the Ministry had bought Henry Begay a 30' x 40' tent, and he had been dubbed the official "Navajo Evangelist." And that wasn't all.

There were two new churches on the drawing board, the Ministry had dedicated a new hogan chapel in Shiprock, and Mr. and Mrs. Don Curley had volunteered for mission service to other tribes. What might have been the biggest step reported was that a dialogue had been initiated with district superintendents in Colorado and Utah to permit the Ministry to invade the Reservation for Jesus in those states. The report, however, put it more circumspectly by stating that the contacts were being made "to reach across conference lines."

Begay received financial backing for his tent ministry. The Four Corners evangelism budget was spread out in the pages of the *Journal* for the members of the annual conference to look at. It showed that Begay needed an organ and loudspeakers to carry his keyboard and guitar music through the flimsy walls of his tent to the ears of passersby. He also had to purchase microphones to carry his verbal message through the speakers. If provided with a used bus and a camper to sleep in, Begay could extend his ministry's range to anywhere on the Reservation. All it would take was money.

Although the annual conference did not fund the purchase of the bus and camper, an unexpected donation was used to buy a used van and horse trailer. The trailer held the tent. Reverend West and Begay called it a "lesson from God on faith."

Largely as a result of Evangelist Begay's tent ministry messages, Navajos were calling for still more churches. The new worshippers needed recognition and help from the annual conference. Fledgling congregations in Arizona were located at Cove, Oak Spring, and Wheatfield. In Utah, churches at Hatch and Aneth were underway. The process of kicking off those new churches had made it obvious to the Ministry that a policy was needed so that more new churches could be accepted into the fold without scrambling to figure out how to do it every time. The board set to work and came up with a model for start-up churches. The Ministry report laid out step-by-step for the annual conference just what was required for a Reservation church to qualify as a "United Methodist Church":

- A new group of worshippers would need a land lease in its name from the Navajo Nation.
- With a lease in hand, the Four Corners Ministry would give the group a maximum of three thousand dollars to put up a church building.

- Local church members would be required to pour and finish the foundation floor.
- The rest of the structure would be built by volunteer work teams arranged for by the Ministry; the teams would erect the exterior and pay for the costs of the materials they used.
- Once that was done, the local members would do the finish work.
- Then, to be a part of the United Methodist connectional system, the congregation would have to connect to other Ministry churches through the "Reservation Mother Church," as the Shiprock church had come to be called.

There were provisions, too, for independent churches, since the Ministry took seriously the admonitions of United Methodist institutional leaders about the importance of being ecumenical. That ecumenical connection could result in an independent but linked church in what was called a "fellowship" relationship to the Ministry. The purpose was to "develop unity, encourage sharing, strengthen teaching ministry, and bear one another's burdens." For these independent churches, the contribution from the Ministry would be limited to three hundred dollars, and Reservation area workers, presumably members of Ministry churches, would lend a hand in erecting the building.[1]

All the guidelines were modified in time, though the core of the model was preserved because it worked. In fact, it worked so well that the activity itself and the sweet aroma of success became a strong evangelical tool. Other Navajos witnessed these new churches operating in connection with the Ministry, watched buildings going up, and listened to Navajo United Methodists sing the praise of the Ministry. All this reinforced the trust of small groups who wanted to become a part of the Four Corners Ministry.

The flurry of activity didn't end there. In 1981, the Ministry's first church planted in the Rocky Mountain Annual Conference's area was completed at Hatch, Utah. It had been erected and paid for by the First United Methodist Church, Big Spring, Texas, and it was "now fully self-supporting." Christian classes were being offered at BIA schools; a home for battered women and abused children had been started; "Surrender Services," a ministry to alcoholics and their families, had been opened; Evangelist Begay was still pitching his tent and preaching about the love of Jesus through those microphones and speakers that had been bought the prior year; and a thrift shop had opened its doors, giving away clothes to fire victims.

Best of all, according to the report given to the annual conference, were the fruits of leadership formation: "The greatest asset of the Four Corners Native American Ministry is its Navajo preachers!" It listed them: Fred Yazzie, Chee Benallie, Raymond Burke (Hatch, Utah), Henry Begay (Window Rock), Lucy Lewis (Shiprock), James Aloysuis (Cove, Arizona), and Danny Dan (Window Rock, Arizona, and Old Sawmill, Arizona).

Some important details did not appear in the report. At the Shiprock church, that hogan chapel which had been built and dedicated was a traditional Navajo structure. It was being used for training sessions, worship, weddings, baptisms, and other purposes called for by a busy church. The little chapel had been built entirely by Oscar Damon, retired layman of that church. He had handshaped the logs and all the wood to perfect fits, explaining, "God did so much for me, I only wanted to do something for Him."

Don and Marie Curley, the couple who had volunteered as missionaries to other tribes, had a story to tell. Don Curley had been called to the Lord's service when he was miraculously healed of high blood pressure, congestive heart failure, and kidney trouble at a home prayer meeting. Marie illustrated the tugs felt by Navajos newly exposed to Jesus Christ. She said that until Don's healing, "we often sat on the fence. Sometimes we would go to the medicine man and sometimes we would turn to the church. But now, we are 100 percent for the Lord."[2] When the couple retired in 1980, they went into full-time volunteer service for the church.

West reported that "the Navajo people continue to dream, and these dreams are becoming prophetic. The Holy Spirit is raising up a solid core of lay leadership and this is our greatest and strongest foundation for the future."

What he could have added was a comment about the solid core of backing the Ministry had behind it in the New Mexico Annual Conference. One of the most solid supporters was Dr. Brodace Elkins, a slow-talking, quick-thinking, former Oklahoman with a love of Navajos and of the Four Corners Ministry that reached out to them, and who would soon be made district superintendent of the Albuquerque district.

CHAPTER TWENTY-ONE

# More Types of Outreach

*All the members do not have
the same function . . .*

—Romans 12:4

By March 25, 1980, Paul West got serious about spreading the Four Corners word around the country. On that date, he sent a newsletter to a broad list of people, including those who had supported him and Mrs. West while they were in Malaysia, family in the Midwest, and others who had been identified as friends or supporters of the new Ministry.

In addition to listing the progress of the Ministry as told to the annual conference, there was also the story of West's visit to a local lumberyard to buy supplies for a new church building under construction. The yardman who greeted and served the United Methodist preacher was a churchgoing, God-fearing Navajo. Only a year earlier he'd been an unemployed alcohol-abuser and wife-beater. He had been rescued from his former life by the Christian alcoholic ministry, Surrender Services, sponsored by Four Corners Native American Ministry. Lives were being changed, and learning about it drew more volunteers, whose lives would also be changed.

These new outreach programs were tangible evidence that the lay leadership of which West had written in his report to the annual conference—a few of those leaders Anglo, most of them Navajo—was reaching out to women and children in trouble, and to men and women abusing alcohol. The outreach was a direct result of the Ministry's recognition of the place of the family in Navajo culture. Families were ripping apart, women and children were abused, and no one was doing anything about it or about the alcoholism that was usually at the root of it all. Having seen the needs, the Ministry acted to use the cultural connection as a basis for Christian spiritual formation.

The energy for the Home for Women and Children, a shelter for those who are abused or threatened, grew from this concern, but it found expression through nurse-turned-stay-at-home-mom Dorcas West. She explained:

> That got started because [husband, Paul West] was sending [women in need] to my house—to the parsonage. And I met this [Navajo] lady who shared her problems. And it seemed like all of them had the same problems.

Mrs. West soon learned that the women had several major problems, including domestic violence, lack of housing, lack of education, and difficult relationships with parents. When the first lady to visit with her kept returning to tell of problem after problem:

> [I thought]—*Get me outta here. I don't know how to solve these things*, because I felt like the government was supposed to be helping people. And here she was. I felt like she had fallen through the cracks in all ways, and that really showed me the need.

So when Dorcas West heard of a community workshop on domestic violence and abused children sponsored by the state Commission on the Status of Women, she went. She hadn't planned to get involved, but Dorcas West couldn't turn her back on all the abuse about which she learned. She watched and listened with the three hundred others who showed for the two-day meeting, the attendance verifying for her that the need was not limited to the few Navajo ladies who had knocked on her door. The Navajo Housing Authority promised the new group a house, and the telephone company offered a free hotline.

In February we got the information on a United Methodist Women's program called Prayer and Self-denial, where it would help women in rural areas. . . . Somebody gave me that information, and said, "Here, Dorcas, you ought to do something about this." I said, "Oh, yeah, sure." But that's how I got into it. And the deadline was within about two weeks.

Dorcas West took the information to the Navajo who was in charge of the workshop. "She wrote this proposal for $250,000—and it was accepted [though not fully funded]. We flew to New York to the Board of Global Ministries, and talked to them too. They were impressed with her, Bella McCabe. Bella Rogers McCabe."

While the application produced only twelve thousand dollars, that was enough to start the project. Dorcas West and a band of Navajo women from the church began to meet every week with leaders of the Shiprock community, hammering out what a home for battered women and abused children should be. "After we got the funding," Mrs. West remembered, "then we asked for the house and for the telephone, and—nothing. Everything started just floating away."

She went to husband Paul for advice. To begin, he suggested, they could pull the mobile home that had been parked at the mission school in Farmington to a Shiprock site for use as the first home. They did this, and had their first three bedrooms.

Not long after that, a young Navajo woman named Evelene Sombrero was hired as the director of Christian education at the Shiprock church. She'd had experience working for Social Services in Gallup, New Mexico, and for a time, she'd worked as church secretary. When Dorcas West started the home, Sombrero interviewed, hoping to put her degree in social work to good use.

In a 2003 interview, Sombrero, who later became the first female United Methodist ordained Navajo clergy, told what it was like in the early days of the home: "I did some counseling work when the home was just starting out. Shiprock was a small community, and people, including husbands, knew where the center was. They would mob the home, which at first was a small trailer on the church grounds."

Shortly after Sombrero's departure, it became obvious that demand had grown so much that the mobile home was no longer big enough to house the women and children. New and larger facilities were needed. Dorcas West and her group went to the Navajo chapter house for help, and they attended workshops. Before long, they were offering counseling, and they opened up the fledgling operation to a broader base in order to get community help. Their aim was to reach out beyond the churches of the Four Corners Native American Ministry to all area women and children who were being abused.

They formed a board, which included a Catholic nun, community workers, church women—and later, a bunch of doctors and doctors' wives connected with the Indian Health Service hospital at Shiprock. The board decided the solution was to construct a building to house all the women and children who came to them. Though the board was independent by this point, in time of need it turned to the Four Corners Native American Ministry.

Paul West remembered what happened next:

> There were sixty acres the chapter had not far from the church. So we asked for two acres. And they said okay. [There was still ten thousand dollars left from the grant, and that money was used to build the foundation and pour the floor.] Then we were broke. Then we had [volunteer] work groups come in and build a two-story structure, about 85 by 36, something like that.

All that from a grant of twelve thousand dollars, and as Reverend West put it, "Well, as you go along in faith, there are good things that happen."

When one of the tribal officials from the chapter saw what was going on, he was inspired to offer some of the tribe's revenue sharing money. Though chasing after it required Paul West to make multiple trips to Window Rock, the tribe came through with sixty thousand dollars. It was used for plumbing, sewer, water, electrical wiring, and for supervision through a tribal training program. The Home for Women and Children opened in its new quarters, and as soon as it took in its first client, it was a showpiece for what the Ministry could do to help families.

But things did not always run smoothly. In November 1987, Dot Steed moved from East Tennessee, with the understanding that she would be paid six dollars per hour to serve as director at the Home for Women and Children. Steed soon found that the funding sources for her pay were not always reliable. Her tenure was a stormy one, resulting in her departure ten months later, in August 1988. Though initially she worked well with staff and with the Wests, disagreements and bickering eventually fractured the relationship, and she began to complain that she had not been paid.

She floated other complaints that were not so specific. She wrote a letter containing a list of grievances and sent it to District Superintendent David Saucier: "All promotion of the [Ministry] portray [sic] the Four Corners Ministry and the Home for Women and Children as one and the same." Yet, in a plea for fiscal accountability made when she was unable to locate certain deposits to the Ministry account, the same letter said she had demanded that "all Methodist funds be sent directly to the Home," seeming to recognize they were one.

Steed found fault with the policy and program management of both the Ministry and the Home, questioning whether the Ministry board even had bylaws (it did). She threw doubt on the religious affiliation of a healing ministry working through the Four Corners Ministry that was spearheaded by a United Methodist couple from Hays, Kansas, who were longtime Ministry volunteers. She questioned whether the Ministry was audited annually (it wasn't, at that time). She asserted that Paul and Dorcas West had forced her to "work with some insubordinate employees who created so much internal dissension that in my case, I was forced into a resignation." She claimed her hands "were tied . . . by the control (often covert action) of the Wests."

Steed's campaign against the Ministry did not end with her complaint letter to the district superintendent. In the absence of a response that she viewed as favorable, Steed enlisted the help of ready allies Shirley Montoya and a handful of other unhappy members of the Shiprock Church. They drafted a petition seeking the removal of Reverend West, and sent it to the presiding bishop, among others. But it drew no positive support.

Gradually, the supporters recruited by Steed lost interest in trying to prove that West was incompetent. Steed returned to Knoxville, leaving the "insubordinate employees," independent-minded Navajos with whom neither the Wests nor the Four Corners board of directors had ever had insubordination or other problems, in charge. The work of the Home ran smoothly once again.

Volunteers continued to come. Word about the spiritual depth of the experience of helping Navajos was getting out in circles from New York to California. Work groups consisting of Methodists and other Christian denominations from all over the country were conducting vacation Bible schools, building churches and other facilities, deworming sheep, and holding dental clinics. The workers were camping out in sleeping bags on church floors, out in the open, and in the beds of pickup trucks. They were eating Navajo tacos, pinto beans, and stew made especially for them from beef or goat, since the Navajos had seen that mutton made the white folks gag. The volunteers were listening to the testimony of open people who loved Jesus, stumbling over the Navajo text of hymns with melodies they sang in their own churches, and making new friends. They were hearing the Rev. Fred Yazzie preach and seeing him demonstrate love. Volunteers were learning patience, and they were discovering that, in the Four Corners, time moves at a slower rate than elsewhere in society. And the volunteers went back home to spread tales of what the Navajos had taught them, although they had gone to teach the Navajos.

But all of it had to be organized. The organizational mind who put it together was Rev. Paul N. West, a man who was not afraid to get his knees dusty while seeking new ways to reach out on the Reservation. One way had not been contemplated when the first plans for the Ministry were laid. Independent churches on the Reservation came knocking on the door of the Ministry, asking to be let in.

The first of the little independent churches to come to the Four Corners Ministry was located at Oljato, Utah, on the western edge of Monument Valley, with its isolated red mesas and buttes and its sandy desert vistas. It came into connection with the Ministry through a path that was surely unique within The United Methodist Church.

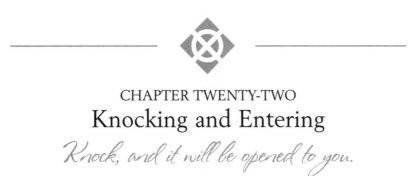

## CHAPTER TWENTY-TWO

# Knocking and Entering

*Knock, and it will be opened to you.*

—Matthew 7:7

In the late 1970s, a Full Gospel evangelist pastor from Albuquerque set up his tent in the Oljato, Utah, area and preached his message to all who came. During his brief ministry there, he stayed at the family home of Cecil Parrish Jr. One night, the evangelist had a dream that led him to get up early the next morning and mark out on the ground the location for a church. Parrish, who knew how to lay bricks, built a church at the very spot he had traced. Parrish acted as its first pastor.

But the church was on its own.

Some months after the church opened its doors, Parrish and the worshippers talked to Henry Begay, the Four Corners Ministry tent evangelist who was preaching in the area. Begay told the congregation about his United Methodist connection and about the Four Corners Native American Ministry. He urged them to check with Rev. Paul West, who could figure out a way that they could become a part of the connected group of churches. He told how the Ministry that backed him was dedicated to starting churches on the Reservation in order to spread the Word of Jesus Christ, and how its people could be depended on to do what they said.

The possibility of hooking up with an organization like that fit perfectly into the beliefs of the church people of Oljato. They asked Begay to get them in touch with the Ministry. He did, and before long West jumped into his Four Corners minivan and drove to Oljato for a prayer session and discussions about whether the group might be comfortable with a connection with the United Methodists, and vice versa.

It did not take much conversation for West to get to the root of what was happening. He explained:

> There's a little independent church here, they begin to see the problem: well, who's going to follow me? If I die, who's going to take over after me? . . . Or they have dreams . . . they go off to visit another church and see they have a Sunday school. And they want one, but they don't know how.

West told the people at Oljato how the Four Corners Ministry could help.

West and the Oljato group concluded they were compatible. While the worship and praise services that the Oljato Christians

*Bible study reenacting the story of Lazarus.*

had been practicing were not exactly what might have been experienced in a large metropolitan church in the Methodist tradition at that time, they nevertheless seemed to be strikingly similar to what could be found in any of the United Methodist churches on the Reservation. The only exception might have been the restrained English-language services in the Shiprock church. In Oljato, hands were raised in praise, belief in the Bible was more fundamental than liberal, "praise God" was a phrase that meant something more than a response mouthed from a hymn book, and Jesus Christ came first. *These people are Christian*, West thought. *And that means that they're open to be made into Methodists.*

But there was some hesitation on the part of the Oljato Christians. The only thing they knew about these United Methodists was that they were behind a tent ministry run by a Navajo fellow named Henry Begay, who could preach, play the keyboard and the guitar, and sing, and that an Anglo who claimed to be a pastor had driven all the way from Shiprock, New Mexico, to talk to them. The explorations began.

One of the first things done was to put all the expectations down in writing, surely an appropriately methodical step for a bunch of Methodists and Methodists-to-be. The document that the discussions produced was called "Contract of Agreement Between Cecil Parrish Jr. & The Christians at Oljato, Utah and The United Methodist Church."

The contract spelled out what the Four Corners Ministry was prepared to do, but only after its first paragraph had acknowledged that the Christians of Oljato agreed "with the doctrines and connectional system of the United Methodist Church principles of Self-government, Self-support, and Self-propagation for mission churches." It then recited what the band of Navajo Christians expected from the Four Corners Native American Ministry: establishing a connection, including Christian fellowship with other United Methodist Churches on the Navajo Nation Reservation and across the U.S.; working to bring the Oljato Christians to spiritual maturity; providing training for the Oljato board, for Sunday school teachers, and for those who wanted licenses to preach; helping with building projects when needed; providing printed material to aid in spiritual growth; and making spiritual oversight available for all church members.

The obligations were to run both ways. The Oljato Christians were to pay their own bills, keep a budget and accurate records of church members and their families, have an annual audit, keep up their buildings, include "United Methodist" in the church name, and take the lease for the church property as The United Methodist Church.

After Parrish retired, his son-in-law, Eugene Chee, took his place. Chee had become a Christian following a narrow escape from losing his life in a flash flood that roared down one of the area's normally dry streambeds. He took the training as a Four Corners lay pastor and was licensed to preach. Pastor Chee is an advocate of the use of electric guitars and snare drums during worship. Chee's church is clear in its theology, persuaded that the old Navajo ways—represented by peyote and the drugs, alcohol, and violence that stem from powwows—lead to hell, while Jesus leads to heaven and eternal life.[1]

The copy of the contract that rests in the New Mexico Conference Episcopacy files does not show signatures. Though the undertakings were indeed carried out, apparently once the agreement was committed to paper signatures became irrelevant. The Four Corners Ministry helped the church build a fellowship hall and start a Sunday school. The Christians of Oljato are convinced that the Ministry is helping to show them the way to heaven.

Despite its success in welcoming the Christians of Oljato into the Four Corners fold, the written contract format has not been used again. Between groups of Christians, verbal assurances and commitments prove to be enough, especially when the word got out among Christians on the Reservation that the Four Corners Ministry meant what it said and delivered on its promises. It also helped that at about the same time as the Oljato church was growing stronger, a church at Dowozhiibikooh, Utah, had been built and was about to be constituted as a full-fledged United Methodist church, with all the obligations that went along with the recognition.

The Dowozhiibikooh community of worshippers, like the Oljato Christians, had also started when a family gathered to pray, sing, and study the Bible. It all began when Charlie and Blanche Burke invited members of their family to join in a Bible study in their living room in Montezuma Creek, on the Navajo Nation Reservation in Southeastern Utah. Ultimately, the increasing participation of local people led the Four Corners Ministry to celebrate another victory before the year 1979 had ended.

The little area of Utah had been home to practitioners of peyote rites for years, and one of the Burkes's sons had hanged himself following a peyote ritual he had attended. Blanche Burke was inconsolable, but her daughter persuaded her to go to a nearby tent revival. Blanche found Jesus Christ there and accepted Him into her heart. She left the revival as a woman with a mission: she would round up the rest of the family for Jesus.

It was Henry Begay who told the Burkes about the Four Corners Native American Ministry. They liked what they heard. But the demands of Begay's tent ministry kept him on the move, and it was two years later that Begay introduced Paul West to the Burke family as a "white man you can trust." The Burkes were open to establishing a connection with the Ministry. When word got back to West, he took three Navajos from the Shiprock church to the Burke home to talk about building a church at Montezuma Creek.

The following year, 1980, a new church building measuring twenty-eight feet by forty-eight feet went up south of Hatch, Utah. The women of the church dug the foundation, and the men of the church poured the concrete. Volunteers from Big Spring, Texas, did the rest of the construction work and supplied the materials.

In the same year, the congregation chose Raymond Burke, second son of Charlie and Blanche, and a full-time worker with Superior Oil Company, as the lay preacher. The worshippers also decided to name the church "United Methodist Full Gospel Church." They had heard the name "Full Gospel" applied to other Reservation churches, and they liked the message it seemed to carry.

The name would not stick, perhaps because some of the congregation felt that mixing the "Full Gospel" connection with the "United Methodist" name might lead to confusion, though West defended the right of the parishioners to name their church anything they chose to. A new name was picked by the worshippers in 1982, the "Dowozhiibikooh First United Methodist Church," from Navajo words meaning "greasewood canyon." In 1983, the church was constituted by the Albuquerque district superintendent, but not without having first run an obstacle course through church politics involving another jurisdiction of The United Methodist Church, another annual conference, and another district. All had authority over Methodist work in Utah. This time, the Ministry also came face-to-face with a cultural and biblical issue: the taboo that warned Navajos against the practice of homosexuality.[2]

The issue came up when a Methodist bishop in Colorado appointed a homosexual pastor to a church in the Rocky Mountain Annual Conference, and word leaked out to the Reservation. Reaction to the appointment threatened to sink the Dowozhiibikooh church just as it was about to be launched. But an alert Albuquerque district superintendent spotted the issue and steered around it before it presented a threat.

During a telephone interview from his El Paso home, Dr. Brodace Elkins told of the troubles in constituting that early United Methodist church on the Reservation in Utah. The predicaments came from the homosexuality issue and from those boundary lines drawn on paper by church law, all issues that were simmering when he took over as Albuquerque district superintendent in 1982.

Dowozhiibikooh, it's in Utah. We had set a Sunday aside to constitute the church there. But Paul [West] called me. Bishop Wheatley in Denver had appointed a gay person to a church in the Rocky Mountain Conference, and that got a lot of publicity on the Reservation. The word that the Denver bishop had appointed a gay swept across the Reservation through radio preachers, who were saying that if [any Navajos] had anything to do with this [Methodist] church denomination, to get out of it. So this created a lot of controversy. We backed off for about two weeks.

Elkins said that the Albuquerque District and the New Mexico Annual Conference then went ahead in Utah with Dowozhiibikooh and Oljato. He mailed an invitation to the district superintendent in Grand Junction, Colorado, and invited him to come and be recognized as the organizing district superintendent. He wrote back that he couldn't come, but authorized Elkins, as an elder, to hold the conference, indicating that the district superintendent from Grand Junction had a role.

Then, Elkins said, "I shared his letter with [New Mexico's] Bishop Schowengerdt, and I told him he should have a conference with the Denver Bishop. So Bishop Schowengerdt did talk to [Bishop] Wheatley."

Elkins thought he had put the issue to rest by his accommodation with the Grand Junction district superintendent. Indeed, relations were so good that a few years later, in 1987, the Rocky Mountain Annual Conference adopted a petition that sought to have the United Methodist ministry on the Reservation "identify with the New Mexico Conference for pastoral appointments, administrative and programmatic structure, spiritual nurture and property management." The action, the petition concluded, specifically spoke "of that area of San Juan County in Utah which includes the Dowozhiibikooh United Methodist Church, located near Hatch, Utah (the Hatch Trading Post) and the Christian Church of Oljato, Utah, when duly constituted as a United Methodist Church."[3]

Nevertheless, questions about the New Mexico Conference's poaching in Western Jurisdiction territory would be raised again after Bishop Roy Sano was assigned to the Episcopal office in Denver.[4] But meanwhile, the Oljato and Dowozhiibikooh churches were firmly in the Four Corners fold, their members taking part in the board meetings, encouraging other United Methodist churches on the Reservation, and supporting one another in the faith.

Reverend West called the Four Corners system for folding existing independent churches, including those like Oljato and Dowozhiibikooh, into the larger fellowship of the Ministry and into The United Methodist Church, "connectionalism in live color." He explained in an interview the way the churches work in connection with each other on the Reservation: "Trust has to be developed. That's true with all the churches . . . because they have never been in a denominational setting, or even in a group setting. I think Navajos naturally are independent. I think that goes back maybe to six hundred years."

West found that the Navajos like their independence and want to preserve it, but they

> haven't experienced the broader fellowship of the church. But once they do, then they want to be a part of that. So that's why, as we made it a connectional church, and made the connection through the Four Corners Ministry, and helping each one of them say, "Now we're connected, now we're connected." They like that. And the help they've gotten with churches [in the Methodist connection] off the Reservation is that they can build up their buildings. And then they wonder, will the white man own the buildings? Or what? And we say, "No, it's all yours. It's yours to work with, yours to pay for utilities, it's yours to do with what you want to do with it. We're not going to tell you what to do." At first, they don't believe you. But after time goes along, it's true. Then they believe you, and then they're gung ho, and they want to work with you more, and they want to be involved.

For consideration by the Four Corners board, West developed guidelines similar to the Oljato contract for taking Christ to the

Navajos through the connectional church of which the Ministry was a part. In characterizing his part in bringing in new churches, as well as in all aspects of the Ministry, as a "minor" role in a 1983 report that made its way into his bishop's files, he split up his work into eleven categories. At the top of the list was "Make the Bible and Christ central in all preaching and teaching." That priority was followed by, "Stress the power of God to work in any situation." Number three was, "Infuse optimism in the church and in themselves." The remaining items included, among others, stepping out in faith, instilling pride, reflecting confidence, dreaming big, stepping back to let the Navajos and God work together, and stressing tithing.

The time had also come to develop a master plan that laid out a strategy for growth. The 1983 report from the Ministry to the presiding bishop spelled it all out. It would plant new churches, evangelize, construct new church buildings, and develop outreach and service projects to serve families. The Ministry needed trained Navajo pastors, and Christian education cried to be developed. New Christians had to be trained in the basics that any American church off the Reservation took for granted: how to be a congregation, how to be Methodists, and how to seize control of their own church's destiny. All this was addressed with specifics in a six-year master plan put together by the Four Corners Ministry board of directors.

Others off the Reservation were watching through the medium of a periodic newsletter sent by the Ministry to its expanding list of friends throughout Methodism. As a result of the word being spread, training for Navajo pastors and congregations eventually got a shot in the arm.

It came from the Middle West, where a group of evangelical United Methodists banded together into an organization in reaction to the perceived failure of the General Board of Global Ministries to place missionaries in the field to spread the Word of Jesus Christ. One of the first undertakings of the unofficial body would be to supply personnel for training indigenous leaders, such as those within the Four Corners Ministry.

The prospect of help was seized with joy on the Reservation. The Rev. Sam Wynn, North Carolina Lumbee Indian missionary to the Navajos, was assigned to coordinate exploration of establishing a training program. Although he had no connection to the new missionary-sending organization, Wynn was not one to let an opportunity pass.

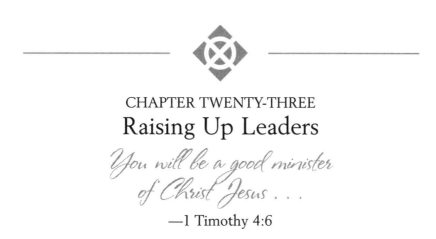

CHAPTER TWENTY-THREE
# Raising Up Leaders

*You will be a good minister
of Christ Jesus . . .*

—1 Timothy 4:6

In February 1983, Rev. Sam Wynn set out to fish for help for the Ministry from the new Mission Society. He wrote to the pastor of the First United Methodist Church in Peoria, Illinois, and one of the Society's prime movers, Dr. Ira Gallaway. The plea was for a full-time evangelist who could speak fluent Navajo, a full-time Christian education director for church school development, a social worker for the Home for Women and Children, and a director for the alcoholism counseling program.

Wynn didn't end his shopping list there. He also wanted full- and part-time volunteers for various kinds of work, a camp director, and a summer intern to work with vacation Bible schools. Wynn's stated hope was that Gallaway "and other evangelical Christians within The United Methodist Church will not overlook the Native Americans," as they matched missionary-minded volunteers to needs in the field. In making his appeal, Wynn identified the nature, needs, perspective, goals, and dreams of the Ministry.

To educate Gallaway, who was uninformed of the ways of Navajo United Methodists and the Four Corners Ministry, Wynn explained that the "'4 Corners Ministry' is committed to a 'life-changing' ministry with the Navajo people." By that time, according to Wynn's letter, the Ministry operated as a "Cooperative Parish Ministry" under the *Book of Discipline*, paragraph 206.

Wynn also reported that the Ministry employed four Native American pastors, one Native American youth director, one Anglo pastor, and one Native American secretary. Its outreach included not only establishing churches, but also the Home for Women and Children, a tent evangelism ministry, a released time study program in BIA schools, and an alcoholism center.[1]

The recipient of this information, Gallaway, had pastored a number of churches in Texas, was a former general secretary of the Board of Evangelism, served on the executive council of the World Methodist Council, and had a long list of other credentials, including his call to First Church Peoria "to try to see what biblical teaching and preaching would do to an old downtown church." He found it increased attendance and giving.

Gallaway responded to Wynn's letter, but it was six years later before he trekked from Illinois to New Mexico to answer a call he had heard to minister to the Navajos. When he retired from Peoria, he answered that call and initiated a training program for Navajo lay pastors and laypersons, while his wife, Sally, worked primarily with women interested in Bible study. They stayed for eight years.

There was a leadership formation program already underway when Wynn wrote his letter. Training had been conducted by Wynn himself, though he had been officially on board only for a few months. Reverend Paul West and Rev. Fred W. Yazzie had put on training sessions, too. The board of the Ministry had also gone to work on the issue. But Wynn figured that if qualified outside trainers could be brought in, the locals would be freed for other outreach.

Dr. Mark Dorff, chair of the New Mexico Annual Conference Board of Ministry, summarized the way the licensing program worked in its early developmental stages in a report he made to the annual meeting of the New Mexico Annual Conference, as reported in the *New Mexico United Methodist Reporter* of July 2, 1982. First, Dorff told the conference that it was the indigenous Four Corners board itself that had set up the licensing program and set the standards. He said:

> The . . . committee [of the Ministry] has developed the criteria and set the standards on the basis of Christian character and actions, gifts and fruits of the ministry, plus required study and class meetings. This examination committee as well as the complete lay pastor project is directed by Navajo United Methodists. We are affirming their desire to set and maintain standards for developing a lay pastorate on the reservation.[2]

It had been months prior to the 1982 annual conference that the Ministry board of directors had adopted the standards referred to by Dorff. They were incorporated into a document titled "Requirements for License to Preach."[3] In it, the board decreed that to earn a license, potential lay pastors would start by reading two booklets, *The Character of a Methodist*, by John Wesley, and *The History of The United Methodist Church*. The curriculum instructed the trainees to read selected chapters from a topical study outline, including studies on "Christ—His Life and Works," "The Three-in-One God," and "Christ was Born as a Man." They had to study *Christ's Death in Man's Place*, see a film on John Wesley, and listen to four tapes on ministering to friends and relatives, as well as the suicidal, the depressed, and those facing death. In addition, they were to attend classes on relating to people and on preaching. Finally, they were to prepare, deliver, and participate in an evaluation of a ten-minute sermon. None of the material had been translated into Navajo.

But, Dorff explained, the licensing process did not end there. There were character requirements to be met. The board had meticulously studied Scripture to come up with a justification for each and every characteristic they wanted every lay pastor who represented Jesus Christ, the Ministry, and The United Methodist Church to possess. Dorff produced a list.

Candidates had to show that they were "blameless." That meant "no smoking, no cheating, no teasing or flirting, no breaking promises, no bad words, no practicing other religions, not superstitious, doesn't overdress, be neat." The list was lifted right out of the third chapter of 1 Timothy.

*Anthony Tsosie and Guy Nez Jr. meet John Wesley at
a pastor's conference at Asbury Theological Seminary.*

Drawn from the verses of 1 Peter were: "living [with] and
married to only one wife . . . open with the people, sober
(serious), self-controlled and orderly, don't lose temper, organized
schedule, organized worship, office, and house, organized appearance and neat."

The aspirants to licensing agreed to welcome strangers
into their homes, not to drink alcohol, not to be violent, not to
love money so as to be blinded to the Bible, to be respected by
family and children, and to be mature in the Faith. There was
a warning that it was sinful and bad to be divorced, and if the
ex-spouse were living, forgiveness should be sought.

Then the list moved on to Christian character and actions.
In that section were listed doing good deeds, friendliness,

gentleness, being a living sacrifice, love, hard work, sharing. The gifts of ministry in the name of Jesus Christ were not overlooked. The lay preachers would be expected to speak God's message, serve, teach, encourage, share, work hard, and show kindness cheerfully. The messages they preached were to be full of wisdom, full of knowledge. Those who delivered the messages were expected to have faith, as well as the power to heal and to work miracles.

Pastors Henry Begay and Chee Benallie were the first paragons able to persevere through the training and the examination into their character, action, gifts, and fruits of the Spirit. They stuck it out to the end; they survived the interrogations of the Four Corners board and were judged to have measured up. At the 1982 session of the annual conference, new lay pastors Begay and Benallie were presented with certificates attesting to their standing in the leadership of the Four Corners Native American Ministry. The write-up of their honor was carried by the conference's edition of *The United Methodist Reporter*, along with an outline of the requirements they had met to qualify for their appointments as lay pastors.

The *Reporter's* account of the requirements drew an immediate response. Lois Jackson identified herself as a "commissioned" layperson who had served overseas for eighteen years. At the time of the annual conference, she wrote, she was the business manager of the Navajo Mission Academy in Farmington. Jackson wrote at length about her irritation, taking up four columns covering one-quarter of the front page of the newspaper. Her salvos are reported here, as representative of the types of criticisms still being heard from critics after thirty years of successes and setbacks for the Ministry.

She regretted the return of the Navajos to first-century church practices. To make her point, Jackson went through the list of Navajo pastoral requirements item by item, disparaging every one of them. She argued that if the same criteria were applied to present-day candidates for ordination, "there would not be enough pure and upright persons left to fill the pulpits or high level organizations of the church."[4] She jabbed the finger of blame for the high standards squarely at "present day clergy," without naming names. She charged the faceless figures with harboring an "elitism attitude," though admitting that many were "humble, good teachers and dedicated servants of God," even if they fell short of the standards set for Navajo lay pastors.

Her closing statement was a rhetorical question that implicitly mirrored condescending assumptions made by others about the Ministry over the years: that Navajos could not think for themselves; that any action they took must have been imposed on them by colonial missionary oppressors who were doing the thinking for them. She asked: "Who are we to make such puritanical requirements of those who are emerging?"

The Ministry found an advocate who stepped up to answer that question, the Rev. Norton Scrimshire of Gallup, New Mexico. Scrimshire responded to the attack by writing that the Native Americans on the Reservation had set their own standards, which is exactly what Dorff had told the conference during the presentation ceremony for Pastors Begay and Benallie, as it had been reported verbatim in the article that prompted Jackson's ire.

At the time of his response, Scrimshire was registrar of the Conference Board of Ordained Ministry, and Dorff was its chair. That gave the two an insider status to the licensing procedures, and thus to knowledge of any dabbling in requirements for Navajos that might have been engaged in by colonialists or others out to impose their will on hapless Navajos unable to think for themselves. Scrimshire's letter added his first-hand testimony, "We heard, and with joy affirmed, the request and requirements for recognition of lay pastors to the Navajo Nation submitted by the Navajos themselves."[5]

Scrimshire's reply told only part of the tale concerning development of the plan and of efforts to get it approved after the Four Corners Ministry board had drafted and adopted it. In performing his duties with the Conference Board of Ordained Ministry, and with the encouragement of Dorff as the board's chair,

Scrimshire had taken the lay pastor licensing program adopted by the Navajos to the General Board of Higher Education and Ministry. That General Board, located in Nashville, was the ultimate authority on licensing United Methodist clergy and lay preachers. The aim of the Four Corners Board of Directors—which had, in turn, become Scrimshire's aim and that of the entire Conference Board of Ordained Ministry—had been to get blessings on the licensing plan at the highest church level possible.

Scrimshire explained in an interview that West had come to the Conference Board of Ordained Ministry to ask whether the *Book of Discipline* permitted "bringing the Native American preacher program into accountability and recognition by somehow recognizing the lay people who preach and serve local native churches." These men and women were essentially lay speakers, according to Scrimshire, and the Four Corners Ministry wanted to bring them in as preachers, with the greater respect that the title carried. At that time, in 1981, "there were two or three persons who fit into that category," Scrimshire said. "We never dreamed there would ever be as many as there are now."

Of his contact with the General Board of Higher Education and Ministry in Nashville, Scrimshire related that while its officials said they understood the problem, they regretted that there was nothing they could do about it. They threw up no barriers, but they did point out that the *Book of Discipline* did not prevent the proposed licensing procedures.

Scrimshire, and the board of which he was a member, took that as a signal to move ahead, even though no one at the Nashville board wanted to say so in writing. The conference board would back the study and certification program that the Four Corners board had set up on its own, and the people in Nashville would not rule it out of bounds.

Scrimshire identified the reason why West, as coordinator of the Ministry, had been charged by the Four Corners board with looking for some stamp of approval to place on the certification procedures. At that time, the educational requirements for the official course of study route to ordination, an alternative to a seminary degree, made it virtually impossible for Navajos residing on the Reservation to pursue. It required that the candidate must have either an associate's degree from a college, or the hours for one, in order to begin the program. Then, the candidate had to earn a degree by the time the course of study was finished. Those living on the Reservation just did not have that education, and they had little means for acquiring it.

Yet, people were being called to preach, and the Ministry had people to listen and pulpits to fill. The board was determined that it would not stumble over technicalities that seemed tailor-made to prevent the taking of the Word of Jesus Christ to those who needed and wanted it, and who lived on the Reservation.

The Four Corners Navajos found enablers in Dorff, Scrimshire, and the conference board on which they sat. These Anglos, who were wired into the United Methodist system, understood that the Ministry had agreed upon high standards of spirituality and leadership for the lay pastors. They also knew enough about the Navajo United Methodists to understand that these were standards that laypersons with little of the white man's formal education could achieve with the help of the Holy Spirit. Scrimshire and the Conference Board of Ordained Ministry also knew that the standards were based on what the apostle Paul wrote to Timothy. The conference board was not persuaded by Jackson that Navajos would be led astray by relying on New Testament Scripture, especially since it was the Navajos' choice.

Scrimshire reminded his interviewer of the importance that the Four Corners Ministry Navajos placed on the warning in 2 Timothy 4:3–4, that says: "For the time is coming when people will not endure sound teaching, but having itching ears they will accumulate for themselves teachers to suit their own likings, and will turn away from listening to the truth and *wander into myths* (emphasis added)."

The Four Corners Native American Ministry, to this day, has its own procedures for certifying its lay preachers. Even in the face of procedures for certifying lay ministers adopted in 2004 and recorded in the 2004 *Book of Discipline*, the Navajos do it their way.

But the Reservation is like no other place in America. Having a license framed on the preacher's wall at home was not enough to satisfy skeptical would-be Reservation Christians of the authenticity of the message or of the messenger. From time to time, when a lay preacher got up to preach in one of the little churches, some doubting person would stand and demand to know by what authority the lay pastor spoke. Answering by saying that he or she was a licensed lay preacher of The United Methodist Church was not enough, the preachers reported to the Four Corners Board. So West came up with a solution. He made wallet-sized copies of the certificates, had them signed by the district superintendent and by himself as coordinator of the Four Corners Native American Ministry, found a local office supply place to laminate them, and the board then presented them to the lay pastors along with the larger certificates. Then, a lay preacher faced with a skeptic could flash the card indicating licensure by authority of an entity of The United Methodist Church, and satisfy the doubter. The feedback was immediate and favorable; the problem had been solved.

With the lay pastors newly confident in their positions and their status, the number of Reservation churches began to grow at an unprecedented rate. But for the Ministry, nothing came without a price. The increasing number of Navajo United Methodists called for more lay preachers. The volunteers who stepped up to meet the call had to be trained. Those who had provided the training up to that point were so overwhelmed with the pastoral ministry and administering the affairs of a burgeoning organization that they had trouble preparing for and delivering grueling, two-day training sessions. Additional time and emotional demands came from the personal counseling that went along with the training.

But for the Four Corners Native American Ministry and its board of directors, hope sprang eternal. It had learned that the concept of Methodist connectionalism extended far beyond the connection among the Four Corners United Methodist churches. That's why it took heart when it heard that the General Conference, the quadrennial legislative session of The United Methodist Church, had considered, and overwhelmingly passed, legislation that instructed the General Board of Discipleship in Nashville to study the issues faced by Native American churches and then find a way to solve them. Would this provide a solution to the need for pastoral training? Perhaps, but the work of starting new churches could not be put on hold while the possibility was explored.

## CHAPTER TWENTY-FOUR

# The Thrill of Discovering Christ

*For to this you have been called . . .*

—1 Peter 2:21

An article by an unidentified writer in the September 1988 issue of the *Newsletter of the Four Corners Native American Ministry* provided perspectives on how life for Navajos on the Reservation differs from experiences within the white, or Anglo, society.[1] Included in the differences was the way Navajos express their Christian faith, and thus how they go about starting a church. For example, no Anglo congregation would sit still for a two- to seven-hour church service, but Navajos expect to worship for that length of time without a single complaint about how long-winded the preacher is. Navajos give generously from their poverty, the article says, while most Anglos contribute sparingly, if at all, from their wealth. Navajos live from day to day, as Jesus counseled in Matthew 6:34 ("do not be anxious about tomorrow"), while Anglos worry themselves sick about the future. Navajos find their security in family life, the article continues, but most Anglos fight for position, struggling to accumulate wealth in different forms—money, real estate, securities, or personal property.

Most directly aimed at the placing of new churches was the writer's observation that "Navajos are experiencing the thrill and excitement of discovering faith in Christ for the first time, while Anglos have been building churches for over 1,700 years." This fact has led Anglos to assume that everyone is a Christian, the article said, but Navajos, with fewer than 15 percent of the Reservation population practicing Christianity, draw a completely different assumption. They are "MOVED BY LOVE," the article said, in capital letters, "to share their faith, especially with their relatives." They want their immediate family and their extended family, which might number in the hundreds, to know about Jesus, and to experience (and there were those caps again) "SALVATION, DELIVERANCE and HEALING."[1]

It was out of that love that five of the nine churches that then made up the Four Corners Native American Ministry had been started, the article suggested. They began when Navajo men and women, moved by love to share their faith, pulled in relatives to hear the Good News. The relative-based churches and their founders were listed: Raymond Burke, inspired by his mother, Blanche, at Dowozhiibikooh, Utah; Cecil Parrish Jr. at Oljato, Utah; Roger Tsosie at Tselani Valley, Arizona; Billy and Sadie John at Blue Gap, Arizona; and Roger and Frank Lee at Tohatchi, New Mexico.

Reverend Fred W. Yazzie described how the Bible-study family churches began: "The groups that form these Bible studies are families . . . But then there are some neighbors who join in because they want to believe in Christ. Or believe in God and worship Him."

To start the church at Blue Gap in 1982, Billie and Sadie John saw possibilities in the lumber from their old house. The siding and planks, augmented by one thousand dollars and lots of volunteer labor chipped in by work teams brought in by the Four Corners Ministry, were used to construct a sanctuary. Its opening was celebrated by a day of preaching, singing, and food, with some eighty area Navajos attending. The mutton stew the crowd feasted on was cooked in an outdoor pot over an open fire. A visiting Anglo said it was the largest cooking pot he'd ever seen— but then, he'd never been to a Navajo family cookout, the Navajo Christians' successor to a powwow.

One of the churches started with love—though not drawing on family to form its initial nucleus—was the church at Ojo Amarillo. "Ojo," as it is often called, is a small community less than a dozen miles south of the site of what was once the Navajo United Methodist Mission School. A small group that grew into a church began there by meeting in homes. Starting it all off was Chee Benallie, who was then pastor of the church at Bistahi. Benallie learned that some of his friends were living in the Ojo Amarillo housing area located on the Navajo Agriculture Products, Inc. (NAPI) Irrigation Project, a federally funded program that promoted the irrigation of thousands of acres of Navajo flatlands, turning it into an agricultural Eden in the middle of the desert.

Pastor Benallie always had an eye open for a way to expand the ministry of the church and of the Four Corners Native American Ministry. He asked one of those friends if he could start a prayer meeting in his home. The worshippers had been getting together, praying, and reading the Bible for over a year when a federal official decided to check out why all the pickup trucks were parked around a certain neighborhood house, particularly on Sundays. When he knocked on the door and was invited to come in to pray and sing, he put a stop to it. The house was part of a federal housing project; religious services were not permitted in federally owned homes.

*Ojo Amarillo, New Mexico, services held during church construction.*

For Benallie, however, that was no more than a bump in the road. He moved the group into the gym of a nearby boarding school while he searched for a permanent location. He nosed around and found that land next to the housing development had been designated for churches in the development's master plan. He persuaded First United Methodist Church, Shiprock, to apply for a site. There was a five-year wait, but then, to Navajos, time passes whether prayers are sent up from a home, a gym, or a church. The application was approved, and the group was given a lease. With a ten-thousand-dollar gift from Newborn United Methodist Church in Indiana, gifts and grants from the New Mexico Annual Conference and from mission groups, and volunteer labor, the congregation built a new, two-story church building with sanctuary and pastor's office on the top floor, and kitchen, bathrooms, Sunday school rooms, nursery, and fellowship hall underneath. Taking advantage of the slope of the land, it was built with ground-level entrances for both tiers. The design of the 5,284 square foot structure was the brainchild of Herb Moushon, a contractor-turned-missionary, who had volunteered to work for the Ministry through the Mission Society for United Methodists. The church was begun in 1982, and was constituted in 1988.

Before the roof was on, the annual conference assigned the Rev. Fred Yazzie to the church as its pastor. When interviewed in his church office, he told about its start: "Work groups came from across the nation, United Methodist groups, young and old. Work groups came and started building from the ground floor on up. . . . And every week there was a team to carry on work until the church building was finally up."

Yazzie explained that two people supervised construction of the two-story building, in succession, after the first one left. "A couple took over the leadership of the man who left. So the work was continuous. We had people who knew construction, they were engineers in that field, so the work continued. It didn't stop, even though there was a change in leadership."

The interview with Yazzie took place on a Monday in mid-June, when school was out. Children were working busily with adults under a shade shelter in the dirt parking lot. The volunteers working with the children, Yazzie said, were from Haleyville, Alabama. Others with the volunteer group of twenty-six people were doing construction work on the church building, renovating a four-head shower annex used by the volunteers during their stays. Other volunteers were making repairs to the parsonage and working on homes belonging to some of the church members and others in the community.

In response to questions relating to the number of children reached by the Ojo vacation Bible school program, Yazzie described the church's problem as too many, not too few:

> We can't use many efforts to bring in the kids. One year we did that, and we had over 300 kids. Over 300 children. It was a large work group of volunteers, and even for them it was almost too much. . . . We have at present 19, 20 children. And we will increase that as we go into the week, but I asked the group to keep that smaller so we will have time to work with each student.

Yazzie estimated that if they were to send out vehicles to pick up children and bring them in: "We could easily go up to three hundred, but we're not going to do that . . . We could handle them, but it's a lot of stress. Even young people who come to us from different churches, they're strong, young, but three hundred is a little bit much." Even with little effort to draw in children, Yazzie figured that before the week was over, fifty to sixty children would be coming every day.

To emphasize the seriousness of a commitment to work as a volunteer for the Four Corners Native American Ministry, whether with a vacation Bible school or with a construction project, the Ministry developed and distributed an application form. It's called *Four Corners Native American Ministry of The United Methodist Church: Work Group Brochure*. In it, the requirements for two types of work groups are spelled out: vacation Bible school groups, and home repair and construction groups. The rules are stringent for both groups, and detailed enough so that any church agreeing to send a work group should encounter few surprises.

But though the volunteer program itself became another sort of outreach, the Four Corners Ministry was not finished with looking for other ways to touch the Navajos. In the tiny communities in which many of the churches were built, the church building functioned much like a community center, not only like a church. The community service aspect of volunteering began to draw persons from denominations unconnected to the United Methodists. The Kitsillie Congregation of The United Methodist Church, for example, placed a "Thanks" in the New Year 2001 newsletter of the Ministry. "We really appreciate those persons who have come out from different denominations to help put the building together," Pastor Kee Littleman wrote.[2] Pastor Littleman also found ways to open the church doors at the slightest excuse, for reasons in addition to holding church services. Many of the uses involved getting together to eat and celebrate whatever occasion came along, with the community invited.

While grateful for the ecumenical help and pleased at the evangelical effects of community outreach, the board stayed focused on the family as all-important. It studied what kinds of ministries might reach out to help families in the name of Jesus Christ, in addition to Yazzie's death ministry. In the early 1980s it settled on adding two: a thrift shop and an alcoholism counseling center.

CHAPTER TWENTY-FIVE

# More Ways to Reach Out

*For the body does not consist*
*of one member but of many.*

—1 Corinthians 12:14

The grocery store building had seen better days. Its roof was failing, the grit carried by the prevailing winds had sanded its siding into a pale shade of gray, and the sun had curled and split its boards into a crazy quilt of geometric patterns. But on the highway north of Shiprock the building was available, and the lessee was willing to let the Four Corners Ministry put it to good use under a sublease. Though the first home for the Ministry's thrift shop would be temporary, providing serviceable clothing to Navajo families at a low cost was long term.

The board figured that if they just had the right person to run it, a thrift shop could help those living in poverty, which was close to 100 percent of the Navajo families on the Reservation. The "right person" would be someone who could keep the place open several hours daily, and who was bold enough to speak up and tell customers that the services were offered in the name of Jesus Christ. With that, the thrift shop could be a tool for outreach, and maybe a few of its customers and their families would not only dress warmly for the winter, but would be led to salvation.

The Ministry's first thrift shop took up residence in the ancient building. It was open for only a few hours, three days a week, but that's all the time that Cecelia Smith could spare. It was enough, however, to let a Ministry-related board of directors overseeing the operation know that they were on to something—

*Lorena Lynch presides at the
Shiprock Thrift Shop.*

people were driving in to buy clothes at give-away prices from all over the Reservation.

In 1984, some four years later, word came from the old grocery store's landlord to move out. The thrift shop's board held a meeting in the lobby of an abandoned hotel on the main street in Shiprock. Paul West had arranged to meet there because he'd already scouted around town and decided that the hotel was probably the only vacant place that might house the shop until a more permanent location could be found.

The problem that the place just wasn't open often enough or long enough remained. So the members looked around the circle of Navajos sitting there in the hotel lobby, and right in the center of the circle was Lorena Lynch. Lynch is a grandmother who walks purposefully, with an erect, confident bearing that makes her seem taller than she is. She keeps her graying hair cut short in the back, swept up on the sides, and she dresses neatly. She could blend into any United Methodist Women's group anywhere in the country. Her face stern, she appears to be a woman who is all business. But then, someone will crack a joke, and like as not, she'll burst into laughter.

When interviewed in 2004, Lorena Lynch remembered the hotel lobby meeting:

> We had to select somebody, and I never knew it was going to be me (*laughing*). They said, "Well, we need to have somebody there who will really work, who can make something out of it." So they selected me.

> That was in March 1984. So I agreed to it. I said, "I'll try. I'll see what I can do. I don't know nothing about running

a thrift shop, or running a business, or nothing. And my kids have all gone out of high school, and I don't have nothing else to do any more." And this was just a perfect time. I was kinda feeling sorry for myself, I'm all alone and don't have nobody to care for (*laughing*).

West received tribal permission to lease the hotel, then the whole operation—lock, stock, and barrel—was moved by volunteers from the old grocery to the equally old hotel.

So they said, "Okay, you have the place, start working on it." So I got in there and cleaned it up, and some ladies helped me . . . So there I am with a whole pile of clothes, didn't know where to start, didn't know what to do.

So I thought, *Well, I'll just let it pile up, and I'll just open my doors* (*laughing*). And I opened up [on] March 20, 1984. And that was the day that I started out. It was slow, but I just had the faith that it [could] happen, that it [could] change; if it's God's will, it [would] happen. So we started writing letters to the Four Corners supporters out of state. We put it in the newsletter that we had a new thrift shop. We were in the UMW calendar . . . Clothes just started coming.

There was another move a few years later, this time to a building constructed by volunteers specifically for the thrift store. It was on the south side of the main east-west highway through Shiprock, on land leased by the Ministry from the tribe.

But selling clothes and other items donated to the shop was not enough for Lorena Lynch. She felt called to a personal ministry, and seeing an opportunity, she grabbed it with both hands. Lynch witnessed and prayed for the people who came in. When it came to marital problems, she could help, because she had first-hand experience. But, she recalled, nothing affected her quite as much as the customer who came in to look for healing.

I've never forgotten the very first time a client came for me to pray with her. . . . When I was working there . . . the preacher [on TV] would [sometimes] pray for people who had leg and hip problems, and then . . . stretch their leg out so [it] would be the same size. And I used to think that it was a fake. But . . . my first client who came in and asked me to pray for her, she said, ". . . Pray for me. I didn't sleep last night because my hip hurt, my leg hurt, and I'm crippled."

And I thought, *Oh, my God! Is it really going to happen?* (*laughing*). And I was hesitant, and I didn't know what to do. And I said, "Oh please, God, this time You're going to have to work. It's going to be in Your hands" (*laughing*). And I started praying for her and holdin' her leg. And you know, when I was praying for her, the leg became the same size. And I thought, *Oh, my goodness! This is what I always thought was fake.*

Lynch laughed and said that she no longer doubts that prayer can heal. As for her patient:

She said, "Oh, I feel so good. The Lord has just healed me. My leg don't hurt any more. My head don't hurt. I can run now." And her legs were the same size. At the time we started praying it was one inch shorter. And that was the start. That was the first test of me, and from there on, I didn't have any problem praying for people, no matter in what condition they were. I even prayed for drunks.

By the day of Lorena Lynch's interview in the Four Corners Ministry Thrift Shop, the operation had been offering its services for almost a quarter of a century. In those years, Lynch explained, there had been some changes. Her daughter, Vivian Farley, secretary for the Four Corners Ministry, now keeps all the books and records in the Ministry office. The operation runs so smoothly there's no longer a need for a separate thrift store board: Lynch reports directly to the Four Corners Ministry board.

She explained that clothes have come primarily from both Big Springs and Lewellen, Nebraska, for the past several years. The Nebraskans became interested in the shop after visiting as work teams. Barb and Dennis Miller became interested, too, and said, "We really need to help you with the clothes and all the items that you sell. We sure can bring you a lot of stuff." And the clothes started coming.

There's something else Lynch has never run out of: the spirit that leads her to pray for her customers while she helps them cope in her own special way with the poverty that grinds down the Navajos. "It's why God put me here," she says.

The Four Corners Ministry now operates another thrift shop in Window Rock. And further west, in Lakeside, Arizona, Shirley John has opened a third.

About the time that the board of the Ministry conceived of and started its Home for Women and Children in Shiprock, it saw the need for another outreach to help families. Most of the women and children who were coming to the Home did so to get away from husbands and fathers whose drinking led them to abuse their families. Once a woman came, it proved to be more than a one-time visit. She would come again and again. It was obvious that more than temporary shelter for victims was needed. Somehow, a way had to be found to end the abuse. The solution would be to treat the abusive husbands and fathers for the alcoholism that was driving them to take out their anger on their families.

While the need was obvious, the solution was more elusive. The Ministry tried several alternatives, but there was no funding for a trained alcoholism counselor. At last, the Ministry found a volunteer within its own congregation at Shiprock. Bill Sellars was a truck driver and an alcoholic himself, though he'd been healed of his affliction by a genuine Christian conversion. The board knew that Sellars had not been trained or educated as a counselor, but from the first day on the job, he was effective in his role as counselor for the new Shiprock Alcoholic Counseling Center. The program he ran included AA meetings, and was successful in bringing alcoholics, mostly men, to life-changing conversions.

The single report that remains in the Four Corners files reflected that through August 1983, the center had counseled 302 people; held 136 AA meetings, drawing fifty-five persons per week; and provided thirteen with Christian witness and prayer.[1] A preface to the statistical report declared that the purpose of the center was to "help those dependent on alcohol to find total freedom from their addiction by helping themselves with God's help." It explained also that the center "is operated by volunteers under Shiprock Community Christian Fellowship, consisting of Southern Baptist, United Methodist, Episcopal, Christian Reformed, Roman Catholic, and Assembly of God, by a letter of agreement with Nataani Nez Community Citizens Concern Committee on an acre of land designated by Shiprock Chapter in a building constructed and donated to the community by the United Methodist Church." The truly ecumenical community program was based, the report said, on 2 Corinthians 5:17 (NKJV), "Therefore, if anyone is in Christ, he is a new creation; old things have passed away; behold, all things have become new."

But the program ran into a snag that masqueraded as a benefit. It was finally able to get federal funding to pay for the counselor's salary and other operational expenses. That was the benefit. The snag was that the government required reports. After several months during which none of the federal forms were prepared or filed, the Four Corners Board of Directors learned that the man who was so successful counseling men wrestling with alcoholism was illiterate. Efforts to find funds from sources that did not require reports turned up no support, though the tribe and United Methodist agencies applauded the concept of an alcoholism counseling service aimed at Reservation Navajos.

A search for a volunteer, literate worker on the Reservation who was able to fill in forms produced no one who wanted the job and had the skills to fill it. There was no alternative but to close the door on the volunteer-built counseling service located on the top of a hill south of Shiprock. But the concept was too sound and the prayers of the board were too earnest to permit it to stay closed for long. In 2001, the Ministry was contacted by the Congregational Methodist Church, a small denomination that wanted to begin an outreach on the Reservation. It saw a

Linda — thanks for
letting me take this
book — Wanted to under-
line & write notes, so
did buy one (many
folded down pages) — so
giving you a new
one —

My cousin who
lives in Albuquerque
read it & found it
interesting — was
surprised at how
political the church is —

He has lived on
Navajo land as a child
& worked for BIA as

a teenager —

Thanks again —
You are a dear friend —
Ginny

*A roadside band draws attention to the newly opened alcoholism treatment center.*

need for alcoholism counseling, and it had the funds to get it going. The Ministry sublet its building to the new group at no cost. Today, the Surrender Service started by the Four Corners Native American Ministry has a new name and a new sponsor, but it's back in the counseling business, healing Navajo alcoholics through the miracle of confrontation with Jesus Christ.

❖

During the same period that the Ministry board and Rev. Paul West were wrestling with the issues of the alcoholism treatment center, the General Board of Global Ministries decided to take a hard look at the Ministry that was functioning so well. With encouragement from Albuquerque District Superintendent Brodace Elkins, the GBGM agreed to the transfer of home missionary Rev. David Warden from his post in Taos, New Mexico, to Shiprock, where he was appointed by the New Mexico bishop to serve as assistant director of the Ministry. Eventually, he would be appointed as pastor of the Shiprock church, too.

Warden apparently met the test for Ministry pastoral leadership that had been set by Bishop Schowengerdt some ten months earlier, following the expression of the GBGM's concern over the role of the Mission Society in supplying volunteers. In the fall of 1984, when the activities of the conservative Mission

Society came to the attention of the GBGM, Schowengerdt addressed West to make clear his hands-off position on the theology of the Ministry:

> [Let] me state that it is not my intention to control the theological orientation of selected persons for the Four Corners Ministry. It is important that whoever is selected have a good working relationship with you and Fred Yazzie. [Once that requirement was satisfied, he wrote,] bring the recommendation to the New Mexico Cabinet and the appointment will be made by me.

But having approved the move of Warden to the Reservation, the GBGM also had another move in mind. That was to position itself to designate West as "head of the Four Corners Native American Ministry," and to make the Ministry an agency of the GBGM. The proposal came from the executive secretary of Ethnic and Language Ministries, Dr. Myong Gul Son. His plan was sent to Dr. Elkins, Albuquerque district superintendent, who forwarded it to West without comment, except to ask him if it was what he desired.

Son's offer proposed that goals for the Ministry would be worked out between the National Program Division of the GBGM and the New Mexico Annual Conference, though Son specified three social goals, as well as the administrative responsibilities of the head of the agency for reaching them. None of them addressed making new Christians in a non-Christian environment or placing new churches, unless the definition of "leadership for Christian witness and faith in action" could be stretched to include such specifics.[2]

West wrote back promptly. He reminded the district superintendent of a recent letter which Schowengerdt had written when the National Division had begun dabbling in Ministry affairs. The bishop had stated with no equivocation that "the Four Corners Ministry is exclusively a New Mexico Conference and Northwest Texas Conference mission project." West suggested that Elkins reject the notion of making the Four Corners Ministry into a National Division program agency, and that he make his comments known to the bishop and his cabinet. West proposed that the cabinet could then reply appropriately to Son.[3]

The response to the executive secretary was made by Elkins. He said that he, Schowengerdt, and West had conferred and decided

> that your proposal concerning Paul does not fit in with the history and the direction of the Four Corners Native American Ministry. This has always been a mission effort of the New Mexico Annual Conference with the Northwest Texas Conference joining in. [It is] not appropriate for the Ministry to become an agency of the National Division which your proposal does.[4]

The Ministry would stay connected directly to the New Mexico Annual Conference, where it had been since the day some ten years earlier that the National Division representative had caught up with West in Illinois and pulled away his home missionary support.

But while these matters were demanding attention from the Ministry board, it also had its everyday business to look after. At the August 31, 1985 board meeting, it set up a pastor parish committee for the Ministry. It was to include two members from each of the five churches, none of whom, by church law, could be pastors. Those two members, plus one other, were also expected to act as the local church's committee. At the same meeting, the Ministry director's job description was approved. It included seven specific responsibilities, beginning with traveling outside the Reservation to raise money. The director was expected to spend two days each month at each church, getting to know the people and pastors. The board assigned him the duty of working with tribal red tape, as well as handling the books, newsletter and general administration.[5]

Meanwhile, the board of the Ministry had not forgotten about that legislation by which the General Conference had directed the General Board of Discipleship to offer help for Native American churches.

CHAPTER TWENTY-SIX
# Training Leaders

*. . . we shall reap, if we do not lose heart.*

—Galatians 6:9

The Board of Discipleship responded to the General Conference's directive to address issues faced by Native Americans by calling a meeting in Nashville in September of 1981. The conclave, called "Consultations with Ethnic Minority Local Churches," offered the hope of training for lay preachers. The Four Corners Ministry sent five of its board members, plus Reverend West, to the gathering. While Ministry representatives arrived full of anticipation and optimism, the whole exercise proved to be yet another betrayal.

The six Four Corners leaders drove all the way together in a minivan, rarely stopping along the way except to gas up, eat, and take restroom breaks. When Henry and Jean Begay (Window Rock, Arizona), Louis and Raymond Burke (Montezuma Creek, Utah), and Stella Lee and Paul West (Shiprock, New Mexico) pulled into the Board's Nashville parking lot, they found that they were part of some 230 local church leaders who had appeared. The crowd represented 112 churches out of a total identified 158 United Methodist Native American churches scattered over 117 annual conferences and five jurisdictions. Few of them, it seemed, had much in common with the conservative and evangelical Four Corners Ministry Navajos, except that all were eager to learn what the Board could offer by way of leadership formation, leadership training, and funding.

The official report of the consultation glowed with satisfaction in describing it as "a historic event." It boasted that "no other agency had gathered such a number of Native Americans for the purpose of listening to what they had to say." The staff of the General Board, all the way up to the acting general secretary, "gave repeated assurances that this was not just another meeting to air needs and issues with no intentional strategies to address the needs."

Singled out for special attention were the Navajo Indians in the New Mexico Conference. They were promised stewardship training, to take place on May 22–23, 1981, at First United Methodist Church, Shiprock. The Navajos present promised a turnout of some 100 to 150 persons, and that they would provide an interpreter to translate lectures into Navajo. The Four Corners representatives drove back home filled with enthusiasm and vigor. Not long after, they received a report confirming all that had taken place.[1]

But the training never happened, for no one from Nashville came.[2]

Navajos have always been known for endurance, patience, and—unfortunately—for expecting white men's promises to be broken, so the breach of faith came as no surprise. But the Four Corners Navajos had the advantage of having a friend in the New Mexico episcopal office.

Three years later, in late 1984, Resident Bishop Louis Schowengerdt prodded the Annual Conference Board of Higher Education to take action on the most current issue facing his favorite mission outreach. The Four Corners Native American Ministry needed to find a way to train its lay preachers, and despite the disappointment with the Board of Discipleship, Schowengerdt was determined to uncover it.

At the stimulus of the bishop, early in the winter of 1985 Rev. O. A. McBrayer, chair of the Conference Board of Higher Education, was commissioned to reach out to the General Board of Higher Education and Ministry in Nashville on behalf of the Four Corners Ministry. According to a report he wrote to Bishop

Schowengerdt in November of that year, McBrayer's assignment was "to secure aid and leadership for a training program for Navajo 'Lay Preachers' of the Four Corners Parish." McBrayer went to work.

For the Four Corners Ministry—calling on the name of the bishop for leverage—McBrayer was able to get a one-thousand-dollar grant from the Conference Board of Ordained Ministry. With that in hand, he induced the Nashville organization to send a representative to New Mexico to put on a lay preacher training workshop. The Division of Ordained Ministry of the Nashville board assigned Rev. J. Richard "Dick" Yeager to do the work. Step one for Yeager was to scout out the territory.[3]

In a meeting held in Albuquerque in November 1986, Yeager took measure of the group that had assembled to orient him. As a rookie in the ways of the Navajo United Methodist, he wanted to know something of the character and education of the lay preachers he would be dealing with.

Among the eleven planning expediters that showed up from Four Corners to meet Yeager, he found three ordained clergy, including Rev. Fred W. Yazzie, Rev. Paul West, and Rev. David Warden, and eight Navajo lay preachers: Chee Benallie, Henry Begay, Raymond Burke, Lucy Lewis, Leonard Begay, Shirley Montoya, Eugene Chee, and Harry Descheene. Five of the lay preachers he identified as holding down other jobs. Among the lay preachers, one (Shirley Montoya) had two years of college, three had finished high school, one had gone through the tenth grade, one through the sixth, and two had stopped their formal education at the third grade level. The three ordained pastors assured the visiting expert that the group of lay preachers was representative of those he would find taking the training he planned to offer, except that Montoya, with her two years of college, had more education than he was likely to run into among the Navajo United Methodists.

Yeager was a careful report writer, though as a newcomer to the Ministry he skewed some of his facts. He correctly recorded that all the lay people who had appeared were involved in the "special license program," though he did not know that it was the Navajos themselves who had designed the program. Yeager, too, persisted in identifying his new clients as "Navaho," unaware of the fact that the Tribal Council decades before had adopted the spelling "Navajo" to eliminate all doubt about how to spell in English what these American Indians were called.

In structuring his teaching program, Yeager's aim was to equip the future attendees to "do ministry within and upon the

WE BELIEVE that

1. Prayers should not be made to "mother earth."
2. The cross and feathers do not go together.
3. The Yei (rainbow or others) represent Navajo gods and should never be incorporated into Christian symbols or pictures.
4. The Indian drum in powwows, tepees, and traditional ceremonies is always considered a spirit (or spirit voice) and should never be used when Navajo Nation Reservation Christians are present.
5. The Navajo word "beauty" may be used to describe the Navajo Christian's experience, but it is never an end in itself apart from Jesus Christ. In worship, the word "beauty" should always add "of God" or "of Christ."
6. Bringing Navajo ceremonies (or parts thereof) translated into English into Christian worship is not only offensive to reservation Christians but also offensive to the medicine man.
7. Respect for other religions and cultures is part of the Navajo way. Reservation Christians would appreciate respect for the way they feel led of God to worship and follow Jesus.

—From "On Consulting with
Navajo Christian Leaders on the Reservation.
Submitted by the Four Corners Doctrine Committee,"
a resolution adopted by the New Mexico
Annual Conference. 1996 session.

reservation." But he also hoped to motivate some "to go into the ordained ministry." Yeager proposed a plan that would culminate in the design of a continuing education program for the Reservation. Yeager reported that West was excited about the whole program and eager to have him finish his planning and get on with it.[4]

Discussions with the Navajos led Yeager, the outsider, to decide that there was no question that the Ministry intended to be an indigenous outreach. A harder question was whether the structure the Ministry took on should be indigenous, or whether it should reflect what Yeager called a "traditional United Methodist form."

District Superintendent Dr. Brodace Elkins had slipped into the meeting. It did not take him long to clarify for the man from Nashville a few concepts that he thought the trainer should know up front, though there was too little time to share with the teacher more than a fraction of what he needed to know. Yeager summarized what Elkins had told him in his report to Bishop Schowengerdt:

> The Navajos [want] to be Navajo although they will not want to bring the medicine man's religion into the process of formulating their Christian theology. They are Christian, not Native American [in theology], although the Native American approach culturally does influence almost everything they do. They function on a different concept of time, and the family is of exceeding importance.

Though there is no way to measure how much of the advice from Elkins soaked in, the counsel was enough for Yeager to make a decision about how his lessons would approach the Methodist structure. He wrote, "Perhaps until the church becomes 'family' the methodical, that is, the United Methodist approach, will not work until this feels like the family has the needs and the time to do things this way." The man from Nashville, though struggling to understand the people he'd come to serve, was replowing ground the Ministry itself had tilled a few years earlier in deciding what would work on the Reservation.

Two months later Yeager was back in New Mexico, but this time he was in Farmington, where he held a three-day pastors' seminar. For this meeting he drew eight lay pastors, one missionary supervisor, two laywomen active in the Ministry, and spouses of four of the pastors. He kicked off his training with a theological inquiry, which included asking what God was calling the Four Corners Ministry to do, and with whom He was calling the Ministry to do it.

When he'd finished, Yeager wrote a ten-page report that outlined each and every topic covered. He closed with listing the "Next Steps," which included contacting a Native American professor at Iliff Seminary in Denver, and contacting his board in Nashville for leadership at future training events to be planned.

Yeager, however, was not invited to return. The lay pastors who had come to learn gave him and his proposed road map for future training a thumbs down. Though it appears that Yeager never knew what had happened, his proposal that the Navajos should ulti-mately be led to change their family values and put first the Methodist value of doing things methodically had butted heads with the Four Corners board strategy to modify the Methodist way to conform to the Navajo culture, and single-mindedly focus on making disciples for Jesus Christ. Yeager's plan to bring in the Native American from Iliff fell flat, too, since the professor was known to hold views of native spirituality that were opposed to the Ministry's views, and to embrace a liberal theology that was 180 degrees away from the conservative beliefs of the Ministry.

Yeager's problem was not unique among outsiders that came to help: when it came to the Navajos and their culture, he had more to learn than he had to teach. One telling point made by someone he interviewed, recorded in the "Problems" section of Yeager's report, told the tale: "Those who would help us from outside the reservation do not know us."

The experience with a representative of the General Board of Higher Education was not the end of pastor training for the Four Corners Native American Ministry, though it marked a new beginning of sorts. The Ministry made a decision: when in doubt, do it yourself. It would go back to in-house training, while recruiting occasional outside teachers who had a feel for the culture and whose theology paralleled that of the Navajo Methodists. The outside educators would be integrated into a program which featured homegrown talent at the teaching podium, and homegrown interpreters to translate English words spoken into Navajo.

During an interview, West outlined the model that evolved for formation of pastoral leadership for Reservation churches:

> They all have a local pastor from their own church with a license to preach—the license we give—and who has had the training. I would say that they're generally from the family that started the church. [The training was initially provided mostly by Fred Yazzie, Roger Tsosie, and myself, who would work up an outline together.] We'd ask ourselves, "Well, what do the preachers need that they're not getting?" or, "What do they need to learn that they don't know?" or, "What kind of two or three year training program can we do?" We'd come up with courses like that.

Since the leaders-in-training would come from as far as 150 miles across the Reservation, training sessions were held in motels so that the Ministry could provide lodging. But things changed.

> Now, we have a master training center at Window Rock. We have a training center there, so we can house them. If we have overflow, they can go to a hotel. So we are now tying more into Cook Training School down in Phoenix. . . . We're working in conjunction with others also.

The Ministry also began to import trainers. Paul West explained:

> I met a man from Hawaii. He's Methodist, but he's with a non-Methodist mission organization. And he came and he brought two or three others of the team. They taught for a week. One session was on preaching. How do you prepare a sermon? How do you organize it? How do you prepare yourself to present it? And things like that. It was excellent.

[The man from Hawaii, named Stan,] brought a series of messages on Moses, and on Aaron, how Aaron lost and how he regained his status as a leader. It was on leadership, from the Bible. We majored on preparing for preaching, because we found that a lot of them got up that morning and put their finger on a verse and they preached from that. But most of them, most commonly, would pick the third chapter of John and go verse by verse in a running commentary. That was the standard for preaching on the Reservation. Just going from verse to verse. So . . . we were doing the training ourselves. Fred and Roger both knew the language and had seminary training . . . We try to have four sessions a year . . . It's starting to work really good. Of course we started this years and years ago. Ira Gallaway, he was helping us for several years.

So the Ministry experimented with various in-house training models when the General Boards of Discipleship and of Higher Education and Ministry struck out with their training proposals. But the Four Corners Native American Ministry had not seen the last of the general boards of The United Methodist Church. And there were issues of culture and theology to be addressed.

## CHAPTER TWENTY-SEVEN

# Preserving the Nonreligious Old Ways

*Why do your disciples transgress
the tradition of the elders?*

—Matthew 15:2

Vivian Farley is a Navajo who is vocal on the issue of preserving native cultural practices that do not carry religious overtones. While she is convinced that the practice of native religious rites and the use of native religious symbolism coax new Navajo Christians back to the old ways, she sees value in preserving the old ways that represent the native nonreligious culture.

A friendly, open young woman, Farley is the soccer mom for the team her grade school daughter, Morgan, plays for—though she hasn't yet figured out how the girl plays soccer, basketball, and all the while keeps up with her award-winning academics. As part-time secretary on the paid staff of the Four Corners Native American Ministry, Farley has a stake in its success, but first and always she is a Christian with convictions that go deep.

Vivian Farley is the daughter of Lorena Lynch, who runs the Methodist Thrift Shop started by the Ministry in Shiprock. When she was a child, her mother had not yet become a whole-hearted Christian. Later, when she reached her teens, her mother sent her to the Methodist Mission School in Farmington. But the instructions Farley had received in the ways of the medicine men and witches while she was a young girl on the Reservation were not easily put aside.

Farley says that accepting Jesus Christ in her life when she became an adult has made a difference in the way she lives.

167

She is no longer gripped by the fears that once made her think twice about everyday activities that made her vulnerable to spells cast by witches or skinwalkers, in the way that medicine men taught her when she was a child. She gave a matter-of-fact example in an interview:

> Take cutting our hair. We would sweep it up and gather it and take it home in a bag and burn it. The witches were so powerful, we thought, that all they need is some part of you, something from the body, to cast a spell on us. Fingernail clippings, too. I would gather them up and flush them down the toilet.

Farley says she no longer worries about the hair, though she still finds herself flushing fingernail clippings, but for a different reason. "It's habit now, not fear, that makes me do it. And owls. Owls brought bad news. Like a death, sickness. We were afraid of owls. There is no fear in the living God I pray to now."

For Farley, though, there is some apprehension that remains. It comes from the temptations in the whispered messages of fear left over from the old ways. The apprehension might be described as an awareness that those messages still call out to one who was brought up to believe that evil powers brought danger. Farley knows that the Navajo Christian who once followed the native religion must always guard against falling back into honoring the old deities and fearing witches. Relax the guard, and there is the risk of being tugged away from the Lord Jesus Christ, in whom there is no fear.

"The important thing about the Ministry and its history," according to Farley, "is that its people have turned their backs on the traditional religion and practices. And that's a miracle." But she warns that especially those who have recently turned away from the old ways are still very sensitive to them. "We call the new ones 'baby Christians,'" she says. "They need extra care and love."

Though she has rejected the traditional religion and practices, Farley is a proponent of emphasizing Navajo cultural practices that do not carry overtones of native deities or witches. Among their number, which was approved by the Four Corners Board, is native architecture, "like the hogan and our brush shelters," she says. "Then there's our native way of dressing, our clan system. Especially the clan system." Others include native foods and ways of cooking, weaving and the geometrical patterns, but not the religious ones, used in weaving, and "our language and our Reservation life. Sheep herding. And don't forget our jewelry. We like silver jewelry, and you go to a Four Corners meeting and you'll see a lot of it." Farley says that sand painting is a cultural practice that is retained, but that native god-figures should not be portrayed. And, "the rainbow is a symbol with Christian significance, but not when you combine it with the yei [native god-figure]."

There were other native traditions and practices that the Ministry set out to preserve. They included love of the living land, concern for physical fitness, respect for elders, generous sharing, and the Navajo sense of humor. In addition to sand-painting and jewelry making, pottery painting as an art is preserved, without religious symbolism. And then there's the practice of community meals at special moments of life, observed at the local Navajo churches at the slightest excuse. All these elements, and more, were to be collected and listed by Mrs. Sally Gallaway during the period when she and her husband were in Shiprock training Navajo lay volunteers.[1]

Vivan Farley is aware that Rev. Paul West has been criticized by those who think he is trying to stamp out the Navajo culture. She says the critics have it all wrong:

> He has helped me in my growth. When I've questioned some things, like Navajo religious ceremonies that some of my Christian friends say I should not be going to, I've gone to Paul to talk about them. He doesn't say don't go. Instead, he's shown me how I can change things to make them Christian.

Farley says that Rev. Roger Tsosie and West have helped Four Corners Navajos put a Christian twist on puberty rituals, for example, focusing on the help God and Jesus can give to the girl entering womanhood:

> [The ritual] is a four-day ceremony with lots of things taking place. Every mom on the Reservation puts her girls through it when it is time for them to be adults . . . One of the things is, the girl has to run. You know, to teach her to be healthy and to exercise. The girl has a mentor, a lady who stands by her for the four days. She is picked by the family as an example of a good woman for the girl to follow.

When she talked to West about participating in the ceremony, she says he told her that the mentor can be a Christian woman:

> She lays the girl on a blanket and shakes her and prays she'll be a good woman. The prayer can be Christian, to the living God through Jesus. The gifts to the girl can be Christian symbols, like a necklace with a cross. Those things can teach the girl how to be a good Christian woman.

Farley goes to those puberty ceremonies with no twinges of conscience. "But when I'm asked to be the mentor—and I have been asked a couple of times—I haven't done it yet. I don't feel that comfortable, even though I know I can make it Christian. Some of these times I will."

Vivian Farley is not the only one to wrestle with non-Christian religious ceremonies embraced by young Christians. A different cultural version of her dilemma was reported in the January 14, 2004, issue of the *Wall Street Journal*. A front-page article reported on a young Methodist girl who told her parents she was ready to convert to Judaism because she wanted a bat mitzvah and the big party that went with it. Her parents compromised. They gave her a big party, but "without the religion." Jews have objected to this making of a religious ceremony into "a pop-culture celebration with no religious significance," the author of the article wrote. Some claim that, "They mock an important spiritual rite of passage."[2]

To date, there have been no reported situations that Christianizing of the Navajo puberty rites mocks the significance of this milestone in a young girl's life. The same cannot be said of the resolution of some other Native American/white Anglo religious and cultural differences.

George E. Tinker is a professor at Iliff School of Theology, Denver, a United Methodist seminary. Dr. Tinker, in his book, *Missionary Conquest: The Gospel and Native American Cultural Genocide*, points out that on some of the Plains reservations, a pipe is often placed on the altar next to Holy Communion by "'liberal' or 'open' white missionaries to usurp native cultural forms into their own repertoires." He finds that, rather than demonstrating sensitivity to the cultural needs of the native community, the placement of the pipe is a tool of the Anglo clergy.

Tinker concludes that "placing a native religious symbol adjacent to [communion elements] elevates the white religious expression of the gospel as superior to traditional native spiritual forms." While the professor admits that the behavior is subtle, it nevertheless emphasizes white superiority. When the pipe is added to the white missionary presence and the "Euroamerican interpretation of the gospel, which is inherently culturally biased . . . the result is to [teach to Indian peoples] that spiritual leadership, like economic leadership, has passed to white people."[3]

Reverend Roger Tsosie has his own interpretation of the purpose of many Native Americans in intertwining the symbolism of native worship into Christian sacraments. He knows that some Native Americans who grew up away from a Reservation and lost connection to the old ways have gone back to practicing some of the ways of the native religion as a way of recapturing their cultural heritage. He explained:

> There's a kind of marginal Indian, marginal Navajos or [from] other tribes. They were not exposed to this type of way down deeper [native] religious life. . . . I guess in order to identify themselves as authentic Indian, they want to . . . have a sense of religious life, additional life, they want to be warmed [*sic*] into that.

While Tsosie understands where these people are coming from, he says that's not for him:

But for me, if I can speak the Navajo language, that makes me an Indian; that makes me feel like an Indian. I don't have to dance in a powwow to make me feel like I'm a full-blooded Indian. I'm already—you know, my skin tells me when I look in a mirror. My hair tells me that God made me this way (*laughing*). That's what I appreciate.

Since he first met West and came to be a part of the Four Corners Native American Ministry, Tsosie says he has heard some individuals criticize West because they believe he is against blending native practices into Christian worship:

I haven't heard [Paul West] say anything about that. I just have a feeling that those people that say those things are the ones that are more like city-raised individuals that don't seem to know much about the traditional life . . . or they're trying to be Indian while they're trying to be in the Anglo world. So that's the way I feel. We are Christian. If I can read the Bible, if I can do what it says and live according to that, I feel satisfied.

Reverend Fred Yazzie is more adamant on the issue of how to worship and how not to, and more firm in preferring beliefs held among the Four Corners Navajos to those of other Native Americans. He said:

They will say that to you that Paul West has brainwashed all the Navajos. But Paul would not do that. It's just our way of believing in Christ that the Caucus doesn't believe in. And in fact, the people in the Caucus have asked us to join their group. And because they're doing drums, feathers, and all of these, the Navajo people do not want to be a part of that, because that's syncretism. They have chosen to leave their former way of worship.

And I know that the people in the Caucus, they do not worship that way. They think they can praise Jesus and worship the old way, but that's—worship in the old ways really means praying to Mother Earth, Father Sun, and still holding on to traditional ways, and they are talking to many gods, where the Navajos feel they should talk to only one God: He's God the Father and Jesus Christ, His Son, who

died for us on the cross. The Caucus doesn't know how to
stand that. That's not in their vocabulary. Their vocabulary
is (*laughing*)—well, they're very liberal.

Lay pastor Elmer Yazzie is unequivocal in identifying the
source of the stance of the Four Corners Navajos against incorporating native religious practices into Christian worship: "We
got together and decided we'd better stay away from the old
ways because we might fall back into them." But Elmer Yazzie is
all for preserving the kinds of nonreligious cultural practices that
Vivian Farley identified on the Four Corners list of acceptable
cultural customs, those nonreligious customs that will not call
baby Christians back to the old ways.

The view is neither new nor unique among Native
Americans. The Rev. Homer Noley is a United Methodist pastor
who, for a time, worked in the offices of the General Board of
Global Ministries and is now director of the National Native
American Center, headquartered at the Claremont School of
Theology in California.

A Choctaw Indian who grew up in southeastern Oklahoma,
Noley authored a book titled *First White Frost: Native Americans
and United Methodism.*[4] In it, he tells the story of Duane Porter,
a Chippewa clergyman who became a Methodist. Porter took
the gospel to the Native Americans in the Upper Midwest before
the end of the nineteenth century. Noley's book seems to
pronounce a judgment on Porter's theology when it records that
"unfortunately, Porter, as did many early Native clergy, believed
that acceptance of Christianity meant giving up the ancient religions." Noley called the following report from Porter a "touching
if frustrating scene":

> On the morning of July 4, 1891, we gathered together a
> company of converts and went inside the lodge, took
> down all the wooden images of birds and animals,
> carried out the drum and threw all these things in a pile.
> Soon many of the old pagan Indians came up the hill
> with their little drums, medicine bags, skins of small
> animals used in the medicine lodge ceremony and threw

> them also on the pile. We then walked around the lodge
> hall singing, "Nearer my God to thee." Some young brave
> touched a match to the pile of pagan relics and a great
> fire consumed them as we stood and watched.[5]

The quote Noley extracted from Porter's tale described the destruction of what Yazzie would call animistic worship symbols. Noley's lament, that to Porter accepting Christianity meant giving up the ancient religions, reflects the NAIC's intolerance of the path chosen by the Four Corners Navajo United Methodist Christians in making precisely the same decision.

In a telephone interview, however, Noley urged only a respect for the Native American belief system, while suggesting that the rejection of that belief system springs from what he calls "frontier fundamentalism." Nevertheless, he concedes that theologically conservative groups, such as the Four Corners Navajos, are probably more effective in making disciples for Jesus Christ than those with more liberal beliefs.

Tsosie is not judgmental. Of those who work the old ways into their Christian religion, he says, "I'm just neutral. That's the way I look at it. So I try to tell my people not to be down on each other because of a certain person who is behaving this way, praising God or being quiet, or so forth."

Tsosie said that when West came to the Four Corners, he asked West:

> How do you want us to worship God? And he told us, "Do
> whatever you want. However you want to please God,
> whatever you're used to, that's the way you worship God."
> He didn't say get away from your traditional custom and
> your culture, your religious life, he didn't say anything. So I
> was pleased with that.

As for the board of directors of the Four Corners Native American Ministry, it adopted a catalog of cultural practices for preservation, paralleling those listed by Vivian Farley and Sally Gallaway. Fred Yazzie added to the list by emphasizing similarities between the place of spiritual healing in the native

*Lay pastor Elmer Yazzie and Rev. Paul West take a break at a training conference.*

culture, and the healing power of Jesus Christ, as well as the resemblance of the Navajo devotion to family and the concept of brotherly love, to the emphasis on both to the follower of Christ.

Sometimes, though, the theological stance of the Ministry has seemed to negatively impact its treasury. The situation seems to have arisen because of reactions by general church boards that shy away from funding Native American missions that elevate evangelistic efforts for Jesus Christ over preservation of the old religious symbolism through what has come to be called "contextual ministry."[6]

Meanwhile, as the Ministry wrestled with the theological issues, the Methodist Mission School was facing problems of its own, and the Ministry was still keeping an eye on it.

Dr. Leonard Gillingham, a former New Mexico Annual Conference district superintendent and former pastor of several large churches, now retired, served a term on the General Commission on Race and Religion from 1992 to 1996. During his tenure, the subject of the Four Corners Ministry came up through Caucus members who served on the same board. "I once got a phone call from one of them asking for help," he said. "The caller told me the Caucus wanted to get rid of Paul West in that Four Corners Ministry out there." Gillingham asked why.

"He said that West was 'Anglo, racist, his theology is not Methodist, he doesn't understand the Native American culture, and he's out there colonializing.'" Gillingham promised to check it out. He did so to his satisfaction, concluding after conversations with Bishop Norris, Albuquerque District Superintendent David Saucier, and others, that the charges had their roots in an individual who was antagonistic toward the annual conference and the Ministry for personal reasons, and "that individual was influential with the Caucus."

Another member of the same board from New Mexico, though he'd lived in Virginia when he joined the board, was Daniel Ivey-Soto, an attorney. He recalled the discussions Gillingham referred to:

> There was a lot of talk over whether Four Corners people honored native spiritual traditions or not. Caucus people thought they should be honored. But a lot of people with the Four Corners Ministry found freedom in rejection of things that had spiritually impressed them in the past. That was the issue.

Ivey-Soto could not say for sure that the Caucus position had hurt the Four Corners Ministry financially since he was not on the Minority Self-Determination Fund Committee that recommended grants. "But it was very political," he said. "And the organization with the political power was the Caucus, not the Ministry."

Ivey-Soto explained that he related well to the Ministry because of lessons he had learned from his mother, who grew up in a missionary church in Latin America. As with people from the Central Conferences who spoke at the 2004 General Conference of the denomination, at which he was a delegate, he knew that, "If you are from one of these non-Christian cultures, if you are a Christian, you live a very different life than those around you." The lesson his mother taught him opened his eyes to the position of the Four Corners Navajo United Methodists.

And so, the debate continues. The Four Corners Navajo Methodists practice their conservative, if not fundamentalist, brand of theology without benefit of native religious symbols and with rare denominational support, and the members of the NAIC practice their beliefs. Perhaps in a few generations the

CULTURE AND CHRIST by Roger Tsosie

The person officiating the baptismal service has to be affirmative that the person he is baptizing has been taught specifically concerning baptism for repentance and that the "teaching and learning to observe all things" the Lord has commanded will continue. Furthermore, the person being baptized has to know that the baptism is being done ". . . in the name of the Father, and of the Son, and of the Holy Ghost . . ." and not in any other deity like father sun, sky or any celestial body, which the Navajos believe as supernatural deity.

To be in full surrender to God will require a purposeful decision to turn one's love from the love of any other gods to the one true God . . . there has to be a change of mind. . . . Many times I have admired many of my Navajo elders, who testify that they have decided to follow Jesus, because for them they were brought up authentically in the Navajo religion and culture. There is a strong Navajo belief that it is taboo, and the gods through natural phenomenon could cause tragedy, for the individual who forsakes the Navajo religious birthright. . .

I recall . . . an old Navajo medicine man who became a Christian . . . because he couldn't handle the power of alcoholism with religious ceremonies. He was very well known all over the Navajo Nation Reservation as a medicine man and a healer. . . . When he gave his life to Christ he gave up drinking miraculously, and he forsook all his religious paraphernalia. . . . He was horrific with nightmares, and evil spirits would invade his hogan.

He was able to fight it off with his prayers until a king owl started haunting him. This owl flew in every evening and sat on his hogan. . . . He felt crazy and had fainting spells. He was just a new convert and didn't know about spiritual authority. . . . One night he went out to curse the owl straight in his eyes, but he forgot what to say so he just said, "I am Jesus Christ. Don't you ever come to my hogan again!" "The owl flew off in a zoom and never returned," he said.

A continuous visitation of an owl represents evil spells, and it can lead to death. There are many other ways spiritual battles can develop when a Navajo turns to Christ, and so it is wise to teach biblical authority with cultural awareness.

—Reprinted with permission from *Newsletter of the Four Corners Native American Ministry*, November–December 1995 powwow, the prayer sticks, the cedar ash and smoke, and the representations of the *yei* god-figure, may come to mean little or nothing to Navajos residing on the Reservation other than a quaint reminder of a long-ago past when there were no Christians on the Reservation. Or perhaps the Caucus Native Americans will come to accept the concerns of those still vulnerable people to whom the native religion exerts a call to return to the old ways by abandoning Jesus.

But for now, at least, the Four Corners Navajos are just too close to the old ways to forget that the traditional religion stands for what Tsosie identifies as "deception," and Yazzie calls "spirit voices." And what new Christian needs that?

While the Four Corners Ministry was treading a theological pathway in the steps of Jesus, to some, the mission school in Farmington seemed to be about-facing to march in the opposite direction.

CHAPTER TWENTY-EIGHT
# Mission School Escapes the United Methodist Corral

*The sheep of the flock will be scattered.*
—Matthew 26:31

With the Navajo Academy in possession of the campus and firmly ensconced in the mission school buildings, in less than two years Rev. Paul West was mailing letters to the board of directors of the Four Corners Ministry to answer their question: "What has happened to our Navajo United Methodist mission school?"

West responded with a Navajo-style parable of an old sheep that escaped the corral, turned bad, and attacked its would-be rescuer. West's tale suggested the owner had four possible solutions: leave the creature for the wild animals to devour; sit by and fret, stew, and complain; chase it down, bring it home and brand it to show ownership; or shoot it and use what you can. He ended with a question: "Which do you think the family [that owned it] did?"[1]

Before long, West and the Four Corners board members were not the only ones asking questions about what was happening with the school. On October 18, 1982, Lula M. Garrett, as assistant general secretary of the General Board of Global Ministries, wrote to Hector Navas to ask why the Navajo Academy personnel seemed to think that the Church would give them the property.

Garrett apparently found this attitude difficult to deal with, as the National Division of the General Board believed it was in charge of administering the operation. Her solution was to demand that the boards of the academy and the school get together and hash out an operating agreement, perhaps a lease. She called on Navas for a budget, clarity on who was paying whom, certainty about who staff worked for, and an explanation of how an academy owned by the Tribe could be paying money for repairing property belonging to the National Division.[2]

While Garrett was waiting for an answer, Navas wrote to West, accusing him and others of stirring up the board of the school to replace Navas as school superintendent with the Rev. Sam Wynn, the clergyman from North Carolina who was under appointment to the Four Corners Ministry.

Though Navas was not removed, Garrett was invited to travel to Farmington. She accepted, and on March 11, 1983, she met with the boards of both the Navajo Academy and the mission school to talk it all over. There, and in a follow-up letter a month later, she promised to make a consultant available to the two entities, and to work to put together a single corporation with representatives from both boards for the operation of the school.

Despite the optimism briefly resulting from the meeting, Garrett's follow-up letter expressed indignation that the National Division's relationship to whatever then remained of the mission school had been misstated. She had taken offense at language in a federal official's plea for funding for the construction needs for the Navajo Academy campus. The official's letter sought funds to refurbish the "physical plant which formerly comprised Navajo Methodist Mission," and it asserted that the Tribe had a lease for twenty years for use of the Navajo Academy, with the right to renew "as long as they use the facility as a school or as some educational institution."

It was all such a surprise to Garrett that she accused the local board and Navas of incorrectly stating the intentions of the National Division concerning the school's operation. She proposed that someone be sent in to protect the GBGM's interests, both fiscal and legal. She emphasized the board's commitment to ethnic people, however, and was pleased with the academy and what it was trying to do for the Navajos, especially its youth.[3]

When it became obvious that her calls for action had been lost in the shuffle, on May 23, 1983, Garrett wrote again, this time to Dr. Dillon Platero, principal of the Navajo Mission Academy. She told Platero of her frustration over the school's total change in direction under Navas, saying she had tried for five years to clarify the National Division's role in the school's operation. She had gotten little response to all her inquiries, and expected little more.

She seemed to have reached the end of her rope. Somehow, under her very nose, the academy had taken over the school. She found she could not send whom she wanted to the campus to help Platero establish a functional relationship with the National Division. Her ending observation was a threat that if matters could not be worked out, Headmaster Platero should consider an alternate location for the academy for the next academic year.

Garrett was a prolific letter-writer, and her letters continued, though it seemed that no one was paying much attention. The list of alternatives she proposed for the mission school, or whatever it had become, grew longer, pleas for a budget escalated, her musings turned to talk of recouping losses, and the frustration level that boiled out from between the lines increased from one letter to the next until she decided to bring in an outside consultant.

At that, Navas confessed his own frustration. He wrote to Garrett on May 23, 1983, telling her that her decision to bring in a consultant brought him "personal pain." He would seek a sabbatical from the mission school board, because, he said: "Ministry to the Navajo people has been difficult for me. Not because of the way others have labeled them as pagan or unchristian, but rather because they have come to know God in an atmosphere so radically different from my own tradition and experience."[4]

It was yet another affirmation of the conclusion drawn by Richard Yeager, the researcher sent to the Four Corners by the General Board of Higher Education and Ministry, repeating an unidentified Navajo's comment: "Those who would help us from outside the reservation do not know us." As it turned out, the new consultant sent by the National Division to try to work with the local mission school board and the academy had not learned the ways of the Navajos either.

CHAPTER TWENTY-NINE

# "The Incredible Experiment" at the Mission School

*Let the children come to me . . .*

—Matthew 19:14

S ome ninety days after the visit of the latest consultant to Farmington, Lula Garrett wrote to Richard Lewis, president of the mission school board, and admitted that the expert she'd sent out had "handled it very poorly." He was being removed. She proposed that the division "streamline our staff to one person," a chaplain, and advised that funds would be cut.[1] Not since the missionary ladies jumped down from their wagon in the shadow of Hogback had the mission staff been so paltry.

The entity on the campus was now known as "Mission Academy." It had resulted from a merger of sorts that permitted the New York board to claim some credit for the academy's academic program. The school's newsletter, the *Navajo Mission/Academy Messenger*, in its June 1984 issue, traced the melding of the academy and the mission school in an article titled, "The Incredible Experiment." Terming the newly named Navajo Mission Academy an integration of "self-determination and the reinforcement of Navajo cultural values" with the "salvation of souls and missionary work," the writer said the end result was an institution made possible when "the consciousness of the missionaries changed from controlling to empowering the Navajo people to help themselves." It announced the transfer of authority from the "appointed missionary," Hector Navas, to the "new missionary," Headmaster Dillon Platero, "appointed by his own people."[2] Platero was not identified as either a Christian or a native traditionalist.

Having turned the academic operations of the school over to a secular organization, Navas, a United Methodist clergyman, declared victory by restating the school's reason for being to something different from that announced by past superintendents, who had focused on Jesus Christ and Christian education. Navas wrote: "We have fulfilled our mandate as a Mission, to further the principal [*sic*] of the self-determination of Indian peoples, as an enabler, sustainer and supporter of people who are trying to help themselves." With that, in the view of the Four Corners Native American Ministry, its split with the school was complete.

Despite the Navas explanation for the reason for dropping the reins of the school, Rene O. Bideaux, having resigned several years earlier from his position at the National Division, shed doubt in a 2004 telephone interview on the promotion of self-determination as the motive for letting go:

> We were afraid of liability issues. Our attorneys were telling us that trial lawyers around the country were stripping away what had protected us against lawsuits like peeling layers off an onion. It was happening to all kinds of institutions, not just Methodist-related in particular. And so we thought of that, and we decided to divest ourselves of hospitals, schools, and things like that.

But the National Division still kept a tenuous grasp on the mission school. A document titled "An Agreement for the Cooperative Administration of the Navajo Mission Academy" was intended to mate the former Navajo United Methodist Mission (NUMM) with the former Navajo Academy (NA) to produce the brand new Navajo Mission Academy (NMA). The pact recited that while the NUMM's purpose had been religious, and the academy's goal had been education, now there would be a common objective. The new entity would exist to develop "leadership among Navajo young people through the processes of religion and education." So the "incredible experiment" began.

The National Division soon arranged to send Deputy General Secretary Bideaux to Farmington for yet more study, analysis, and conversation, including review of the feuding between the school and the Four Corners Ministry-related Concerned Committee.

Bideaux was no stranger to the Four Corners area. The year before, he had brokered a settlement of issues that had led the General Board of Global Ministries to threaten to cut off denominational funding to the Four Corners Ministry because of fears that the Ministry was being taken over by the Mission Society. When Bideaux's on-site investigation of the facts turned up only a misunderstanding, the New York authorities were calmed, and Bideaux left New Mexico with a reputation as a problem solver.[3]

Minutes of the March 1985 meeting of the board of the surviving remnant of the Navajo Methodist Mission School contain revelations by Bideaux about the relationships among the school, the National Division, the Four Corners Ministry, and Rev. Paul West. Bideaux admitted that GBGM had been "exclusive theologically." Adding to the admission, Bideaux said that "the stance theologically and Methodologically [*sic*] of Shiprock & Four Corners Native American Ministry is somewhat distant from the Mission at Farmington." The split between the liberal school and the conservative Ministry, he added, "belies inclusiveness and the diversity we are called upon for."

Calling the situation he found in the liberal-versus-conservative struggles in Farmington and northern New Mexico a "Micro-Cosom [*sic*] of the Total National Mission Context," Bideaux laid the burden for implementing mutual respect at the feet of the New York Board of Global Ministries.[4]

There was a second confession in the minutes. Despite verbal affirmations of the importance of indigenous leadership for the school and of "empowerment," the National Division had moved out one board and brought in another "without consultation." Having done so, then the Board of Global Ministries failed to have "greater involvement" with this second, all-Navajo, board.

Bishop Schowengerdt was in attendance. He reported that the style of the approach taken by the General Board toward the school was not just local, it extended to the whole United Methodist Church and beyond. CBS's *60 Minutes* and the *Reader's Digest* had carried stories on the Board of Global Ministries, and had found that it "had a narrow and limited view of missions."

After Rene Bideaux had returned home, issues came to focus on the local board's decision to hire Cordelia Candelaria to succeed Hector Navas, and on the extent of the board's authority. Dr. Candelaria was given a contract, but then Bideaux nixed the pick: the board had taken diversity too far when it found a person of the Baha'i faith to hold down the position of Superintendent.[5] If the board persisted in its independence by hanging on to Candelaria, Bideaux decreed, he would see to it that school funds were frozen. That was insult enough for Candelaria. She asked for a buy-out of her contract, and George Hartzog III was chosen to fill the job.[6]

At virtually the same time, Schowengerdt reinforced the position of West, thus implicitly approving his actions, by giving him a "Special Appointment" as director of the Four Corners Native American Ministry. West viewed the step, and reported it to his charge conference at the Shiprock church, as "a big step forward by the New Mexico Annual Conference, to see that The United Methodist Church continues to grow on the Navajo Nation Reservation." West characterized the year 1985 as "a time of great struggle, trial & testing, and transition." He viewed his bishop's affirmation as a mandate to move on toward more new Navajo churches, more evangelism, more Christian workers, and stronger Navajo leadership.[7] And there would be no slacking off of efforts by the Ministry to save the United Methodist presence on the campus of the former mission school.

Hartzog's time at the school surpassed that of Navas in the quantity and length of his correspondence to and from the Four Corners Native American Ministry. West continued to write to question the direction the school was taking, and others jumped on the bandwagon. Part of the reason was the difficulty in getting a handle on what the role of the Methodist Mission School was, because the school operating on the campus was now known as Navajo Mission Academy (NMA), and a Christ-centered presence was all but invisible.

The new direction of the school was confirmed when NMA dedicated a newly renovated Alumni Hall on September 30, 1986. The dedication ceremony featured singer/medicine man Frank Collins of Church Rock, New Mexico, who performed a Navajo Blessingway ceremony. The program described the ceremony as "the foundation of Navajo religion," and explained that the name Blessingway meant "the way of beauty, harmony, good, blessedness." The day after the ceremony, West wrote to Bishop Schowengerdt to describe the occurrences, noting, "No Christian ministers were invited to the dedication."[8]

At its fall meeting in 1987, the Board of Global Ministries recommended that the Women's Division and National Division grant "up to" $450,000 to the mission school to supplement its budget for 1988. A representative sent by the National Division to Farmington to determine how the sum would be used returned to New York, and wrote to Superintendent Hartzog to tell him that next time he needed money, he should find alternative sources.[9]

At least fifty thousand dollars of the promised funding was paid, though the board of the Navajo United Methodist Mission School (NUMMS), on August 21, 1987, authorized its attorney to file suit to remove the Navajo Academy from the campus. The academy contested the eviction, claiming it had the right to occupy the campus rent-free because it had spent so much in capital outlays for improvements to the facility.

The "incredible experiment" was dead. Though there were efforts to resuscitate it, at least on paper, they failed. No students wanted to board on the old mission school campus while attending Farmington municipal schools for college prep studies.[10]

On March 13, 1989, Lula Garrett and Joyce Sohl jointly sent a letter to Richard Lewis and George Hartzog to tell them:

The National Division will no longer recognize Navajo
United Methodist Mission School (NUMMS) as a national
mission agency related to the national Division and will so
advise the appropriate organizations of the denomination
which control the solicitation of Advance Specials.[11]

Though the lawsuit would continue for a time, the academy
eventually came out on top, receiving a final affirmation of its
lease until 1991 from Judge James Brown. The court ruled that
an immediate eviction would destroy the academy's program
and "cause a major setback for Navajo education." A publicity
release distributed to the *United Methodist Reporter*; the board of
directors of the General Board of Global Ministries; a newspaper
in Farmington; and *Newscope*, a United Methodist newsletter,
quoted Garrett: "The mission school is not a school. There is no
program." At last, in August 1995, the division sold the school
building and eighty acres of land, valued at around three million
dollars, to the academy for about $573,219.[12]

The seller retained for itself thirteen acres with a scattering
of small buildings at the north end of the campus. It is there that
it hangs on, operating an off-reservation program called New
Beginnings, a service to abused and substance-abusing Navajo
women. Pleas from the Four Corners Native American Ministry
that it rework its logo to remove or revise a representation of the
Navajo yei deity, considered offensive to the Navajo Nation
Reservation United Methodists, are ignored.

During all the activity going on at the campus and in the
courtroom in Farmington, there were jurisdictional issues of a
different sort in Shiprock playing out for the second time. These
struggles would never have come about had the Four Corners
Native American Ministry not been so successful in making
disciples and in opening new churches while the Methodist
Mission School was slipping out of the Methodist corral.

## CHAPTER THIRTY

# Issues of Theological Correctness

*Can you find out
the deep things of God?*

—Job 11:7

In the spring of 1987, the outreach of the Four Corners Ministry into the Western Jurisdiction states of Arizona and Utah began to draw reactions in the Desert Southwest Annual Conference offices in Phoenix.

The cabinet and representatives of the Conference Board of Global Ministries of Desert Southwest were puzzled, they said through their spokesmen. Their resulting unease was spelled out in a letter jointly written on May 6 of that year by two conference officials and addressed to an officer of the Methodist Church's Native American International Caucus (NAIC).

The letter said that those in Arizona did not understand how the Four Corners Ministry related to the Native Americans in their state, though the writers denied any desire to subject the people of the Navajo Nation to state lines drawn by white men. The letter pleaded for help by way of advice from the Caucus in assisting the letter-writers, and presumably the cabinet and board whose concerns they said they were expressing, to understand the place of the Four Corners Ministry in their state.

The starting place, according to the letter, should be some kind of a Four Corners consultation. It would be held under the direction of the Caucus or of the National Division of the General Board of Global Ministries, perhaps to be held in Farmington. Included would be Bishop Schowengerdt of New Mexico, and

Western Jurisdiction bishops from Phoenix and Denver. The aim of the consultation would be to assemble all the persons who should be occupied with ministries among the Navajos and the Hopis. [1]

Three months later, after the Caucus executive committee had met and decided to hold a planning meeting to address the work of the Four Corners Ministry, the NAIC president sent a copy of the letter to New Mexico's Bishop Schowengerdt. The transmittal letter reported that the Caucus had already enlisted Rene Bideaux and Dr. Negail Riley, both of the National Division in New York, to organize the meeting.

It was all news to Schowengerdt, to the coordinator, and to the board of directors of the Four Corners Ministry, the results of whose missionary zeal and effectiveness had prompted the proposed consultation.

In the three weeks following his receipt of a copy of the letter, Schowengerdt met with the bishops from Phoenix and Denver in the Western Jurisdiction, as well as with Bideaux. Their encounter happened during a break in a meeting of bishops held in New Jersey.

When Schowengerdt returned to Albuquerque from New Jersey, he responded to the Caucus by a letter dated September 1, 1987. He reported the New Jersey conversations as well as his subsequent talks with various leaders in the South Central Jurisdiction and some in New Mexico about what he'd learned back east. He explained that all of those leaders had wondered why the Desert Southwest Conference and the Rocky Mountain Conference had passed resolutions affecting the Four Corners Ministry without a word to anyone in New Mexico, including its bishop, and why the National Division seemed to be backing them up. After expressing disappointment at the way the planning had been handled, he added, "all [the leaders in the South Central Jurisdiction] strongly urge that any consultation be composed of at least 60% Navajos."

Schowengerdt affirmed the respect in which the New Mexico Annual Conference held the Navajos and how it was committed to helping them in their journey to faith. He followed the affirmation with a lesson in how to deal with the indigenous peoples whose Reservation included parts of New Mexico, Arizona, and Utah: "I think it would be a major mistake for those of us outside the Navajo Nation to tell them what they need or how they need to relate to The United Methodist Church."

The New Mexico bishop then elaborated on his demand that if there were to be a consultation, the voting odds must be tilted heavily toward the Navajos. He set a requirement that there should be one or two representatives from each annual conference, one or two from the Caucus and the National Division, and "approximately forty from the Navajo Nation." The meeting should be chaired by Rev. Fred Yazzie, then the only ordained Navajo United Methodist elder.

He added a suggestion from his South Central Jurisdiction consultants that maybe it was time that the Western Jurisdiction developed a ministry to the Hopi. "Because of the territorial dispute between the Hopi and Navajo tribes, it would be better for some conference other than the New Mexico Conference to develop this ministry." No one needed to be told that the Hopi Reservation was entirely within Arizona of the Western Jurisdiction or that the Hopi were not the subjects of any noticeable United Methodist mission outreach, just as no one needed to be told that the New Mexico Conference was the only conference in New Mexico, Arizona, and Utah with substantial work among the Navajos.

Schowengerdt's closing paragraph addressed an aspect of the conservative theological stance of the Four Corners Ministry, whose importance in the minds of the Navajos had been proven to the New Mexico bishop. If the principle involved were not embraced by the officials of the Western Jurisdiction, he knew it would rule out the effectiveness of any outreach they might try to aim at the Navajos, if indeed they were to initiate Reservation activity.

> There is a Navajo radio preacher speaking every day to the Navajo people criticizing the United Methodist Church and stating that we support homosexuality. I have checked

with various members of the Navajo Nation and they all tell me that homosexuality is taboo in their culture. As you know, our formal principle is that homosexuality is incompatible with Christian teachings. It is absolutely essential for the work on the Navajo Nation that all participating conferences support this position in every regard or it will be extremely detrimental to our work with them. [2]

Unexpressed was the fact that the Rocky Mountain Conference had recently appointed a homosexual pastor to a local church [resulting in that fiery radio campaign against those responsible]. Known to Schowengerdt, too, though the information had not been widely circulated outside the Reservation, was the fact that the board of directors of the Ministry had three years previously, on April 9, 1983, adopted a proposal on the issue of whose jurisdiction they wanted to operate under. It read:

The Navajo church members have a dream. We dream that the whole Navajo Nation Reservation will be under one Annual Conference. And we dream that all future Navajo Mission work will be under one organization: The 4 Corners Native American Ministry. [Closing with an expression of desire,] Our Navajo churches are in a multiple charge parish under the New Mexico Annual Conference and we wish to stay that way.[3]

The vote for the proposal had been unanimous.

Meanwhile, questions about jurisdictional issues resulting from lines drawn on maps by white men as affecting the churches at Dowozhiibikooh and Oljato, in Utah, had reached the other Western Jurisdiction bishop involved in the consultation plan, Roy I. Sano, who had replaced Bishop Wheatley in Denver. The matters that came up would surely be discussed should a consultation ever come about.

Dr. Brodace Elkins, the Albuquerque district superintendent, believed he had put to bed the concerns over the Ministry crossing state lines to the satisfaction of the Rocky Mountain Annual Conference when he had worked the matter out with the district superintendent in Steamboat Springs, Colorado. His optimism faded, however, when he received a call from Sano. He told of their first conversation: "But later [after the Dowozhiibikooh Church had been opened] Bishop Sano called me. He seemed upset. 'What are you doing organizing a Methodist Church in our conference?'"

Elkins explained:

> I told Bishop Sano the D.S. [in Grand Junction] had author-
> ized it—he recognized the problem, and I said I was happy
> that the Grand Junction D.S. was helping with this church.
> Bishop Sano said, "What are you trying to do with those
> Navajos?" I said, "Help them do what they want to do."

Nevertheless, Elkins said:

> I told Paul we were decommissioning those churches as
> United Methodist Churches. So we did—made them into
> independent mission churches, and that's how they're
> carried today in the *Conference Journal*. Paul West did a
> magnificent job. He thought like a Navajo.

Following his telephone conversation with Elkins, Sano wrote him to record the solution they had struck for resolution of the jurisdictional dilemma. He began by reciting that the Rocky Mountain Annual Conference "celebrates the outreach ministries of the Four Corners Ministry, including its work in southeastern Utah." He called that outreach "an opportunity to challenge" his own conference to pursue outreach ministries among Native Americans. He confirmed that the channel for such efforts would be the existing structure of the Four Corners Ministry.

In the same letter, Sano addressed the issue of Four Corners-related churches that had already been planted on the Reservation in Utah. "There seems to be no reason to formally charter the Navajo congregations in southeastern Utah as United Methodist churches," he wrote. He listed the reasons for his conclusion.

First, he and his conference had gained "an emerging under-standing of the processes of fellowship and mission churches being chartered United Methodist Churches." The congregations planted in Utah seemed to him to be in that process, though that conclusion appeared to ignore the fact that the Utah churches had already been "chartered" as United Methodist Churches of the New Mexico Annual Conference with the cooperation of the Grand Junction District Superintendent.

Second, he suggested the New Mexico Annual Conference call the "fellowships and congregations 'Christian churches' in the broader sense of that phrase." while indicating that they were part of the Four Corners Ministry. There was no suggestion that any United Methodist connection be disclosed.[4]

Elkins then wrote back to confirm Sano's summary:

> Since the Rocky Mountain Annual Conference did not wish to have any connection with the two churches at Oljato and Dowozhiibikooh in Utah, I met with representatives from those two churches at the Council meeting of the Four Corners Native American Ministry and explained they would be a part of the Four Corners Native American Ministry as Independent Christian Churches. They will be listed as a part of the Four Corners Ministry in our *Conference Journal* and will be a part of all publicity in the future as independent congregations.

The Elkins letter thanked Sano for his support of the Ministry, asked that all work groups for the Utah churches be scheduled through Rev. Paul West, and promised that in literature relating to the Advance, the churches would no longer be carried as "UMC churches."

In closing, Elkins reminded the Colorado bishop of the furor created on the Reservation when the Navajo radio preacher had railed against Bishop Wheatley of the Western Jurisdiction for appointing a homosexual clergy. Those incidents, he wrote, "might pose a serious problem for the Four Corners Native American Ministry" if representatives of Sano's Conference were named for participation in the proposed consultation with Navajo leadership.[5]

The implication was clear. Elkins knew that the Four Corners Ministry Navajo lay leadership would not participate in a consultation about their future if the Rocky Mountain Annual

Conference were represented. The consequences of the solution advanced by Sano and accepted by Elkins were also clear: the churches at Oljato and Dowozhiibikooh would have their charters withdrawn in favor of an independent mission church designation, and no more United Methodist churches, as such, would be formally chartered through the New Mexico-connected Four Corners Ministry in the parts of the Reservation lying within Utah, or presumably, within the part of Arizona west of the fifty-mile strip previously agreed on as part of the New Mexico Annual Conference.

Despite the assurance of the letter that had started the clamor for a consultation, denying any interest in subjecting the Navajos to state lines drawn by white men, Sano's plan as agreed to by Elkins had done exactly that. It continues to influence the structure of indigenous Navajo churches established through the Four Corners Ministry on the Reservation even today.[6] Nevertheless, it explicitly legitimized the model for allowing Ministry churches to be planted without regard to the annual conference boundaries, thereby enabling continued outreach without bureaucratic interference. Though apparently there was no formal communication with the Desert Southwest Annual Conference about the plan, the Ministry continued to reach out into Arizona as though that Conference were also a party to the accommodation.

Elkins reported that the *Conference Journal*, as of the date of his interview, still carried the Utah churches as independent mission churches. Currently, they are listed alphabetically in the church directory of the *New Mexico Annual Conference Journal* with other United Methodist churches. However, following their church names there is no UMC listed, as with other churches. They are not labeled as independent mission churches, nor do they carry any other distinguishing words.

The news that the Utah and western Arizona churches would be called independent mission churches was received with good graces in the Four Corners Ministry. Everyone with the Ministry board understood that soon the people in New York, Denver, and Phoenix would move on to something else and forget all about the Navajos, but the Ministry would endure. For the Ministry Board of Directors were all Navajos; they all knew that time was on their side, and that time erases everything.

Since 1991, or perhaps earlier, all of the Four Corners Ministry churches are clearly United Methodist churches. All display with pride the distinctive cross and flame of the denomination. Some of them are "fellowship churches," some "mission churches," and some "constituted" churches within the Ministry, but none deny that they're United Methodist. That's the way the Navajos of the Ministry want it, and the New Mexico Annual Conference supports both the Navajos and the Ministry.

After the agreement between Sano and Elkins had been struck, West wrote to Marvin Abrams, NAIC president, on February 1, 1988, to acknowledge that he had been given a copy of the letter to Abrams proposing a consultation that had started all the hubbub. He offered whatever services might be useful to the Desert Southwest Annual Conference, including an invitation to visit the Four Corners staff, churches, and projects.

West's letter included a few statistics. He noted that on the eastern side of the Reservation, the part in which the Four Corners Ministry did its work, "around 15% are Christian. Whereas on the western side of the reservation 5% or less are Christian." Most of the population centers, he added, are in the eastern section, and "the western part is a lot more rural," making mission work "more difficult."[7]

As the serious business of who would have jurisdiction over churches started by the Four Corners Ministry in areas of Arizona and Utah within the Western Jurisdiction, and how they could be accommodated to the Ministry working under the New Mexico Conference was being renegotiated, Bideaux unintentionally provided an interlude of comedy.

On November 18, 1987, Bideaux wrote to Schowengerdt to bring to his attention a "delicate matter" that those in New York "no longer can allow unchallenged." He charged that West had been seeking funds for the Ministry through the Mission Society for United Methodists, rather than through "channels of the New Mexico Annual Conference." The offense was one that "would remove it from the concerns of the GBGM and the Benevolence Program of the U.M.C." It was a not-so-veiled threat to cut off funding for the Four Corners Ministry if West did not pull the Ministry away from support by the Mission Society.

Bideaux had proof positive of West's transgression, a copy of which he sent to Schowengerdt. It was a letter from a person in the West Ohio Conference who had worked as a volunteer for a Four Corners church construction project. She complained that Paul West himself had gotten up before a group of the volunteers and "said he represented the Mission Society." (Underlining was provided by the accuser.) To nail down her indictment, she attached an exhibit, a copy of a page from *Good News* magazine. It was labeled "advertisement," and was set up as an article entitled "Missions." The picture in the ad, the accuser said, was the very person she had heard make the statement. She identified the smiling face as belonging to Paul West, and the building he stood in front of as the self-same church she and fellow West Ohioans had worked on for Four Corners. It was all so very clear that the hanging rope should be readied.

But the accuser had fingered the wrong man.

The picture was not of Paul West at all; it was of a lay volunteer named Herb Moushon. A construction expert, he had been recruited by the Mission Society to work at Four Corners and had supervised various church construction teams in New Mexico and Arizona over several years while he lived in a camp trailer provided by the Ministry. He was there "seeing to completion a number of important projects," according to the ad that featured his picture.

Apparently, Moushon's zeal for the work for the Navajos had led him to ask for funds for the organization that had recruited him to serve and was responsible for his presence in Shiprock. The ad in which Moushon's face appeared had been placed by the Mission Society as a solicitation for volunteers to work in any of several United Methodist–related ministries, from Shiprock to Ghana.[8]

None of the statements attributed to West had been made or approved by him. The accusations against him fell by the wayside, though the fact that the Mission Society contributed money and volunteers to the Four Corners Ministry continued to be a burr under the GBGM saddle.

CHAPTER THIRTY-ONE
# The Evaluators

*It is the Lord who judges me.*
—1 Corinthians 4:4

Instead of the consultation the Caucus and the National Division had planned to hold in Farmington at the urging of the Desert Southwest Annual Conference, the GBGM sent two staff researchers to New Mexico in late 1987 to check out the work of the Ministry among the Navajos. The results of the investigation were written up by Douglas W. Johnson, director of research, and published in 1988 in a fifty-nine-page booklet titled "Research on the Four Corners Area and Churches in the Navajo, Hopi, and Ute Reservation and the Denver Urban Ministry."[1]

Johnson recorded that his work had sprung out of "requests from staff following a meeting with Bishop Roy Sano (Denver) and Bishop Elias Galvan (Phoenix) and conversations with Bishop Louis Schowengerdt (New Mexico)." The requests, he wrote, sought data about population for the purpose of helping the Desert Southwest and Rocky Mountain Conferences that border or include parts of the reservations (Ute and Navajo) under study "make decisions about the potential for mission." Despite the report's title, it devoted only a few pages to data, the Hopi, the Ute, or the Denver Urban Ministry. The balance addressed the Four Corners Native American Ministry and its churches.

Among those interviewed during the study was Rev. Fred Yazzie. The report writer called him "one of the most vocal proponents of an uncompromising Christian perspective." He was described as opposing the "Native American Church (the Peyote Church) and the singing of Navajo American Church songs and pow wows [*sic*] and other old practices." Although Yazzie was not asked to verify the accuracy of the description of him, he did so in the copy of the report provided to the Four Corners Ministry. Yazzie emphasized that he was *not* opposed, he wrote, to "the singing of Navajo American Church songs," but to the singing of "*Native American Church (peyote) songs*." He was *not* opposed to "old practices," but to "old *religious* practices." The researchers had failed to pick up the distinctions.

The evaluation of the Ministry described it as a "model of church mission extension." It nevertheless criticized the Ministry as "unable to critique itself in the face of opposition." Troublesome to the reporter was the Four Corners stance on syncretism, a term referring to the incorporation of native religious symbolism and spiritualism into Christian practices and worship. In drawing his conclusions, the report writer apparently relied on Ministry member Shirley Montoya for the pro-syncretism view, and on Yazzie as spokesman for the Ministry board, leadership, and the church members. Ridiculing the Navajo United Methodist negative view of native religious ceremonies that honor and respect native deities and spirits, and that call on them for healing and spiritual guidance, the report discussed the differences.

On the syncretism issue it said:

> there are differences of opinion on syncretism and acculturation. One of the key questions is, for example, "Can you be a true believer and go to Pow-Wow [*sic*]?" For those who grew up in a culture where Boy Scouts have pow-wows [*sic*] at the YMCA and are still considered American, such questions are as absurd as asking, "If the Pope dances a Polka, can he still be Catholic?"

The comparison was offensive to the Four Corners Navajo United Methodists. Likewise, it was insensitive and naïve in measuring the Navajo powwow against a Boy Scout meeting with parents hovering in the background. The Ministry view was described in comments made later by both Yazzie and

Roger Tsosie. One pointed out the disturbing religious element of powwow; the other, the negative social impact.

Tsosie described temptations at a Navajo powwow that could not be dreamed of by adolescent Boy Scouts, and which had been ignored by the researchers from New York. "With us, some of us have been brought up with those social ceremonies, like powwows and other things. It kinda reminds us where we're coming from. There's a lot of deception, a lot of drinking and partying and stuff like that."

"Stuff like that," according to Tsosie, refers to drunken assaults on women, drunk driving, and illegal drug usage. That's why, he said, it's best for Navajos to stay away from powwows: to avoid the call of alcohol and to sidestep an environment where drinking and drug use is socially and culturally acceptable for a people who have felt the adverse effects of alcohol more than any other ethnic group on the continent. Better to go to church family gatherings where songs are sung and big pots of food are cooked and shared around a communal table, and the drink of choice is coffee or soda pop.

Yazzie attacked the spiritual element of the powwow: "The Indian drum, powwows . . . traditional ceremonies [are] always considered a spirit, or spirit voice."

The report criticized the "leadership" of the Ministry (a euphemism for Rev. Paul West) for not being more self-critical and for failing "to be open to some of the diversity that exists especially as it relates to tensions between the old traditions of spirituality and the new embracing of the Christian faith." It suggested that the limitations could be overcome if personnel from the very agency Johnson worked for could just get into a position in the Ministry so that they could bring "a wider range of theological perspectives." The report lamented that while Asbury and Fuller seminaries were "well represented," people from Iliff Theological School, a seminary espousing a more liberal theological viewpoint, including embracing the use of native religious practices, "feel left out of the dialogue and planning for Christian mission."

Left unexplored was any connection between the growth of the Ministry and its roots in the conservative and evangelical

theology that put Jesus Christ first—ahead of native deities, native
religious ceremonies, and their incorporation into Christian
worship. Left unexplored, too, was the justification for paternalistic
interference of outsiders coming in to promote changes to the
evangelical theology of a single cooperative parish.[2]

Despite the occasional criticism of the Ministry, the report
written by Johnson gave it overall high marks. Its recommenda-
tions section drew this conclusion:

> The Four Corners Ministry represents an excellent
> example of faithfulness and creativity that has worked out
> in a particular context over the last several years. This
> model may have general applications for future mission
> development among other indigenous peoples.

Lifted up as especially important was the Ministry's practice
of beginning "in the field," such as through tent revivals. The
growth in the number of church buildings was a plus, including
especially the use of volunteers as builders, giving the locals an
ownership stake in the constructed worship or study center. One
of the results of this practice, the report said, was the low cost of
operating the Ministry. Another positive was the success of the
local churches in their spiritual and numerical growth, their self-
sufficiency, their focus on starting new churches, and their
missional outreach to their communities. Finally, the report
pointed out, all this was being done with indigenous leadership
recruited and developed from the local churches.

Johnson offered the National Division of the Board of Global
Ministries as a "pool of personnel, resources, and capital" for the
Ministry he described as a model for other mission outreaches.
The situations in which the Division could provide help included
education opportunities through an Iliff-related Reservation
seminary branch for training lay speakers and lay workers, and
help for youth ministries for Henry Begay's church in Window
Rock. It suggested exploring other unspecified means for starting
United Methodist churches in addition to the one it recognized
as so effective.[3]

The praise was welcomed by the Ministry as encouraging recognition by other United Methodists. But all the suggestions for liberalizing the theology that the Ministry had chosen as its own fell on deaf ears, beginning at the level of the office of the resident bishop and extending all the way down the ecclesiastical and organizational ladder through the Four Corners Ministry Board of Directors to its laypersons in the local churches.

◈

The College of Bishops of the South Central Jurisdiction sent another evaluator to the Reservation a year following the Johnson visit. The investigator was Dr. Earl B. Carter, the executive director of the South Central Jurisdiction, whose office was in Dallas.

Carter was commissioned by the South Central College of Bishops to respond to a letter written by Dr. C. Leonard Miller of the General Council on Ministries, Dayton. The letter had addressed Native American ministries within the South Central Jurisdiction, and suggested that the Jurisdiction should "give consideration to ways in which they (the Jurisdiction) can enhance ministry to Native Americans in those geographical areas in consultation with Native Americans in the development process." Carter made visits to the Four Corners and to the Oklahoma Indian Missionary Conference.

Carter sounded an alarm in the cover letter to the report he wrote for the General Council on Ministries:

> We may be facing a crucial situation at Four Corners. If the work among the Navajos in eastern Arizona is removed from Four Corners the results will be devastating. The ministry of the past 25 years could "go down the tube." The Navajo people have a strong sense of family and clan relationship. Such a division or separation is almost incomprehensible to them and much beyond their range of experience. I am afraid we could lose our ministry to a large group of people.[4]

At the time of Carter's visit to the Reservation, he wrote in his report, he found fifteen licensed lay preachers, five constituted churches, and seven mission churches. Carter supplied the General Council with a twelve-item list of "what is being done, with, by, and from Native American Ministries" in the Four Corners. He included the two thrift shops, the home for women, and the alcohol rehab center, then added a recently begun foster home program for children and youth, "adequately trained lay preachers," trained leaders who had been "invited to Indian Reservations in Canada to assist in evangelism," and a movement away from tent evangelism to "Kinship or Clan evangelism." He identified "about 30 Volunteer in Mission work teams a year" that came to help with facilities, annually contributing some twenty- to twenty-five thousand dollars to the work. He told of vacation Bible schools, youth attending United Methodist–related McMurray College, a voluntary missionary who itinerated five government schools to teach Indian children religion and worship courses, and a woman being trained to itinerate the churches to strengthen Sunday schools.

Carter also identified a handful of needs: the Ministry could use approximately five thousand dollars per year to train lay pastors; it hoped for money to train local church officers but called for only five hundred dollars per training session; the Ministry had no office space of its own; it needed books for the lay pastors; it was short on vehicles and looked forward to, preferably, passenger vans; it lamented the lack of guaranteed funding for its two-hundred-thousand-dollar annual budget while pointing out that its Advance Special goal was sixty-five thousand dollars, and that the GBGM had once "cut us off at mid-year and we nearly went under."

As Carter finished his report, he added a section of "Suggestions and Referrals for Follow Up," which reported that the people that Carter had interviewed were well-informed about jurisdictional issues between the South Central and Western Jurisdictions of the Church. They were concerned about the possibility of the Desert Southwest and the Rocky Mountain Annual Conferences assuming authority over the Ministry activity in their geographical areas. They begged that the Ministry and its churches be kept as a unit. They pleaded, "do not divide us. We are well-pleased and happy with our relationship with the New Mexico Annual Conference.

1991 APPOINTMENTS [relating to the Four Corners work]
ALBUQUERQUE DISTRICT
FOUR CORNERS NATIVE AMERICAN MINISTRIES:

Director. . . . . . . . . . . . . . . . . . . . . . . . . . . . Paul N. West
Bistahi . . . . . . . . . . . . . . . . . . . . . . . . . . . . [Lucy Lewis]
Blue Gap . . . . . . . . . . . . . . . . . . . . . . . . . . [Billy John]
Dowozhiibikooh Christian . . . . . . . . . . [Raymond Burke]
Minister of Leadership Development . . . Ira Gallaway (R)
Ojo Amarillo. . . . . . . . . . . . . . . . . . . . . . . . . Fred Yazzie
Oljato . . . . . . . . . . . . . . . . . . . . . . . . . . . . [Eugene Chee]
Shiprock. . . . . . . . . . . . . . . . . . . . . . . . . David Warden
Tohatchi . . . . . . . . . . . . . . . . . . . . . . . . . . [Albert Lee]
Tselani Valley . . . . . . . . . . . . . . . . . . . . . (Chee Benallie)
Window Rock . . . . . . . . . . . . . . . . . . . . . [Henry Begay]

( )–Local Pastor
(R)–Retired
[ ]–Lay Pastor

—From *New Mexico Annual Conference
1991 Journal*, 98–100

This relationship is based on trust. We do not want to lose that. It will be like breaking up a family. If we are taken away from the Four Corners Ministry, we will feel abandoned." They called for prayers for the Ministry.[5]

Dr. Carter had heard their pleas, proving himself to be the exception to the maxim that, "Those who would help us from outside the reservation do not know us."

In another two years the General Council on Ministries, to whom Carter had written, would send yet another team to pay a call. By then, the Ministry included seventeen churches in its portfolio, including five constituted churches, seven listed internally as Mission Churches, and four as "Possible Mission Churches interested in joining Four Corners Ministry dependent upon their request."

The Council's team consisted of six persons with undisclosed qualifications, who visited the Reservation for three days in

October 1991. Their observations were published in a booklet dated fall 1991, and titled *General Council on Ministries Member Experiences with United Methodist Native American Ministries.* The publication devoted four pages to the Four Corners Ministry, one of which was a Reservation map showing seventeen churches, another written by West to explain the Ministry, and one-and-a-half of observations by the visitors.

Observations made by some of the visitors were inaccurate, such as: "This ministry is located in the New Mexico Annual Conference and is not connected to the Annual Conference" and other misstatements. One observer concluded that the only native language service held in Ministry churches was one in the Shiprock church, even though the other sixteen churches then in the Ministry all held services exclusively in the Navajo language.

Yet, overall, the visitors were impressed with the work being done. Some expressed sensitivity to the problem of alcohol and the Navajo culture, others noted the buildings under construction, one observed that this was the only ministry for two hundred thousand Navajo people. Still another expressed regret that local churches in her conference were not involved in Native American ministries. Another observer noted:

> There is a struggle between ideologies at Four Corners. Most of the people we met represented the more mainline UMC perspective. My impression was that the ministry is directed under the influence of Good News/Mission Society which in most ways was white male dominated and patronizing of the Native American population.

There was no indication how the impression was formed.[6]

As far as communicated to the Four Corners Native American Ministry, no action was taken as a result of the visit.

Although Dr. Carter's overall view of the Ministry was a positive one, and though the General Council on Ministries' team reacted positively, the Ministry did not lack critics. Some of them came right out of the Ministry itself.

CHAPTER THIRTY-TWO
# Critics

*. . . by their fruits.*
—Matthew 7:16

---

**B**y their fruits you shall know them," she said. The comment from the Rev. Shirley Montoya was not intended as a compliment.[1]

The Montoya paraphrase of Matthew 7:16 was a postscript to a telephone interview, added after she pointed out that three ordained clergy had come out of the Four Corners Native American Ministry since its inception some twenty-six years earlier. Two of them, she said, both women, had been "kicked out of the New Mexico Conference and ordained in the Desert Southwest Conference." (The remaining Navajo clergy was Rev. Roger Tsosie, Rev. Fred W. Yazzie's ordination having predated the Ministry).

Since the mid-1990s, the Ministry has had two frequent critics. Both are ordained United Methodist clergy, both are Navajo, both came out of the Four Corners Ministry, both are graduates of Iliff School of Theology. They also share a common theology, beliefs unsuited to the conservative leanings of the Four Corners Navajos. For both, the road to the ordained ministry was as rocky as the landscape of the Reservation.

For anyone, the path to the ordained United Methodist ministry is a long and arduous one, mapped out in detail, step by step, over sixty-three pages of the *Book of Discipline of The United Methodist Church.*[2] Not only are the educational requirements grueling, but there is an obstacle course of psychological testing, local church recommendation, examinations into fitness by a special committee set up for that purpose, and repeated verifications of the call by God to the ordained ministry. Some survive to ordination. Many don't.

Comparisons to the numbers of clergy produced by other denominations serving the Navajos are often irrelevant: many have far more manageable educational demands for those desiring to serve in ministry, more like the requirements for lay pastors in the Four Corners Ministry than the demanding education demanded by United Methodist ordination steps.[3] And yet, through both the low educational requirement procedures of those denominations and through the Four Corners Ministry's lay pastor certification steps, have come dedicated servants of the Lord who are effective in carrying the Word to Navajos residing on the Reservation.

One of the three Navajos to be ordained began her connection with the Four Corners Ministry not long after it was organized. Evelene Sombrero is known as "Tweedy" Sombrero. In 1978, Sombrero went to work for the First United Methodist Church, Shiprock, as director of Christian Education. When the Home for Women and Children opened shortly after she took the Christian Education job, she applied to work as a counselor, hoping to put to use her degree in social work. But she felt a tug toward the ministry, and that led her to leave to take a job in Kansas City, Missouri, and enroll there in course work at the International School for Native American Ministries. Thus began a journey that ultimately led to a seminary degree and ordination.

It was a circuitous route, one that led her to explore seminaries in Kansas City and Oklahoma City and jobs in other cities. She stated during an interview that Rev. Paul West reached out to her while she was going through a difficult time, offering her summer employment in Shiprock, and she had jumped at the chance to go back home. By September of 1985, Sombrero and her daughter had moved to Denver, where she enrolled in Iliff

*Bishop and Mrs. Louis Schowengerdt flank the first ordained female
Navajo clergy, Rev. Evelene "Tweedy" Sombrero.*

School of Theology, a United Methodist seminary. It was at Iliff
that she found the motivation to keep at it until her graduation.

The September 1988 issue of *The United Methodist Rural
Fellowship* newsletter carried a front page picture of a black-
robed Reverend Sombrero standing next to New Mexico Bishop
Schowengerdt above a caption which read, "First Navajo Woman
Ordained." Of her bishop, Sombrero said when interviewed, "I
related well with him, though I did not know him very well."

But before the picture was taken, there had been a
disagreement over what the deacon-to-be would wear at the
ordination ceremony. It was resolved by an understanding with
the Conference Board of Ordained Ministry. As a result, for the
ordination she wore her native dress under the traditional
United Methodist black robe. Immediately after, she took off
the robe and put it aside.

At the time of her ordination, there were "no appointments
available in the New Mexico Annual Conference," so she
accepted a position as director for Safe Home in Flagstaff as an
appointment outside the annual conference. Safe Home was the

only center against domestic violence in northern Arizona, and she was there for two years.

Sombrero said: "Then I was invited to join the Desert Southwest Annual Conference, and Bishop Norris [who had replaced Bishop Schowengerdt] urged me to accept. They probably thought that since I was working in Arizona anyway, that would be best." Bishop Galvan was the Arizona bishop then, she explained. He asked her to pastor a church in Phoenix. She was there for eleven years. During that time, she was ordained a full elder in the Desert Southwest Annual Conference. Currently, she serves churches in Holbrook and Winslow, Arizona.

Sombrero came out of the Iliff School of Theology with a personal theology more liberal than that she had held while she worked for the Four Corners Ministry. Today, she views practice of the native religious ways as posing no threat to a dedicated Christian, at least not to one with a seminary education. She is comfortable in the Desert Southwest Annual Conference, which she describes as more liberal and less evangelical than the New Mexico Conference, particularly than the Four Corners Ministry. Except for a single episode, she has kept a distance from the Ministry since she moved to Arizona.

The one incident occurred when she accompanied an independent video crew from Tucson that came, unannounced, to shoot footage of the Four Corners Ministry work at the Tselani Valley church started and pastored by Roger Tsosie. Pastor Tsosie, who would later also attend seminary and be ordained, was out of town. Since he, as the lay pastor in charge, was unavailable, the crew interviewed a white husband-wife visiting volunteer missionary team, accusing them of "cultural genocide" by teaching Sunday school. The TV crew demanded that parishioners throw out the volunteers. The church members refused, and some of them cried. Sombrero stood by and watched, though two weeks earlier she had paid the little church a visit with others from her annual conference as "brothers and sisters" of the people of Tselani.[4]

It appeared to the Ministry that the television people had been deliberately confrontational in order to try to provoke the Four Corners Ministry into a response, and that Sombrero, who provided commentary when the piece aired in Tucson, had been their tool. Nevertheless, she had kind words for both the Ministry and West when interviewed for this book:

> Most Navajos must establish trust. The People who have not had the gospel brought to them have no trust. They question what they want to take with them. But they see Paul's thirty years there, and the People think, "this guy really means business" . . . Anglos, they think, change, but this guy stays the same.

When asked if she could identify the source of the conservative theology that keeps the Four Corners Navajos away from the native deities once they accept Christ, she grew thoughtful again:

> I can't say for sure if Paul taught that or not. Probably, he did not. It probably came from Fred Yazzie and Chee Benallie. They made people think that in order to be saved, you can't go to the medicine man . . . You have to understand that with these Indian people, the pastor is the most important person, the pastor is in an elevated position. Fred and Chee were strong people, very influential.

When asked why her adoptive annual conference had apparently turned over work on the Reservation to the Four Corners Native American Ministry of the New Mexico Annual Conference, she explained:

> No one was doing ministry on the Reservation, even in border towns, when Four Corners was established. Conference borders were the state lines between New Mexico and Arizona. Then it was moved to fifty miles inside Arizona, with the understanding that Four Corners would do its ministry up to that line. But there was a need beyond the fifty-mile limit. Desert Southwest was not interested.

So, Reverend Sombrero carries on, ministering to two largely Anglo congregations in Winslow and Holbrook in an annual conference that seems to have little interest in reaching out to the sprawling Reservation in its living room. She makes occasional trips to the Four Corners area to see relatives, but never stops by the offices of the Four Corners Ministry to say hello.

❖

The Reverend Shirley Montoya makes no secret of her disagreement with the theological beliefs held by the people of the Four Corners Native American Ministry nor of her antagonism toward the Rev. Paul West.

Although Montoya was ordained through the Desert Southwest Annual Conference, her path to the ministry started at the First United Methodist Church, Shiprock. "I spent nineteen years as a volunteer at Shiprock, and it was my church," she said when interviewed. "But there was nothing done with people in the community."

But having dismissed West, she had more to say:

> The theological difference was they wanted me to stop being Indian if I wanted to be Christian. That came from Bishop Schowengerdt, but it was from top to bottom in the annual conference. It came through Schowengerdt to [Bishop] Norris [successor to Bishop Schowengerdt], to [District Superintendent] Saucier—he was the main one in seeing that I did not get ordained in New Mexico for the future. It was Norris who invited me to go to Arizona. Saucier also violated my religious rights and those of Tweedy Sombrero, for which he could have been sued.

The Montoya theology is on the opposite side of the line drawn by Lay Pastor Elmer Yazzie when he said of those who believe as Montoya does, "They're more interested in being Indian than in being Christian." But Montoya says that she was not the only one in the Four Corners Ministry who was open to practicing the native rituals:

> Some of them told me, secretly, that they practiced the old Navajo ways. They'd say things like, "I went to a Blessingway ceremony." God made me Indian, and why is it so bad for Navajos to embrace their culture? God made us all different, and that should be okay because He did it.

The transfer to Arizona still rankles Montoya, but the first sensitive wound had already been inflicted when her very own church, First UMC, Shiprock, voted not to support her when she asked it to recommend that she be continued as a candidate for the ordained ministry. The vote did not take place until she had graduated from Iliff School of Theology, later in the process than is usual for ministerial candidates.

By that time, Montoya had publicly declared her attitude toward the Four Corners Ministry. While a first-year student at Iliff in 1990, she coauthored a paper aimed at a research report on the Ministry by Douglas W. Johnson, of the Research Office, National Program Division, General Board of Global Ministries.[5] Johnson's report had had some complimentary things to say about the Ministry, including suggesting it provided a "model" for ministries to indigenous people. Montoya and her co-author set out to prove the report was wrong.

The Montoya section of the paper identified her "main concern" as "a total disregard and disrespect for Native American (Navajo) culture, traditions and religion by the United Methodist missionaries on the Reservation." She stated her point: "I can be Navajo and Christian at the same time; in worshiping God, I can affirm my Navajo spirituality."[6]

The paper made no inquiry into the sources of the theological stance of the Ministry, assuming without saying so that it came from Anglo missionaries, and that the Navajo United Methodists, including the ordained one who had been preaching and teaching on the Reservation before the Ministry came into existence, surely could not have drawn their own beliefs from the scriptural references they quoted so freely. The paper was circulated within the Ministry.

Approximately two-and-a-half years after the paper was written, the Charge Conference of the Shiprock Church voted down Montoya's request for approval of continuation of her candidacy for the ordained ministry on December 7, 1992. The vote was three in favor of continuation, twenty against, with one ballot invalid.

In the surviving minutes and tape recording of the meeting, the passion and sincerity of the speakers comes through, both in support of and against the candidacy of the new seminary graduate, who had been selected as Iliff's student of the year. One church member said she was proud of Montoya, another questioned how she could represent the Shiprock church Navajos who had turned away from the old religion when she had just described use of some of the old religious ways as "one way to get close to God." To that comment, Montoya responded, "I'm not trying to drag in medicine men. All I'm asking is that you respect people in the way they worship."

Another church member told how disappointed she had been on one occasion when she came to the church to hear Montoya talk, only to hear her say how she (Montoya) "underwent a Navajo ceremony," when "I thought you were going to talk about Jesus." To the question of whether she was using cedar ash in worship, Montoya said, "No, not at the present time, but in the Bible the Greek people use ointments in their worship."[7] She added in a later comment, "there are all kinds of references to uses of incense and the sacredness of cedar trees in the Bible."[8]

At the time of the Shiprock Church Conference, the pastor of the church was the Rev. David Warden, a home missionary under assignment from the National Division, appointed to the church by the New Mexico Annual Conference. Toward the end of the debate, when the outcome seemed inevitable, Warden apologized to the candidate and her family for "failing you," saying, "We worship in different ways."

The New Mexico Board of Ordained Ministry likewise turned down Montoya's application for approval of her track to the candidacy for the ordained ministry, though District

Superintendent Saucier gave her a recommendation after extracting her promise that if ordained, she "would not create any problems for the Four Corners Native American Ministry."[9] After a five hour meeting, the board decided not to recommend her for either probationary membership or for deacon's orders. Reasons had to do with the rejection by the Four Corners Ministry Navajos of her continued practice of the native religion. She failed to appear at a second meeting she had asked the Board to grant, although in advance the Board had offered her the likelihood of probationary membership.

The setbacks did not change Montoya's mind as to her belief that "the fundamentalist view [as held by the Ministry] lays claim to superiority, which also implies that native ways, culture and tradition are inferior. Did God make inferior people in His image?"[10]

Months after the Church Conference, Montoya was still defending her views, though in another forum. She was quoted in the April 8, 1993, issue of the *Farmington Daily Times* as telling a wellness conference in Shiprock that "Native myths are just as important as Biblical stories." Then, according to the newspaper report, she elaborated. "Scriptures are not just the Bible, they're the teachings of our elders."[11]

From 1992 through mid-1996, while still an Iliff student, Montoya chaired the NAIC, whose beliefs closely matched her own. She served as a director of the Board of Global Ministries, the General Council on Ministries, and of the Board of Higher Education and Ministry. Currently, she is pastor of Shepherd of the Pines United Methodist Church, Overgaard, Arizona, having gone from the Northern Arizona Native American Ministry in Kayenta, Arizona, to appointment to an Anglo church in Tucson, then to a church in Patagonia, Arizona, then to Overgaard.

Of her time in Kayenta on the Reservation, and her inability to get a United Methodist church started there, she explained, "But there was no building or place to build. No land. . . . The problems the Methodists have is that they must have a chartered congregation before they start a building, and on the Reservation there are no empty buildings." Later, she added criticism of the Ministry practice of building churches "on individual land," providing opportunities for the individuals to leave the church and take the buildings as their own.

When confronted with the observation that the Four Corners Ministry manages to build and operate churches and to grow despite those obstacles, she dismissed that fact with: "In the Third World that happens. Christianity comes in with a magic formula in which the Creator makes things better, and people come in. But the gospel should be enabling, empowering."

In the same interview, she criticized Four Corners for its lack of connectionalism. When asked if it were not by being connected with the General Church that work teams are sent to build Four Corners churches, thus solving the problem that had stymied her in Kayenta, and whether it is not through frequent connectional meetings that the churches of Four Corners support each other as United Methodist believers in Jesus Christ, she said that if she had had a church in Kayenta, "people would have come. But what is lacking at Four Corners," she said, changing the subject, "is education for the people. The Bible is taken literally. They use a fear tactic, and I have a problem with people who interpret the Bible to use it as a fear tactic."

Lorena Lynch, who runs the Ministry's thrift shop, says she voted against Montoya at the Shiprock Church conference meeting:

> I have no hard feelings against her, again, but there are some things we left behind as Navajo people when we accepted our Lord Jesus Christ and now have only one God. Our parents or elders were using a traditional way of ceremony—with medicine men. They worshipped mountains, they worshipped idols, they worshipped feathers. Some of us have left those behind. That's the reason why we disagreed with her.

Although Montoya served an Anglo congregation in Tucson, and also later churches in Patagonia and Overgaard, she admits Anglos, too, have frailties:

There are also a lot of anti-women-pastor attitudes in the Church, in addition to anti-Native American attitudes. And then, you put those two together, it is difficult. There are some churches that are open to women and Native Americans, like the one [where I served] in Tucson. I [was] well-received.

But what about the criticism that the Four Corners Native American Ministry has produced only three ordained clergy? Perhaps a comparison to the Catholic church might provide some insight, since it, too, has stringent educational requirements for the priesthood.

The Franciscan friars were alongside Don Juan de Oñate in 1598, when he took possession of all the "lands, pueblos, cities, villas of . . . New Mexico and all its native Indians." At that time, New Mexico included all of present-day Arizona as well as much of what is now West Texas. Though it was not until some time in the late 1800s that the Franciscans got serious about the work of planting churches in the lands now within the Navajo Nation Reservation, in all their years in the Southwest, according to Father Cormac Antram, O.F.M., not one Navajo has come to the priesthood from the Reservation. "Perhaps it has something to do with the celibacy requirement," Father Cormac said when interviewed. "But that doesn't explain why we've been able to produce only one deacon in those years." Deacons in the Catholic Church are allowed to marry, he explained. "We had another Navajo who got close to deacon's orders, but he decided not to go through with it."

So maybe the fruit realized by the ordination of three clergy in twenty-six years isn't such a paltry crop—especially after factoring in over fifty licensed lay pastors—some men, some women—plus twenty-seven new churches and a handful of outreach ministries aimed primarily at families.

CHAPTER THIRTY-THREE

# The Day the Support Collapsed

*I have suffered the loss of all things . . .*
*that I may gain Christ.*
—Philippians 3:8

---

No letter beginning "We regret to inform you . . . " ever contained good news. The one received by the Ministry from the General Board of Global Ministries, dated November 7, 1991, was no exception.

The letter was signed by Marilyn W. Winters, who identified herself as "Interim Deputy General Secretary." It broke the news that the Ministry would no longer be approved "for recommendation to the General Advance Committee of the General Council on Ministries." If the decision held up, the action would sound the death knell for the Ministry, because its work among the Navajos was heavily dependent on contributions from friends all over the country who funneled their gifts through the New York agency.

The writer gave no reason for shutting down the support from United Methodists. As far as Winters went was to recite how difficult it had been to make the decision. While she said that there had been "over 200 Advance applications," there was no word why the Ministry had lost out in the competition, or what it was that lifted others above it.[1]

The whole thing bewildered Paul West, puzzled Lorena Lynch (who was then the chair of the Ministry Board of Directors), and baffled the entire board. To express their distress, West wrote to Cynthia Kent, a Native American of the Southern Ute Tribe, from

Ignacio, Colorado, just over the New Mexico border and about seventy-five miles northeast of Shiprock as the crow flies. She was the person in primary charge of Native American affairs at the GBGM offices in New York, and it was to her that the Ministry had sent its application for approval of Advance funding. West reminded her that the Ministry had "met all the criteria." He asked for the reason for the rejection, and told her he assumed it "was a communications mistake and can easily be corrected."[2]

There was no response.

In light of the way those who donated to the Ministry had poured funds through the Advance for years, the Ministry's befuddlement was understandable. Though Kent's cover letter with the application form sent to Shiprock for 1992 funding had said, "Projects which have been in the Advance catalogue for several years without generating funds will probably have a difficult time getting funding," it was obvious that the warning did not apply to an over-subscribed project like the Four Corners Ministry. For, during the fiscal year in which the letter was written, Ministry supporters had sent over eighty thousand dollars to the Four Corners Ministry, making it one of the Advance's best fundraisers. Its Advance budget was fully funded. It had been approved for fifteen straight years; it was the fastest growing Native American ministry in the entire country; its board was 100 percent Navajo, and self-determination for Native Americans was a National Division priority.

West sent a copy of the notice received from Winters to his bishop. Schowengerdt called in his secretary, Patty Posey, and fired off a letter to Winters in New York. It was typed and mailed on November 20. The letter reminded Winters of the good work being done on the Reservation. After reciting how proud the Navajos were of being part of the Methodist connection, the bishop ended by stating he was "jolted by the denial of the Advance Special for this vital work." He asked for a phone call or for a letter of explanation.[3]

He didn't get either.

Frustrated, he placed phone calls to the Global Ministries offices in New York, only to reach the telephone answering staff. The calls were unreturned.

A year or so after the Winter letter turned the Ministry upside down, Lynch was to record the action she had taken when a copy of the Winters letter reached her. "My daughter and I wrote letters to Cynthia Kent at the General Board of Global Ministries, Dr. Randolph Nugent [GBGM general secretary], and Anthony Shipley [director of the Advance] and sent them by certified mail, asking to know about this." Neither Lynch nor her daughter, Vivian Farley, netted a single response.[4]

West drafted a newsletter article describing the frustrations the Navajo people were feeling, the attempts to find why the money was being cut off, and the lack of any reply from New York. The article asked supporters on the Ministry mailing list to bypass New York and send their contributions directly to Shiprock. The flow of money through contributions made through the Advance, he explained, would continue only until December 31, 1992. After that date, the Advance would be closed to the Ministry, and the Advance would return gifts to the donors.[5]

West, however, deleted his article from the newsletter before it went into the mail. He knew the Navajo United Methodists were sending prayers up to their Lord Jesus Christ, asking for a change in heart in New York. He heard those prayers at every meeting he attended. He decided to rely on them rather than on written newsletter pleas.

In the spring of 1992, Cynthia Kent paid a visit to the Four Corners Ministry to talk about salaries for Four Corners pastors, she said, as she ducked questions about the Advance. She left, having worked out some short-term salary assistance for lay pastors, but leaving Advance issues festering on the table.[6]

Later that year, Vivian Farley, the secretary of the Ministry, wrote about the meeting with Kent:

> We tried to question her about the General Advance Special and she told us she knew nothing about it, and yet

in previous acknowledgments that came from New York, they stated that Cynthia was our liaison—someone we could talk to if we had a problem. [She said] this was not the purpose of the trip . . . Since the application was submitted directly to Cynthia, how could she not have known anything about it.[7]

The New Mexico Annual Conference, in its June 1992 session, adopted a resolution directed to the National Division. It summarized the good works of the Ministry, held up the "amazing grace" exhibited by the Navajos in the face of the elimination of support, recorded its approval and endorsement of the Ministry, and asked the National Division for a "fair and open hearing so that [the Conference and the Ministry] might rebut and correct any misinformation on which the National Division might have relied." Bishop Schowengerdt sent the resolution to the deputy general secretary over the National Division, the two bishops assigned to the GBGM, its general secretary, and Cynthia Kent.[8]

No one answered.

On August 15, 1992, the Four Corners board of directors, with thirty-three Navajo persons present, met at the Cove Church to consider options. Handwritten minutes of the meeting recorded the comments made and the actions taken.[9]

Discussions began with speculation that the General Board had cut off the Advance funding because the Navajo United Methodists did not participate in the NAIC. It was retaliation, and an effort to bring the stubborn Navajos into line.

Fred Yazzie suggested a possible solution: maybe Navajos could attend Caucus meetings on a rotating basis, so no one person would need to go all the time. "I would be willing to go once in a while," he said.

Chee Benaillie had his say. "I would like to get back on NAIC and speak the truth and see how they react to it."

Lucy Charley was firm, and the recorder of the minutes showed her verbal emphasis by using both underlining and capitals. "If we go [to NAIC] to witness, I say I'll go. But if we are going to be forced to worship with feathers, I would say <u>NO! NEVER!</u> I will never worship with a feather in my hand or smoke a peace pipe. I don't believe in it. It is wrong for me!"

Lucy Lewis had a different opinion. She thought the General Board had tied up the purse strings because the Ministry director was a white man. "Why do they say that we can't have white people here?" she asked. "We need white people to teach us."

Roger Tsosie spoke up. "We don't know why New York treats Indians like they are all the same. As Navajos we are different." It was enough to prompt a motion.

Rev. Fred Yazzie stood to move that the group send a Navajo petition to New York; that it ask "Why we were refused?" and have everyone sign it. It also asked for a hearing by September 30 on the Advance funding cutoff for 1993, with a chance for the Navajos to respond. Lorena Lynch seconded, and the motion passed unanimously.[10]

On August 17, the next business day, West's secretary typed up the "Navajo Petition." West attached to it the sheets with the signatures of all thirty-three Navajos who had voted for it at the Cove Church two days earlier. He then drove to the Shiprock post office, where he mailed it to New York.

Four days later there was a response.

Early on the morning of August 21, William Carter, who identified himself as "Advance Director," called. Because of the time differential, no one was yet in the office when the Ministry phone rang, but the answering machine picked up. "The National Division is continuing the Four Corners Native American Ministry as a General Advance," Carter said, giving the two Advance numbers. "I think you will be happy to know that."[11]

West called Carter for confirmation, and was actually able to get past the phone answering staff. Carter said everything was set, but the Advance funding for facilities was "conditional." Since Carter didn't know what that meant, he'd have to ask Cynthia Kent.

West drafted a memo addressed to "Dear Pastors and Navajo leaders." In it, he told "what happened to the 'PETITION' you voted on in the last Four Corners Ministry Board meeting on August 15, 1992." He then attached a copy of the transcription of the William Carter phone message, adding, "This is just what we prayed for!!! Praise the Lord!!!"

He provided even more news. West had been told by Carter that "staff from New York" would arrive in the Four Corners in November, but before then the Navajos would meet with their new bishop, Alfred L. Norris.

The resolution of the funding problem called for an appropriate celebration; the memo ended with an invitation to attend such an event.

> HENRY C. BEGAY AND I ARE CALLING FOR A "DAY OF PRAYER" ON THE MOUNTAIN TOP AT LUKACHUKAI PASS FROM 8:00 TO NOON ON OCTOBER 3 (SATURDAY).[12]

And they came.

That was not to be the end of the questions or suspicions. While the funding had been restored, trust had not. If trust were to be rebuilt, it would have to happen at the November meeting with the staff from New York, because the Navajos were still asking why.

On September 28, 1992, Bishop Norris, who had by then replaced the retired Bishop Schowengerdt, along with the conference director of Mission and Administration, Dr. Milton R. Chester, and the Albuquerque district superintendent, Dr. David Saucier, met in Shiprock with lay pastors and other representatives of the seventeen churches of the Four Corners Ministry.

One of the conference officials present wrote an article about the meeting for the *New Mexico United Methodist Reporter* of October 9, 1992. The article said that after a dozen Navajo United Methodist Christians had stood up to speak of their faith and about their belief in Jesus Christ, and how He had changed their lives by saving them from alcoholism, illness, and peyotism, Bishop Norris spoke: "I am deeply moved by what I have seen and heard here today . . . I will be back. I do stand with you."

The article ended with a statement that the Ministry "is approved for advance special gifts," and asked for contributions to the Ministry through the Advance.[13]

So there it sat, but whenever Four Corners United Methodist Navajos gathered, they asked questions, voiced suspicions, or started rumors. The prevalent buzz was talk that what had been behind the money cutoff was a New York–led plot to get rid of Rev. Paul West—and that the plot was still alive and well. After all, the General Board had often repeated its policy that Native American programs should be headed by Native Americans, and West was an Anglo. In the eyes of the General Board, according to the circulating gossip, that was enough to convict him as an "oppressor," regardless of the facts or what the Navajo people wanted.

The imagined plot had a second phase: after West had been dumped, the General Board would move in Shirley Montoya, who was then the chair of the NAIC, and put her in charge. There were few kind words spoken for Montoya, though there was much speculation about how, if she were put in charge, she would probably force the use of drums, feathers, ash, and smoke in the Four Corners churches. All this spawned fear that Christianity among the Four Corners Navajos would die—not by starvation for lack of money, but by toxic reaction to the return of the old religious ways to people who had not been Christian long enough to have developed an immunity to their lure.

To the outsiders, it was all surreal; to the Navajo Christians, it was all too real. The initial silence from New York added fuel to the conflagration and credence to rumors that could have been extinguished by a phone call.

Though funding had been restored, reactions were still being heard from beyond the Reservation. Over two months after the phone call from Carter, Yazzie received a letter from a volunteer supporter in Laguna Hills, California. She asked what the problem was with "a split in your people," and wanted to know, "what are your intentions with our funds and in the future [*sic*]. Since this is and will be a concern of our people here at Laguna Hills."[14]

Her letter prompted responses from both Yazzie and West. The letter from Yazzie set out his understanding of the reasons why the Ministry's Advance Special standing had been cut off, and they went far beyond dollars and cents into theological issues:

> First, it is really the Gospel the Navajos (and I) love so well that is under attacks. The life of Jesus in us is being maligned again. . . . There are people on the Navajo Nation Reservation who believe in the traditional religion of animism or the Peyote Religion also known as the Native American Church. Their view is that "Christian Navajos" have betrayed their own people by going to Jesus and His Church. . . . There are people, American Indians and non-Indians, who also believe that we Navajo Christians have "missed the mark" by being loyal to Jesus only—these people I am referring to are in the United Methodist Church nationwide.

Yazzie's second point was that Navajos were accused of being "just 'clones' of the white missionaries, especially Paul West, when really we want to *follow Jesus only.*" The missionaries, he said, had "provided right and correct direction for us. That is why we have grown at a phenomenal rate."

Finally, his letter said that:

> Some Indian individuals and groups within the United Methodist church want our Navajos to "compromise" our Christian faith. They want us to syncretize, bring two or more religions together as a means of worship. . . . We don't want to go back [to the Native religion] because JESUS IS THE ONLY ANSWER TO ALL OUR NEEDS; HE IS TRULY LORD, SAVIOR, AND GREAT PHYSICIAN . . . we do not want to compromise.[15]

So the Four Corners Ministry, leadership and membership alike, did not resign itself to an inevitable fate at the hands of the outsiders. Whatever the reasons for the alienation from the General Board, as long as there was prayer, there was hope.

**AN HONOR ROLL**
The Navajos who signed the "Navajo Petition" on August 15, 1992, at the Cove Church, inducing GBGM to reverse its decision to cut off Advance funding for the Ministry.

| *Name* | *Church* |
|---|---|
| Henry C. Begay | Window Rock |
| Adella Yellowhorse | Cove |
| Pat Sandoval | Ojo Amarillo |
| Carol P. Yazzie | Ojo Amarillo |
| Bessie Coty | Cove |
| Albert J. Coty | Cove |
| Phillip Sala | Pinedale |
| Nelson Zuni | Pinedale |
| Elizabeth Silver | Cove |
| Anna M. Aloysuis | Cove |
| Sarah Zuni | Pinedale |
| Rose Mary Zunie | Pinedale |
| Alice Sorrelhorse | Ojo Amarillo |
| Evelyn Yazzie | Cove |
| Lucy Lewis | Bistahi |
| DeWayne Sponar | Rocky Point |
| Irene Parker Moore | Rocky Point |
| Mary Moore | Rocky Point |
| Mattie Skeets | Rocky Point |
| Albert Juan | Lake Valley |
| Susan Juan | Lake Valley |
| John Tsosie | Many Farms (West) |
| Chee Benallie | Shiprock |
| Anna Mae Benallie | Shiprock |
| Beatrice Dee | Cove |
| Ari Whallti | Kitsillie |
| Sonny Whitslan | Kitsillie |
| Grace C. Pete | Shiprock |
| Marilyn Charley | Shiprock |
| Lorena Lynch | Shiprock |
| Fred W. Yazzie | Shiprock |
| Stella Lee | Shiprock |
| Herman Lee | Shiprock |

CHAPTER THIRTY-FOUR

# Standing Up for Jesus

*Do not be ashamed then of testifying*
*to our Lord . . .*

—2 Timothy 1:8

---

W hile the pot was still simmering, Cynthia Kent confirmed that a meeting to talk things over would be held in the Four Corners area on November 10, 1992. The agenda, she wrote in a letter dated October 20, would have three parts, including: the "purpose of a General Advance," discussion of "the work of the Four Corners Native American Ministry," and dialogue about "next steps." Kent invited Bishop Mary Ann Swenson of the Rocky Mountain Annual Conference (Denver), Bishop Norris of New Mexico, a handful of New Mexico Conference officials, and Bishop Galvan of Desert Southwest, Arizona. Half-a-dozen or more top officials from the New York offices of the General Board were also going to be there.

The Four Corners board figured that if Kent and her associates had asked to "hear about the work," they'd give them an earful. So the Ministry mobilized, and notices went out to all seventeen churches. One notice read, "Give your WITNESS to people from N.Y. CITY, DENVER, AND PHOENIX. Stand up for JESUS!!!" "Don't be ashamed of the testimony about our Lord," was highlighted at the bottom of the page. The Navajo United Methodists of the Four Corners were rallying to fight for Jesus, for Paul West, and for their very Christian lives.

When the day for the meeting came, the Navajos were ready, and the fact that neither Swenson nor Galvan came did not dampen the fires burning within the Navajo United Methodists. Vivian Farley and Lorena Lynch were carrying the position papers they'd written, ready to read them to the visitors. Others had written out what they wanted to say, too.

Several of the papers written for verbal delivery survived in the Four Corners files. In one, the unidentified author was hopping mad. The paper expressed both fear and resentment in speculating that the New Yorkers would come to remove West. It said:

> We have every right to request the Bishop to transfer or discipline our director. Let it be known to everyone, that we are not slaves held in bondage of fear or ignorance. We are free to speak our mind, to confront our leaders and our accusers, and make our own choices. Some call us shy, but when pressed in the wrong direction, we are anything but shy. And we have something to say now.[1]

Fred Yazzie prepared a handwritten memo to outline the position he urged be taken. "Don't underestimate their Zeal or Sincerity," it said. They "may not always be right. Saul in persecuting the church believed he was right, until God undertook." Yazzie counseled caution: "We should not take an air of superiority. . . . Have a sympathetic heart. Anger or revenge do not win." Then he demonstrated his compassion: "God's love should reach out to them—through us. Pray for them! They have barriers to overcome. Don't try to understand them—that just frustrates . . . Eventually, they will be brought to shame . . . Eventually being in God's own time."

When the meeting was called to order, the fellowship hall at First United Methodist in Shiprock was packed, and everyone wanted a say. One of the first to stand and speak was Vivian Farley. Weighing on her heart was the effect those artificial conference lines drawn by white men were having on the Ministry, and she was determined to bring it up. When told to hush because she wasn't on the agenda, she reminded the visitors she was Navajo, and they were now in her country, Navajoland, so she was going to have her say. And she did just that, proving it was not the visitors who were in charge.

Her typed copy of the address was kept in the Ministry files. "The Navajo Nation is a sovereign nation, we are one," she said. "We all abide by one law, one police task force . . . How can you contemplate splitting the tribe into 3 different conferences? What will be gained from that?"

Then she answered her own questions:

> We as Navajos will not gain anything from it. We want to stay as one, and it should seem evident to all of you that we want to stay with the New Mexico Conference. We are not referred to as Arizona [Navajos], New Mexico [Navajos] or Utah [Navajos]. We are of one Tribe, no matter what our location . . . someone is trying to destroy the very thing that sustains us, upholds us, teaches us, and fills us with unconditional love—Four Corners Native American Ministry and the people that work for the Ministry.[2]

Years later, Dr. Milton Chester of the Conference offices described the meeting in an interview:

> It was kind of funny, actually. But very moving. There were all these Navajos. And they got up, one after another, and they gave their testimony. How they'd been saved; what the Ministry had done for them; how without Paul West and his influence they'd still be following the old ways. They wouldn't stop. There was just no way to get them to be quiet. And Cynthia Kent and the rest, they were just overwhelmed. They hadn't expected anything like that.

Chester said that he had talked to Kent at the meeting. He'd been as skeptical as the Navajos about the stated purposes of the trip that all those out-of-state people had made to a far corner of the New Mexico Annual Conference. "If this meeting is really about how to account for Advance money, as you've said," Chester told Kent, "you could have handled that by telephone with a couple of people on the line." Chester's skepticism hadn't gone away by the time the meeting adjourned.

The Navajo witnessing went on for so long that there was no time left to talk about "next steps." And there was no promise extracted from the "people from N.Y. City, Denver, and Phoenix" that the Advance funding was, in fact, secure. But a lot of people had gotten heavy loads off their hearts from the chance to speak up. Afterwards, since little seemed to have been resolved, there was nothing to do except wait for the next shoe to fall.

There were to be two more visits paid to the Four Corners area by the people from New York before the matter was put to rest. On December 11–12, 1992, Cynthia Kent and Deborah Bass met with the Ministry board at the church in Ojo Amarillo to go over the Advance Special application. They told the group that some changes in accounting for Advance Special monies needed to be made to assure that facilities donations were used for facilities, and program donations were used for program purposes, in the same way that they had been asked for in the application for approval of Advance funding.

With that issue addressed, the Global Ministries representatives sat in the little Ojo Amarillo church and listened while Stella Lee, chair of the Ministry steering committee, pleaded for more money. Her steering committee, she said, had increased the amounts sought for allocation to the Ministry from New York in the past because "We added programs to spread the gospel. We need help. The Navajos are poor and in poverty . . . We praise the Lord for these people coming in that are in need and asking for help from these programs."

Kent's response was wooly. "It's not guaranteed that you'll receive the funds, but submit your application to Global Ministries, to Cynthia Kent."[3] But equivocation was better than the flat rejection of the Ministry's prior application, and Kent decided she needed to visit some of the churches. She planned to return, though she didn't make it until September 14–17, 1993.[4]

On July 18, 1994, Vivian Farley, treasurer of the Four Corners board, sent a report to Kent about action prompted by her return visit. The board had established a General Advance Special Committee of twelve people to take care of all money coming in. It had opened a new bank account, established rules of operation and guidelines for applications for funds, and would be audited annually. The letter was cordial, in the Navajo way, assuming that from there on relationships between the Ministry and the General Board would be free, open, and friendly.

❖

So was there anything to the rumors that the cancellation of the Advance funding was a part of a plot to get rid of Paul West and substitute Shirley Montoya? Phone calls made to Cynthia Kent and others at the General Board in an effort to obtain interviews produced no one willing to talk. The rare persons who finally returned calls pleaded lack of both memory and records. Ultimately, William Carter, still the head of the Advance, made himself available for a brief telephone interview. Carter said that he thought the Advance had been cut off by "temporary personnel" who had made a mistake, and that Marilyn Winters had been one of the temporary people. He couldn't say when the mistake had been discovered, or why no one would talk to the New Mexicans. Winters had retired, but refused comment.

As far as the Navajos of today are concerned, the rumors that the National Division was out to change the director of the Ministry probably originated with the fall 1991 visit to the Reservation by members of the General Council on Ministries. The booklet the Council published following their return to Dayton, *General Council on Ministries Member Experiences with United Methodist Native American Ministries*, inexplicably listed Shirley Montoya as the contact for the Four Corners Native American Ministry. The publication received wide circulation in the Ministry.

Several board members and others wrote to the general secretary of the Council to ask why the then-student at Iliff Seminary, living in Denver, was listed. The letter sent by District Superintendent David Saucier drew an answer. General Secretary C. David Lundquist wrote: "We requested Native American leadership with our Native American Concerns Committee to suggest persons as contacts for all of the sites. It was in this way that Shirley Montoya was suggested as a contact for the Four Corners Native American Ministry." The persons on the Native American Concerns Committee were not identified, but on the Reservation it was known that none were Navajos representing the Four Corners Native American Ministry.

Today, over fourteen years after the day the Navajos stood up for Jesus, the survival of the Ministry, and Paul West, the Advance is still in place, and still supporting the Ministry. It's still funded by local churches and individuals throughout the United States. The Ministry and its spin-off entities receive funds under Advance numbers 581254 for program gifts, and 581255 for facilities gifts. The Covenant Education Center, the child care and day care center operated by the Ministry, receives funds through Advance number 581262. The Home for Women and Children contributions are sent to Advance number 581337. All four continue to receive support, although 2005 hurricane-relief collections have temporarily eaten into donations to the Ministry. On the Reservation there is never enough money to cope adequately with the grinding poverty or the challenges of making disciples in a culture that is hostile to the "white man's religion."

Ultimately, perhaps the Navajo response to the episode could be counted as an example of the self-determination the GBGM had so often verbally promoted: indigenous people standing up for themselves in the face of bureaucratic interference and the real or imagined colonial arrogance of distant functionaries—Navajos expressing their living faith; United Methodists fending off a threat to the Ministry through which they served their Lord Jesus. They had their say. Eventually, they were heard, though some continue to wonder if there was a place for an evangelical ministry in the scheme of The United Methodist Church.

As a home missionary appointed as pastor to the church at Shiprock by the New Mexico Annual Conference during this time, Rev. David Warden probably provided the most balanced evaluation. From the church he was serving in the Red Bird Annual Conference, he recalled in a telephone interview:

They sent out Cynthia Kent and Deborah Bass, and they did reinstate the Advance Special. I feel they were trying to be helpful, and we overreacted. . . . There were problems in communications, though. They wouldn't tell us, or Bishop Schowengerdt, why the Advance Special had been cut off. And so the Navajos were hostile. I did feel that ultimately the General Board bent over backwards to make things right. I think there were sources of antagonism between the Board and the Conference that went back many years, that had nothing to do with the Four Corners Ministry.

So the Navajos of the Four Corners Native American Ministry went back to work to make up for the ground they'd lost in starting new churches and bringing Navajos to Jesus Christ. One of the thrusts was a youth program carried on in a most unlikely place.

CHAPTER THIRTY-FIVE

# The Motivating Power of Love

*Love never ends . . .*

—1 Corinthians 13:8

Anthony Tsosie is a man driven by love. He is the youth director at his church, which has been a part of the Ministry since 1999. It's copastored by his brother-in-law, Eugene Thomas, and by Daniel Jones, both of whom are lay pastors.

Tsosie's church is perched in an unlikely location: up the south, rough side of a mountain covered by smooth rocks the size of basketballs, continuing up to boulders as big as houses—though the north slope of the same mountain is rock-free grassland. Alongside the asphalt road that circles the foot of the mountain is a weathered, hand-painted sign that reads "Roughside of the Mountain United Methodist Church," with the United Methodist cross and flame symbol. An arrow points the way.

The road to the church is unpaved, except by those basket-ball-rocks half-buried in a clay soil that becomes icy-slick when it's wet. Wet or dry, the road is a natural speed barrier. At more than ten miles per hour, parts begin to shake off a vehicle bouncing up or down the hill. The trail is no wider than a single car, creating a dilemma for a driver unlucky enough to encounter a vehicle going the other direction. The landscape is dotted with scrub juniper and cedar among the rocks, with occasional tufts of grass, cacti, and not much else. There are no signs of human habitation until the church comes into view on the uphill side of a postage stamp size, dirt parking area. The road ends abruptly at its front door.

The church itself is a low, double-wide mobile home converted into a single room. Inside, opposite the entry is a platform elevated six inches above the plywood floor, which seems to rest on the earth. On the platform is a trap drum set, keyboard, microphone and other sound equipment, and a pulpit. Banners line the sanctuary. Seating is in the form of folding metal chairs.

The youth center is a single-wide mobile home, a hundred feet or so west of the sanctuary and straight up the mountainside, connected by a rock-strewn footpath. There are three or four other structures in the little enclave there on the mountainside—an unpainted wood house, a corral with a couple of horses peering through the rails, and a pair of weathered outbuildings.

It is in this unlikely setting that the most successful youth ministry in the Four Corners, and possibly within the entire New Mexico Annual Conference, operates. Arguably, dollar for spent dollar, it's the most effective youth program in the entire United States. And the man who makes it go is Anthony Tsosie.

Tsosie is a big man: big in stature at six feet four; generous in girth, too. And big in heart. It seems doubtful that the meager facilities and resources he uses in his ministry could ever be made to function except by a person with a big heart. To Tsosie, though, the power and the force of Scripture in the Holy Bible he carries with him are what level the playing field.

During an interview, he sat in the Roughside church and talked in a barely audible voice. "Last year," Tsosie said, "I had sixty-four kids in the program. But a lot of them graduated from high school. Some went into the army or the marines so they could earn more money. Mostly, they were all here every Sunday."

As to how the young people make it to this lonely spot high above the plain below: "Some ride horses. Sometimes parents drive them, and pick up other kids who ride in the backs of the pickups. And some will walk. As far as five miles. Yes, up the mountain. Yeah. When it's cold. Most of the time, somebody will give them a ride home. But not always."

*Roughside of the Mountain, New Mexico, youth group leaders.*

And what does he do with these Navajo kids who are willing to walk ten miles round-trip for his program? "Mostly, they like to sing," Tsosie said. "And I talk to them about alcohol. About how it's dangerous, and why they should stay away from it."

He's had pretty good luck keeping the youth from drinking, which is always a temptation for kids on the Reservation. There's too little for youth to do—no employment, no recreation, nothing but getting together and guzzling beer or the harder stuff. Like Tsosie himself did when he was younger.

The fact that he was once lost to alcohol leads the youth to pay attention to what he says. Tsosie told how he was saved at a tent meeting when he was little more than a youth himself. He and a friend had been out in the woods drinking, and both of them passed out. They were wakened by the sound of music. They knew from the kind of singing they heard that there was a tent revival somewhere near. The two young men figured they could get something to eat at a revival, so they followed the sounds. Sure enough, they were asked in, despite their alcoholic state, and invited to stay to dinner. They did, but Tsosie got more than he'd bargained for. He had a religious experience, and he says he's never tasted alcohol since—that was over a decade ago.

"But now," he said, "my health is bad. I'm losing my teeth. I think it's from all the drinking I did when I was younger. And I've got a lot of other things wrong with me for that reason, too. So I tell the kids about it."

But that's not all he tells them. "I teach Bible to those kids. One part I like best is Isaiah's message found in the fortieth chapter. I talk about that a lot. It tells about comfort. And Isaiah says the rough places will be made into a plain." Tsosie swept his arms in a gesture that took in all the rocks around him, and he smiled, proving that he is indeed losing his teeth. "And he says that youths shall faint and be weary, but that the Lord will renew their strength so that they will 'mount up with wings like eagles.' I really like that."

He sat quietly for a few moments, staring into his lap, thinking of those youth. "I had a failure this year," he confessed. When he looked up, his eyes were teary:

> There was this young man. A fine young man. I thought he'd never drink again. He told me he wouldn't. But one night, he was walking along Highway U.S. 666, and he was hit by a car. He'd been drinking, and I guess he wandered into the traffic lane. He died. He was seventeen. I lost him, just when I thought he'd straightened out.

Later, Reverend West explained that such pedestrian road deaths are not uncommon. People who've been drinking walk alongside Reservation highways at night, especially 666 between Gallup and Shiprock. They stray onto the traveled portion of the road, only to be hit by vehicles whose drivers can't see a person in dark clothing in the black of a Reservation night. Not until it's too late. That's one reason the state of New Mexico recently gave the highway a new number. Residents of western New Mexico, including those living on the Reservation that the highway runs through, wanted to get away from the apocalyptic message that the 666 number sent.

This year, so far, there are approximately thirty youth in the program. "But we'll grow. More will come," Tsosie said.

He was right. At a Four Corners training session just six months later, he reported that his group of faithful was back up to sixty who attended regularly. And he is still talking the Bible to them, and the dangers of alcohol.

There's little doubt that the youth program that clings to the side of the mountain at Roughside bucks a trend. Interviews of annual conference officials identified weak Four Corners youth programs as a flaw in the Ministry's efforts to reach the Navajos, in the opinion of some. No one there had heard of Anthony Tsosie or of his youth program. Most were not quite sure whether there really was a church called "Roughside of the Mountain," or whether it might have been a joke of some kind.

There are other youth programs in Ministry churches. And there's an effort to get land from the tribe for a youth camp in the mountains that should boost the appeal of church-related programs to young Navajos. If only the Tribal Council would get around to considering the application.

Four Corners young people occasionally go to the annual conference camp in the Sacramento Mountains, east of Alamogordo. Now and then, the Four Corners newsletter reports a youth activity such as a wiener roast at Teec Nos Pos, followed by a two-mile hike into a box canyon for the kids to cool off under a waterfall that's a few hundred feet high. It's not the kind of United Methodist youth recreation time that would be found in a city church. In those churches, though, it would be quite a challenge to find young people who would walk along a cobbled dirt road five miles up a mountain in the dead of winter to sing and to listen to someone talk about the evils of alcohol. But then, it's different on the Reservation, for both adults and youth.

## CHAPTER THIRTY-SIX

# Signing Up to Volunteer

*Whatever is right I will give you.*
—Matthew 20:4

O ne of the many churches that routinely sends summer volunteers to work on the Reservation is First United Methodist
Church, Canon City, Colorado. Review the list of churches giving
to the Ministry through the Advance, as shown on a link on the
GBGM Web site, and Canon City's name appears again and again.
A call to the pastor to ask why his church seems so devoted to the
ministry to the Navajos produced some words of wisdom.

Reverend Denny Sillamon has found that, "A long tenure
helps. I've been here twenty-one years." He explained that's
enough time for continuity in programming, eliminating flitting
from one project to another and losing focus.

Sillamon has invited Rev. Paul West to speak to his people in
Canon City.

> He's been here, and he's made an impact. And we've had
> people come up from the church we help the most. That's
> Blue Gap. Billie and Sadie John. They're the pastors there.
> They've come up to speak. And now, we know the people
> at Blue Gap. We've been there and they've been here. And
> we've seen their needs, and we want to help.

When it comes to churches helping, or "adopting," Four
Corners churches, West says it can be a mixed blessing—though
a pastor with long tenure at the adopting church adds to the
blessing side:

Sometimes [West explained in an interview, though not referring to the church in Canon City], a United Methodist church somewhere . . . wants to "adopt" a church out here on the Reservation. But it's usually a problem because no one knows what adopting a church is. And if the Anglo does the defining, it may not be what the Navajos have in mind, or want to agree to. But they will give in to see what happens with it.

West said that it always starts with good intentions on both sides:

But it's usually pretty one-sided. I think some of those churches have the idea that they'll come out here and visit those Navajo churches, maybe have a vacation Bible church. [They say,] "Then those Navajo people can come visit us, and they can share their witness with us, and that'll inspire us." But it goes sour when they realize there's a dramatic economic difference between where their church is and where the Navajo church is. Also a dramatic difference in their history.

This Navajo church is so young that they don't really understand how the whole system works. And our Four Corners people, when they go to visit, some of the churches they visit become judgmental. "These Navajos don't know anything," they'll tell each other. "They're not Methodists." So it starts falling apart at both ends.

These people go out from the Reservation, and they see a good Christian smoking on the church steps. The Navajos feel you can't smoke and be a Christian. Well, already their faith is shaken. Or, they go in a home, and in the refrigerator there's a bottle of wine. And already, this is not what they expected to see as a Christian witness. Then the sponsors in the Anglo church find they have to pay to get the group out there, pay for them to get back, and pay while they're there, and the Navajos may ask for more money while they're there because they ran out of money, and they may want to do things before they get back, like see the arches in St. Louis, so the Anglos find they're forking out more money. They can't grasp the poverty the Navajos live in.

Then, when our people get back home, they may ask for
something. And that Anglo church says, "Well, what do
you need? We'd like to help you." So the Navajos come
up with the things they want. And the church back there
says, "They're asking for a TV-VCR combination, and
they don't even have electricity. Where's this going to
go?" And the answer is, "Well, in the pastor's house." And
the Anglos say, "Wow, we're not paying for this for him,
we want it to be used for the church." So they find things
aren't operating here as they want them to be, and the
trust level goes down. And our Four Corners church says,
"Yeah, we're adopted but the adoption didn't work out,
so we got a divorce."

In the thirty-plus years that West has labored in the Four
Corners vineyard, he's seen it all tried—volunteers coming, going
home, and adopting churches. Volunteers coming year after year,
working at a variety of churches. Volunteers coming and trying it
once and finding it's too strenuous, or the weather is too hot, or
their backs hurt from sleeping on concrete with only a sleeping
bag and an air mattress. But most are inspired; many keep
coming back. And as a result, the board of the Ministry has
worked up a plan that's effective.

The plan recognizes that the Four Corners Ministry couldn't
function without its volunteers. A work group brochure distributed by the Ministry explains how volunteering operates: "We
accept about 20 groups for construction projects and about 20
groups for Vacation Bible School Projects," the folder says. The
groups can consist of families, adults, high school or college
youth groups, and mixed generational volunteers. There's an
explanation of the duties the groups can expect to perform,
beginning with the admonition to "get on our calendar early."
Vacation Bible School (VBS) teaching volunteers are asked to
select and buy the materials used. Though it's not said, used
workbooks are out, up-to-date, new material is in.

Volunteers for VBS must "lift up Christ in everything you
do," and make the teaching simple, since "some of the children
will be learning English and lack grade level reading and writing
abilities." The teachers must do some of their own recruiting by

going house-to-house in the area served by the church on the Sunday afternoon before VBS starts, announcing that it will start the next day. Finally, the group should pay the church for use of its facilities, but not more than two hundred dollars.

Requirements for construction groups are also spelled out in the brochure. The would-be carpenters and concrete workers must bring enough money to pay for the materials they'll use, provide a group leader with knowledge of construction, and bring their own tools, gloves, paint, hammers, caps or hats, and sunblock. Construction groups, too, are asked to pay the church for the use of facilities and utilities, with a suggestion of two hundred dollars.

Even with all the hardships, it's still necessary for the Ministry to alert potential volunteers to sign up early. Wait, and the jobs may be filled, is the warning, because the pay is in a spiritual currency that is hard to find back home sitting in the pews.

## CHAPTER THIRTY-SEVEN
# The Volunteers

*I by my works will show you my faith.*
—James 2:18

Bonnie Posey presents seminars on missions in Alabama. It hasn't always been that way.

By 1994, Posey, a pleasant-faced, gray-haired grandma and ex-nurse, had chaired the mission committee at the First United Methodist Church in Haleyville, Alabama, population around four thousand, for several years. She and the rest of the congregation thought they had a wonderful missions program going. Once a year, they invited a missionary couple to come talk to them, they took up a collection, and chairwoman Posey wrote to the missionaries now and then to pat them on the back and tell them what a great job they were doing.

Then they got a new, brash, young pastor. He told his congregation:

> You're doing a good job in taking care of yourselves. But you're not taking care of anyone else. And Christians of the United Methodist variety take care of others. I want you to see some of the need in this world. You are going to the Four Corners, where some of you will teach Navajo kids at a vacation Bible school. Others will wield hammers and saws and build whatever the Navajo United Methodists need to have built.

So they did. But only after they'd howled and moaned about how hot and primitive it was in New Mexico, and how hard the concrete floor of a church would be to sleep on. They came, though, thirty of them, and they brought with them a gift of one hundred Navajo-language Bibles they'd purchased on sale at five dollars each, because their new pastor had said they should go bearing gifts for the people.

Since that first summer in New Mexico, Posey and the Haleyville crew have built a church in affluent Jackson Hole, Wyoming, where there had been none; they've sent teams to the Cherokees in the Carolinas and to the Kentucky Mountains;— and six times they've gone back to the Four Corners, because they love it there.

In the summer of 2003, Bonnie Posey brought not only her husband, Merle, but their son and his wife and two sons, ages sixteen and fourteen, who live in Florida. Plus, a team of thirty others out of a congregation of about five hundred from the Alabama church volunteered to teach vacation Bible school, build, and do whatever else they could to help. That summer, Posey's grandsons worked on the Ojo Amarillo parsonage, did home repairs, and poured a handicapped ramp at the church. They also taught Bible stories to the kids under a shade shelter in the sand-and-dirt parking lot, and played games with them.

During the years in which they've spent their vacations in the Four Corners, Haleyville teams have included professionals who check the teeth of any Navajo who asks for a checkup, and a nurse has overseen taking blood pressure and blood samples for cholesterol checks. They've even brought a veterinarian and driven out to sheep camps to vaccinate sheep and clean the worms from their mouths. And they've given out—and received—a lot of love.

As for those one hundred Bibles: the name and address of the Haleyville Church was on a label inside. One of the Navajo-language Bibles made its way to a jail in Aztec, New Mexico, where an inmate wrote and asked for more copies. Posey sent them, and wound up sending them to other Navajo inmates in other jails and prisons, because letters kept coming in to ask for them. By 2003, the count of Navajo Bibles the church had given away was up to six hundred (by then they cost twenty dollars each). And the mission committee that once consisted of only Bonnie Posey had grown to a couple of dozen regulars, noted Posey during an interview. The church which once struggled to meet its budget now regularly tops it because people want to help other people, so they give. And Posey gives seminars on how to do it.

At sixteen, Bonnie Posey's grandson Will Posey made his fourth trip to help with the Haleyville work teams at the Four Corners during the summer of 2003. "I like the way it's like a family of kids, of brothers and sisters who always watch out for each other. The older ones always look out after the younger ones. Like big brother and big sister, and they always look out for each other." Will said it's not that way in Florida.

In 2003, Will said, "I got to go out to sheep camps and vaccinate sheep." Out there in the vastness of the high desert, helping give shots and deworm sheep, Will has seen how strong Navajo family ties are. He's also seen a lot of geology in those remote areas of the Reservation. "It's like having Monument Valley for your backyard," Will said. But what has impressed the sixteen-year-old the most is the people he's met:

> It's so neat to come out here, and hear the testimonies of the Navajos. They give their background, maybe from peyote, or worshipping native gods. They come to Christianity, and it's neat to see the strength of their faith, how strong it is. And how firm a foundation they have. They just won't waver, and they put complete and total trust in God. And I have complete respect for every individual out here, with that faith. And they can do so much work and things with nothing.

That's not all Will has learned from the Navajos:

> It's humbled me . . . I've found I'm not asking for a lot of things any more, and I think this has a lot to do with it, because you appreciate what you have a lot more. And you don't need more things. You learn to appreciate the simple things. You find something when there's nothing.

His fourteen-year-old brother, Wes Posey, found something in the Four Corners, too. Wes recruited his parents to come to Ojo Amarillo with his grandparents' work team in 2003. "I brought them," he said. "They hadn't been here before."

During his four trips [as of 2003] to New Mexico with the volunteer teams from his grandmother's church, Wes primarily worked on construction projects at the Ojo Amarillo church and in the community. "It's helped me back home," he said. "Now I do work for neighbors and friends. I learned how to do it here."

But the greatest thing Wes has learned is the Navajo Christians' practice of their faith. "They're not like people where I'm from. They're dedicated. These people are 7-days-a-week, 365-days-a-year, 24-hours-a-day Christians."

Speaking about the Navajo United Methodists, Grandma Bonnie Posey summed it up for her family and her church in a slightly different way. "We help these people. But they help us more."

But how objective was Posey when she claimed that helping the Navajos had helped her church? The pastor of First United Methodist in Haleyville added his observations during a telephone interview. On the day of the interview, the church's Helping Hands committee was meeting, Rev. Terry Bentley said. Every Tuesday morning at nine, committee members interview people in the community who need temporary help with their rent, heating bills, a car payment, diaper purchases, anything at all to help tide them over a hard spot. Now, in addition to making its mission budget, the church in Haleyville fills its outreach kitty with about a thousand dollars a month to be spent helping the needy. During the first ten months of 2003, Haleyville UMC had spent over $37,200 in what it calls "monetary outreach." And that's after it had raised its missions budget.

As to why his congregation reached out, first to the Navajos, and then to others, Bentley said:

> I didn't get it started here. It began with my predecessor, who moved on to Birmingham. But I've been here seven years. And a long tenure helps in keeping things like that going.

It's enriched us as a congregation. We've been enhanced in our work here because people recognize opportunities to serve that they never recognized before, and we understand that all people have the same needs. We are closer to people, and we have gone beyond cultural barriers. We're here in the South, and there have been all kinds of cultural barriers.

Bonnie Posey wasn't exaggerating. The United Methodists in Haleyville are living out their faith, not just with the Navajos but also in their community, meeting needs they'd never opened their eyes to before. Not until the Navajo Christians came into their lives.

◄⊗►

But Bonnie Posey and her group are not the only volunteers. Each summer there are about a thousand others. Like Cecil and Mary Grace Regier, from Dumas, Texas. On a hot summer afternoon in June 2003, they stood on a rock-strewn rise in Shiprock, behind the thrift store and next to the skeleton of what would become a new home for Ministry offices and for dormitory space to shelter volunteers and visitors. Cecil Regier explained that the volunteer crew he was supervising was lounging in the shade of a lone tree because a lumber shipment from Gallup had been delayed.

Regier, a retired research scientist with Texas A&M University, and his wife, Mary, a retired accountant, came to Shiprock for the first time nine years earlier as part of a Texas work team. Their first project was the church at Pinedale, where they paid for the materials they used, as all work teams do, and laid the floor. They had just retired, and that first trip convinced them that this was a mission they wanted to help. The next year they were back to supervise work teams for five weeks. In the summer of 2003, their plan was to stay through August, stretching their work to over ten weeks.

It took them four summers to build the fellowship hall at the Pinedale church. Then, for two years, they worked on the pastor training center and thrift shop at Window Rock. At Dowozhiibikooh, they built a youth center.

Mary Regier handles the correspondence, keeps the records, and lines up materials. Before each summer's trek from the Texas Panhandle to the Four Corners, she spends a week or so getting estimates for the materials that her husband has determined they'll need, and also arranging for deliveries. Most everything is bought from a lumber yard in Gallup. "We have a good relationship with the people there. They provide it at their cost and add 10 percent," Mary said. When the work teams arrive, the Regiers know each group will have brought money to pay for the materials they'll use. For the Regiers, there has never been a glitch, and no work team has ever failed to show up.

The Regiers and their fellow church members began as Four Corners Ministry volunteers when their pastor was looking for a project in which to involve his congregation, and he showed a video on building churches. The Regiers came with that first group, and they kept coming because they fell in love with the Navajo people.

"We've made hundreds of friends," Mary Regier said. "From all over the country." The summer of their interview, they expected about two hundred people to come out and work in teams that they would supervise. "We can make two hundred more friends," she said, smiling—and scanning the highway for that load of lumber that was late.

The volunteers that come to the Reservation each year are from such varied places as Halstead, Kansas; Irving, Texas; Wytheville, Virginia; the Central Texas Conference; the Amarillo District; Richmond, Indiana; Lubbock, Texas; the Holston Annual Conference, with workers from Virginia and Tennessee; New Port Richey, Florida; Madisonville, Kentucky; San Francisco; the Texas Annual Conference; and from other churches located coast-to-coast.

Some have come to work long-term; a few of those have received a pittance of pay to help defray their living expenses while they managed the day care center, or oversaw long-term construction projects, or undertook to fill other posts.

Sharon Endicott was a seminary student from Methodist Theological School in Ohio. She felt the Great Commission had instructed her to offer herself to the world as one of God's people, and found her opportunity in the Home for Women and Children, where she worked as director for a year during a break from the academic world.

Herb Moushon spent almost three years overseeing construction projects and designing church buildings until the Ministry ran out of challenging projects worthy of his skills, and only after his volunteer crews finished the two-story church at Ojo Amarillo.

Chuck and Karen Short came to the Four Corners area in March 2002, and in September became part of the Ministry. They coordinated teams that served in vacation Bible schools and worked on home and church repairs.

Melody Auxier came from Kentucky to act as director of Christian education. She put on Sunday school workshops in many of the Ministry churches during 1987.

Another who came to direct the Home for Women and Children was Dot Steed (Knoxville, Tennessee).

CHAPTER THIRTY-EIGHT
# Sister Shirley Gets a Church

*. . . lead a life worthy of the calling to which you have been called . . .*

—Ephesians 4:1

By the mid 1980s, while the mission school was experiencing its turmoil, Shirley John had turned her back on the peyote rituals, alcohol, and symbols of a religion that no longer appealed to her. She had embraced her Lord and Savior Jesus Christ. The compulsion to preach soon became irresistible, and before long she was spreading her message from the pulpit of George Davis's independent church in Lukachukai, the Amazing Grace Church. The drive back and forth from her home in Lakeside was dangerous when it was icy or rainy, and she soon felt an urge for a church of her own. She set out to get it.

In starting the church at Lakeside, Arizona, John followed the route traveled by other Navajo lay pastors who had gone before her, inviting family and friends to prayer and Bible study meetings in her home. The group grew, and she eventually needed a building for meetings. That's when her brother-in-law, Eddie Arthur, helped her persuade Tom Dolaghan (who later would coauthor *The Navajos are Coming to Jesus,* reflecting his years of research and ministry on the Reservation) to build her a tiny chapel that connected to her mobile home. A volunteer group from California arrived and got to work, building on her home lease site.

John pastored the small congregation she drew as an independent church. She also acquired a tent for use in an evangelistic outreach tent ministry, preaching in both Apache and Navajo, acccording to the audience. But something was missing, and a number of people told her what it was. "People kept encouraging me for some years. They would say, 'You should go have a fellowship with some church, you know. In some church. Don't just be by yourself.' I said, 'No, I don't want to be with any church.'"

It was then that John found a soulmate. "But this lady, you know, the one that passed on from Spider Rock, Angie. She was one of our prayer warriors at Chinle. I used to pray with her." Angie Segay had already encountered Roger Tsosie and the Four Corners Ministry. She knew that John and the Ministry would be a good fit:

> She said to me, "You should go over there to the Four Corners people. You might get help through them. You can't do it yourself." I said, "No, I don't want to." And she kept encouraging me.

> Finally, I went up to Shiprock. It was during Christmas time. I told them I needed help. And I told them there at that meeting [of the board of directors] I wanted small children to be educated, I wanted some schools of some sort, some sort of mission schools, Sunday schools, out where we're at. . . . And so, I went to the board meeting. I said I wanted to join the Methodists.

> [I was told at the meeting] "You have to come to these board meetings. You have to take the training. You have to show us you're really interested in being part of the Four Corners Ministry, and that you love the Lord."

She told them about her tent ministry, and how she'd already worn out two tents and needed another one. She didn't miss a board meeting, and when training sessions were held, Shirley John was there with her Bible open. When she'd complied with all the requirements, they voted her and her little flock into the Ministry. After a time, the church was accepted as a mission church, and it has appeared in the *Annual Conference Journal* since 2003.

John found that the people of the Four Corners Native American Ministry keep their promises. In the summer of 2003, a work group from Sardis, Mississippi, came and started building a church. They finished it in 2004, and also built a thrift shop on a concrete slab that was already in place. The chapel that the work group from California had built next to her home, she figured, could be used by her congregation as a fellowship hall, for Navajo United Methodist Christians are incomplete without a place to eat, sing, and fellowship together.

John expressed her thankfulness for the Methodists: "They're preaching from the Bible." Then she brought up another issue close to her heart:

> Those [Navajo religious] artifacts. Some still have them. Moses, you remember, took off his shoes approaching the Lord. We need to get rid of those artifacts, because they have demonic forces. Just look in Acts 19:19. People who practiced magic arts burned their magic books in everybody's sight. And that's why the word of God grew and prevailed.

And John has never forgotten the "Begone!" to graven images she found in the book of Isaiah.

> Some Anglos, you know, [John said, recognizing an issue the people from New York had, time and again, looked right past] they come out here and they say, "Let's go to a yei dance, and let's go to a squaw dance." And you know, they don't know what's behind this. When you beat on those kind of drums, the peyote drum, the evil voices are there. They come together with the drums.

John became a member of the board of directors of the Four Corners Native American Ministry, and in 2003, was elected its vice chair. When she was elected to fill the top spot a year later, John was ready. When asked what she'd do if elected, she didn't have to think for long before coming up with some changes she'd advocate making. "I would like for our pastors to be paid. They need insurance, travel insurance every time they travel. I know there's no money now, so we'd have to go to the conferences and ask for it."

◈

What is to be made of questions raised by critics of the Ministry because of its experiences with Christians like Shirley John, who came to the Ministry from an independent church after giving up the native ways? And what about those eyebrows raised at independent churches that have elected to come into connection with The United Methodist Church through the Ministry? Some ask if these people are really United Methodists.

Church growth and administration authority, and also a United Methodist clergyman, Lyle E. Schaller, has something to say about changing church denominations. Schaller wrote in 1987 of the difficulties of pastoring in the 1980s. He explained that, while institutional and congregational loyalties were a strong cohesive force in churches in the 1960s, "institutional or brand loyalties" had eroded by the '80s. He attributed the change to

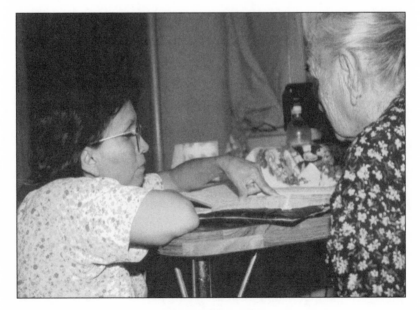

*Home Bible study.*

different attitudes: a particular church is no longer a "destination on a religious pilgrimage," it is a "way station"; and "competition is greater"; the churchgoer has become a "comparison shopper." What people look for is a church that can give them what they need, not one with a particular label.[1]

Schaller wrote in 1992 that "new generations of church-goers" are looking for "a church that is responsive to their personal, religious, spiritual and family needs." In such a church, they find that "their lives have been transformed by the power of the Gospel."[2] That is what Navajos have discovered of their connection with the Four Corners Ministry, as illustrated by Shirley John's thankfulness for the Methodists. Of course, Schaller was writing about the dominant culture in both of these books, not life on the Navajo Nation Reservation.

Yet the churches at Lakeside and Oljato were not the only churches coming into the Ministry.

## CHAPTER THIRTY-NINE

# The Church at the Sheep Camp

*Feed my lambs . . . Tend my sheep.*
—John 21:15–16

Ⅰn 1974, just after Evelyn Yazzie was saved, James and Anna Aloysuis decided they knew the perfect place to locate a church—it should be where people would come. And people were used to coming to the sheep camp outside a collection of half-a-dozen or so dwellings called Cove. So that's the place they picked. They were led by a prophetic vision their daughter, Trisha, had seen and had described to her parents and all their Christian friends: "White men from the east will come and help us build a church."

The sheep camp wasn't on a main highway or a broad boulevard; it was at the dead end of a dirt road at a location that would never support a megachurch. But for the Navajo families that James and Anna Aloysuis planned to reach, it was perfect.

They began by inviting family and friends to meet for worship in their kitchen. Then they added a shade house and, next, a room as a church meeting place. All the while they waited for the white men from the east to come with help.

After a time, one summer afternoon the women worshippers decided they needed a tent as a cool and comfortable, if temporary, meeting place. They went to work, collecting old and cast-off clothes: a grandmother's dress, a brother's shirt, a friend's blouse. All were cut up into eight-inch squares. While they cut fabric, the women prayed for the person who had worn the garment. They later learned that one young man prayed for was saved from suicide; and a young mother lived long enough to prepare her children for her death from cancer and to find homes for them. Praying also helped the sewers with the patience to keep stitching away.

Finally, the "tent of many colors" was finished, and they spread it on the ground out on the hillside in the clean, clear air. They sat on it in a circle, and as they gathered there, hand-in-hand, the worshippers prayed that the twenty-three families in the fellowship might meet beneath its protection "to praise God and put everything in His hands." Up went the tent, hoisted on poles made by the men. They used it for two summers, and under it the people found the Spirit of God.[1]

Tom Lovett, a volunteer for the Four Corners Native American Ministry, had been going from BIA school to school, offering released time Bible instruction to the children. When he stopped by the Cove Day School, Lovett learned what was happening on the hill. Each time he was in the area, he made it a priority to go up to the old sheep camp and tell whoever he could find that they should build a church there. But then he took it several steps further. Lovett drafted a petition and went around getting people to sign it. It asked the Cove Chapter of the Navajo Nation to get behind a lease for a church at the old sheep camp.

The worshippers at Cove knew that everything would work out, and they were confident that Trisha Aloysuis's vision was about to become reality. Before the petition had stopped circulating, men and women alike had begun digging down to solid ground where the sheep had milled around, getting ready for the construction of that church by white men who would come to help.

Finally, when the signature list was long enough, the chapter approved it and submitted a resolution to the tribal government. By then, the members had the foundation dug and some of the concrete poured.

James Aloysuis died in 1988, a victim of radiation from the uranium mines where he had worked. So many men in the Cove vicinity had labored in those mines that the families in the growing congregation were primarily headed by widows, one of whom became the pastor of the little congregation. Evelyn Yazzie, who was converted from the old ways into Christianity in 1974, had been with the worshipping group ever since.

It was not until 1989 that the first of the "men (and women) from the east" came, in the persons of Paul and Dorcas West, and lay missionaries Wayne and Sharon Hatfield. They met with Evelyn Yazzie at the site. She, however, didn't want her congregation to join with the Four Corners Native American Ministry, and she didn't want to become a United Methodist. She didn't want to link up with any denomination, for she feared that she would feel its authority. "I was afraid that some would say I had a rope around my neck, and that the Ministry was in control," Yazzie explained. She and her congregation had their own church, though it was built of poles and rags.

Yazzie soon realized that if the church stayed independent, going it all alone, there would be no one to step up and pastor the congregation when she could do it no longer. So she went to a Four Corners training session in Gallup. Anna Marie Benallie was invited, and she said that God would take care of them, and then there was that vision of the men from the east. Yazzie decided that the Ministry might not put a rope around her neck after all. Maybe, instead, they'd bring church builders.

The Four Corners Ministry sent out groups of volunteers, all of whom were from the east. They constructed a sanctuary and a connected fellowship hall. A group from St. John's United Methodist Church in Santa Fe laid pipe and buried a drain field for a septic system. When they finished, everyone gathered around to sing with the Navajos of the Cove Christian Church, United Methodist. The next day there was a worship service with fifty Navajos present. They shared a meal of Navajo tacos and fellowship with the workers from Santa Fe.

A group of representatives from the Cove church drove to a Four Corners task force meeting on March 9, 1991. Among those making the trip to Gallup were Bessie Cody, Albert Cody,

Lorencia and Anna Mae Aloysuis, Tish Dee, Evelyn Yazzie, and others. After reporting to the task force about the dedication of the Cove Christians, the group listened while Roger Tsosie explained what a connection with the Four Corners Ministry would mean. After everyone had their say, Henry Begay got up and moved to recommend the Cove Christian Church for membership with Four Corners as a mission church. His motion passed unanimously, and the people went home happy.[2]

The Cove Church is big on celebrations. In 1997, it sent its church band to the twentieth-anniversary celebration of the Four Corners Ministry, where it played sweet music. On the Sunday that Pastor Evelyn Yazzie was interviewed, March 23, 2003, the congregation still filled the fellowship hall at 3:30 in the afternoon. The hall was decorated with balloons and streamers, and the band had just put away its music. There had been a birthday celebration, and everyone had stayed for the feast and fellowship—though the teenage boys were fellow-shipping on the concrete basketball court outside, playing three on four. Behind the church, a trailer was parked. In it was the Cove Church's evangelism tent—a real canvas tent, not a homemade one. The Cove evangelism team pulls the trailer all around the area to hold revivals wherever they think people will come; the band plays, they do a lot of singing, and Yazzie preaches and exhorts.

The church celebrated the tenth anniversary of its acceptance into the Four Corners Ministry in 2001. One Anglo was present: Paul West, who understood only the five words of English that were spoken the entire day, when an elderly gentleman stood up to give his testimony. He began by saying, "I'm glad I know Jesus." Then he switched to Navajo.

People celebrated Jesus that day, rather than the passage of time as a church. Time will pass no matter what, but Jesus in the heart cannot be taken for granted on the Reservation. The church had just bought a new evangelistic tent, this one measuring 38' x 56', and Yazzie was looking forward to putting it to use. She had been training successors such as Richard Silver, who'd preached that morning, with the help of the Four Corners Ministry pastor training program. Yazzie had found she wasn't being throttled by a rope around her neck.[3]

In the fall of 2004, there was a celebration of a different kind at the Cove Church. Pastor Evelyn Yazzie, at age fifty-two, was off to Broken Arrow, Oklahoma, to study for two years at the RHEMA Bible Training Center. The sanctuary was bright with streamers, and several speakers got up, stretching the worship service to three hours. Nobody complained, because they were happy that Yazzie would learn to be an even better leader, and they knew that when the service ended there would be a feast in the fellowship hall.

The menu had been selected by Yazzie herself. Knowing she would have no genuine Navajo food for several months, she had asked for roast mutton, providing a sheep from her own flock. There was also mutton stew, boiled white corn on the cob, fresh squash, cucumbers, chilies, fried bread, blue corn meal mush, and sumac berry dessert. Around a hundred family members and friends sat down to eat together in the best Navajo tradition.

Though Navajos do not give up their families easily, Yazzie's mother stood up and said that her daughter should go and do what she wanted—and then come back home. There were tears in her eyes, and in the eyes of everyone in the congregation. Others stood to say that it was all like the banquet in heaven at the marriage feast of the Lamb. Nobody had to ask what that meant, because Yazzie had been preaching from the Bible and encouraging Bible study since 1974.

Carrying on in her absence is Wilma Todacheeny, acting pastor. She'll get the same love that Yazzie got, for she's preaching the same message.[4]

The board of Four Corners Ministry was happy that Yazzie agreed to accept the scholarship they offered, funded by a gift from the Lane Foundation (which had awarded its first scholarship earlier to Roger Tsosie) and from matching contributions from the New Mexico Annual Conference. Yazzie's scholarship was the first given since Tsosie went off to the seminary at Fuller. But it would not be the last.

In the fall of 2004, three more Navajo women from Four Corners went off to study on scholarship gifts made from donors giving for the purpose of training and education. Charlotte, Lilly, and Marjorie Tullie left for Cook College & Theological School in Phoenix. At the Presbyterian Christian school for Native Americans, the three ladies from the Blue Gap church study to be Bible teachers, Sunday school teachers, and Christian educators. They are related by marriage—two are married to brothers, and the other is married to an uncle of the brothers. But if you ask them, they will say that, in Christ, they are sisters.

CHAPTER FORTY
# A Leader for the Times

*Let him . . . take up his cross daily and follow me.*

—Luke 9:23

What kind of a leader has Paul West been for the Ministry and its Navajo members?

When he came, was his agenda to make the theology of the Navajos match his own by taking the "colonialist" approach of stamping out the native religion and molding these independent people into theological clones of himself? Has he pulled the wool over the eyes of Vivian Farley, Rev. Fred W. Yazzie, Rev. Roger Tsosie, Lay Pastor Elmer Yazzie, and others previously quoted as saying that West did not and would not tell them what to believe?

Or are those who criticize Ministry theology right in their criticism, justified in describing West as a "white colonialist," and in imposing on him a verdict of "guilty" of intentional cultural genocide?

There's another question that might also be asked. That is, with the conservative, evangelical theology so prevalent among Protestant Navajo Christians that it was a given on the Reservation at the time of West's arrival, should his leadership be judged at all based on some subjective standard of theological correctness that weighs evangelistic outreach against perceived social values of the day?

More objective standards could be developed. Those standards might include such measurables as counting churches,

fellowship halls, and other structures to attract Christians; new
Christians added to the Ministry; congregations brought in;
lives changed; work teams recruited and the lives of volunteers
enriched; or funds raised. Such standards would have to be
examined in the context of the politically and religiously inhospitable Reservation in which the counts increased, as well as in
comparison to the work of other annual conferences in the
same cultural and geographical area.

There is no doubt that the conservative brand of Christian
theology was alive and thriving on the Reservation before West
arrived. Dolaghan and Scates included a chapter titled "Navajo
Churches and Missions: A Brief History" in their 1978 book,
*The Navajos are Coming to Jesus*. Though the authors do not
specifically examine the nature of the theology that developed,
they do provide some insights into it. They quote a Navajo
pastor, J. Thompson, as telling them in 1977, "When they say to
me the missionary has destroyed the old religion, I say no, it
was not the missionary. It was the wine bottle, the *bich'ah
lichii'ii*. When you drank it and fell in your hoghan [*sic*] upon
your medicine bag, the power left you."[1]

Their research counted the Protestant churches planted by
each denomination on the Reservation from 1950 to 1977. Well
over half were clearly conservative in theology: Indigenous
Pentecostals, Assembly of God, Pentecostal Holiness, and Baptist.

Prior to West's arrival on the Reservation, Navajo Pastor Fred
Yazzie was preaching a conservative theology that held no
sympathy for the native religion, animism, or the fear of spirits.
Yazzie himself was a product of that conservative bastion,
Asbury Theological Seminary, and even before that, of an evan-
gelical college, Taylor University in Upland, Indiana. His initial
Christian experience was at the Methodist Mission School in
Farmington, which at that time was devoted to a mission of
carrying Christ to the Navajos.

Though one former NAIC officer suggested that Rev. Fred
Yazzie's educational background led him to introduce into the
Reservation a sort of second-hand colonialism, Pastor Elmer

Yazzie explained that the path taken by the Navajos in rejecting the old religion and its symbols—including the drums, smoke, and prayers to inanimate objects—was all their own choice. "The Jesus Way is better," he said. "Better than practicing the old ways."

There's little doubt about support for West within the ranks of the lay pastors. Lay Pastor Guy Nez Jr. wrote in an annual pastor's report, carried in the Ministry newsletter in 2003, "I have been praying for a church for 15 years. My prayers were answered through my brothers Roger Tsosie, Paul West, and [work teams] from Mississippi. . . . With the help of my brother Paul West, we've built the shell for the fellowship hall."[2]

The public thanks of Lay Pastor Kee Littleman of Kitsillie to West for putting together the church building for his community were reported in a 2000 newsletter. Over the years, similar testimonials have appeared. At virtually every meeting of the board of directors of the Ministry, a variety of Navajo lay pastors stand to give their thanks for Paul and Dorcas West and what they've done for them. But those aren't the only assessments available.

In 1983, the General Board of Global Ministries sent Nelson A. Navarro, a senior writer, for two weeks of observation of the Four Corners Ministry in Arizona and New Mexico. With him was a video crew from the Nashville-based United Methodist Communications office, as well as other mission development staff. When Navarro returned to New York, he wrote an interoffice memorandum summarizing his visit. After commenting on the "extraordinary physical effort" it took just to get from one Four Corners church to the next, Navarro told of his personal response to the Ministry and how impressive he found the positive attitudes of the missionaries. "Paul West, for example," he wrote, "is one person who has taken the effort to really know the people he is serving—their history, culture, lifestyle, etc." He described West as not out to simply "save" the Navajos nor holding a "patronizing attitude" towards them. Instead, he wrote, West was very aware of the dynamics of the

Navajos, which might not agree with the way others might conceive of the mission being run.

Navarro concluded his report by urging that "people like Paul West ought to be heard from more by the church," because he has much to say about integrating with the "aspirations of the people" ministered to.[3]

Another person with something to say about West's leadership is Dr. Ira Gallaway. The venerable Dr. Gallaway, former general secretary of the Board of Evangelism, later renamed the General Board of Discipleship, looked at West's management from the perspective gained during the eight years he spent training lay United Methodist pastors on the Reservation. Much of Gallaway's work was done on the grounds of the First United Methodist Church in Shiprock, where he had regular contact with West. The Ministry coordinator's office was in an unpretentious single-wide mobile home parked on a corner of the sand parking lot of the church.

A conservative, a founder, and board member of the unofficial Confessing Movement within The United Methodist Church, and a perennial thorn in the side of the General Board of Global Ministries, Gallaway had this to say about West and his leadership style:

> He's very orthodox. And he's the most non-directive leader I've ever seen. But, he's a leader. He leads without leading. . . . Paul is not a forceful A-type personality. But he's a leader. He plans. Paul and Dorcas are a very loving couple that really love the Navajos. . . . Paul is a biblical Christian. He's not a narrow Christian. He's not a fundamentalist, he's not a literalist, but he's a biblical Christian.

When asked if he believed West had brainwashed the Navajos, Gallaway responded, "I don't believe that at all."

There are other factors that add to any evaluation of the worth of West's service, including the views of the people whom he serves. Few examples are as dramatic as the occurrences when the Ministry was confronted with the cutoff of its lifeblood through the Advance for Christ. Ministry members stood up to be counted as supporters of Paul West.

Fred Yazzie gave credit to West for providing the direction that resulted in the Ministry growing at such "a phenomenal rate." And West's work, he added, was in the face of accusations that he was "dictatorial, paternalistic and committing cultural genocide."

Some of the miracles that led to that growth came through West's patience in working with the tribe, learning the ropes for obtaining church leases and tribal approvals, and in working to find alternative ways to build churches when approvals stalled. While other annual conferences with Reservation jurisdiction wondered what to do with the Navajos in the face of hand-tying regulations and church jurisdictional rules, West was figuring out how to work around those restrictions—bringing in volunteers; building churches, fellowship halls, thrift centers, and a training center; and filling them with Navajo Christians, postponing until later the dotting of regulatory i's and crossing of bureaucratic t's.

For a ministry with no fixed support from the annual conference, the GBGM, or any other source, the fiscal environment in which the Ministry has operated must be another element in any evaluation. On the poverty-stricken Reservation, with a membership with too few resources even to support themselves comfortably, contributions to the Ministry fall far short of providing even marginal maintenance. A review of the Ministry's board minutes discloses one financial crisis after another. But the study also reveals the persistence of the faith that West brought to the operation of the Ministry, evident especially when finances came up short.

In 1983, West wrote to his district superintendent, Brodace Elkins, "Since the 4 Corners Ministry is in a crisis financially, I have taken the following (or will be taking) steps. . . ." Four handwritten pages listing fifteen specific measures followed. While two of the items involved cost-cutting by taking Chee Benallie and Gilbert Badoni off the payroll, thirteen of the listed items were positive actions, aimed at the generation of additional income and support from all over the country. The final solution was "to plan future." Regrets, hand-wringing, and self-pity had no place on the agenda.[4]

Austerity measures had to be put in place in 1989, too. In that year, West wrote to the Navajo lay pastors: "We are facing shortages of funds for the operation of the 4 Corners Ministry and it has been going on for some time this year. Since our funding is based on faith, we never know what to expect."[5] What the Ministry came to expect was a series of crises, but that each one could be navigated by the faith that sustained its director.

A mammoth task in itself is the annual recruitment and coordination of three or four dozen (or more) groups of volunteers, hundreds of people pouring into the Reservation annually to build and teach. West is always willing to pack up on short notice and leave for the East Coast, the Deep South, big cities or small, to tell the tale of the Ministry and explain its needs to whatever United Methodists are open to hearing the story.

What of the charge that West would stomp out the Navajo culture? Charges of that nature seem to ignore the distinction between the Navajo culture and the Navajo deities and religion. West fights for preservation of the Navajo culture while putting Jesus Christ first. He sees a difference between culture and religion, a distinction his critics refuse to make. He recognizes that it is the old religion and the old deities that tug the people he loves away from the Christ they have found.

Sally Gallaway was not idle while her husband trained Navajo United Methodists to be lay preachers. She worked with Navajo women, helping them to improve their skills as Bible teachers and Sunday school workers. During her time spent on the Reservation, Gallaway became so interested in the Navajo culture, as viewed by the Navajo ladies she taught, that she asked them to list the cultural elements they wanted the Ministry to preserve, and asked them to discuss the religious elements of the native culture that they wanted to exclude as calling Christians away from Jesus Christ. Despite daily contact with the women,

Gallaway could not conclude that exclusion of religious symbolism such as the drums, ashes, and smoke, had originated in white missionary influence from West.

If one adds the time that West has spent under appointment as pastor to the Navajos of the First United Methodist Church in Shiprock to his years as appointed head of the Navajo-oriented Four Corners Native American Ministry, he stands as the longest-tenured clergy to a single constituency in the history of the New Mexico Annual Conference: thirty years and counting, under four separate presiding bishops. It's a measure of the value attributed by the conference to the quality of Reverend West's leadership.

## CHAPTER FORTY-ONE

# The Shepherd of Tselani Valley

*Feed my sheep.*
—John 21:18

The first, small voice of a call to the ordained ministry whispered to Roger Tsosie when he was just a young boy hanging out near a mission church in the tiny settlement of Tselani Valley, Arizona. It was long before he or anyone else had envisioned anything like the Four Corners Native American Ministry. In those days, Roger was a shepherd, a Presbyterian shepherd.

The local missionary was a newly ordained Presbyterian pastor from Pennsylvania, a woman who'd followed her call to the Reservation right out of the Princeton Theological Seminary. Tsosie's family attended the church regularly, and it was the boy's haunt, not just on Sundays but during the week. But things change.

The journey Tsosie took to follow his call of starting a church and his struggling on to seminary and to clergy status in The United Methodist Church is one that rivals the adventures of Old Testament prophets. "I was a sheep herder. Started from a real down-to-earth family. We lived off the land, and didn't know anything about the English world, the Anglo world, and didn't know a word in their language," Tsosie said.

But young Tsosie was persistent, and he learned to speak the English language and learned the knowledge the Anglos had. "And I developed those. And I went through the training. I never dreamed I would go through or past high school, but I fit into that, and I went to seminary, the University seminary, and then I got ordained."

The Four Corners church at Tselani Valley was begun by Tsosie in the 1970s, when he was a young school teacher. His hometown, if it can even be called a town, is so small that it doesn't rate a flyspeck on the map of Indian Country. Tsosie described it:

> Back when I was a little boy, it was real remote. It didn't have very much there. It didn't have a school, or a shopping area. The nearest one was Chinle, about twenty, thirty miles away. Mostly hogans, wagon trails. It's gradually developed now. They've got power lines, a water system there now.

When Tsosie's dream of going off to school finally came true, he left for Arizona State University, in Tempe. He said:

> Some time after going away to school, after going away to universities and finishing my college and becoming a teacher, after a long time I got back to my community as a teacher with the Bureau of Indian Affairs.
>
> And so when I got back in my community, the Presbyterian church, the mission church, was no longer there. . . . So I had to go down about twenty, thirty miles to go to church. In between, I felt like maybe I should start a church, you know, a church that was there.

The new teacher didn't have any idea of how to start a church. But, with the call, the urge to try was irresistible. "Eventually, I gathered some of my relatives together, and we started having services in my living room, around my mother's place, or under a tree. We just had Bible study, prayed together, and things like that. Sang together." And more and more people came, relatives and others.

"Then, after a while, about half a year later, people started thinking about building some shade, just a brush shelter to meet in. And we started doing that." But there was a problem. "We felt alone, and we wanted support from a major denomination, a major church. Somebody to support us."

Tsosie came up with an answer:

So I kind of asked my small congregation to pray about it, about what denomination we could join, what church could support us . . . And we went to the Presbyterians. And they said, "We've already tried there, we can't go over there any more." Then I approached the Mennonites. That church was a distance from our place. But they didn't have any money to support us. So we just kind of continued praying.

It was at this time that Reverend Paul West challenged the lay preacher at Bistahi, Chee Benallie, to set out on a mission. Armed only with a tank full of gas, good intentions, and his Bible on the seat beside him, Benallie drove from Shiprock, where he also served as outreach director, with an assignment from West to find a place on the Reservation that needed a church.

Tsosie explained how fate, in the person of Chee Benallie, caught up with him.

It so happened that same day, that one of my sisters, she didn't have a car. She hitchhiked to Chinle, that was about twenty miles, to the hospital there. [The young woman was taking her baby to the Chinle hospital for a checkup.] And she hitchhiked down there. And it takes about three, maybe four hours, from Shiprock to get to Chinle. So that preacher started driving that morning, and my sister went down to Chinle and had her baby treated there. [After the checkup, Tsosie's sister walked down to the main road.] And just when she stood at the road, here came the preacher, picked her up, and gave her a ride. And from there on, you know, he took her back to her place, and talked about whether there was anybody that wanted to start a church. And she mentioned my name, and it took another month or so until he could find me, because I was teaching in another place, in Piñon. And so that's how we got acquainted with the Four Corners Native American Ministry out of Shiprock.

Before long, the Ministry started to help the little group of worshippers:

And instead of having that brush arbor, the next summer we had a vacation Bible school, and later, some group from California, a mission team, came out and helped us with running in the power line, and the Four Corners built us a

double-wide unit, a mobile unit, and they took it out there
and we started meeting in it.

After some six years of working as a part-time lay pastor and
full-time teacher, Roger Tsosie, with a scholarship inspired by
the Lane family, left his ancestral home for Fuller Theological
Seminary in California. He picked Fuller because a friend whom
he admired had gone to school there.

The Lane Foundation is a charity funded by a fortune made in
the furniture business that included manufacturing and nationally
marketing cedar chests and other fine furniture. B. B. and Minnie
Lane, from Virginia, had been working as volunteers in a service
agency in Phoenix. The United Methodist couple was keeping a
lookout for a Navajo whom they might help get a seminary education through the family foundation. They asked around in
Phoenix, and were directed to the Four Corners Native American
Ministry in Shiprock.

When they drove to Shiprock, West told them there was no
one at the moment who was ready for seminary, but there soon
would be. What he didn't say was that the candidate he had in
mind had not yet made his final decision, though West knew he
was on the brink. West figured the scholarship would likely be
enough to tip the scales.

The Lanes were patient. Two years later, Tsosie decided he
was ready. With scholarship funds in hand, he set out for
Southern California and the Fuller Theological Seminary.

The Lanes later offered to set up a permanent endowment
for scholarships for United Methodist Navajos who wanted to
make the Church a vocation, if the conference would match the
foundation's donation. The conference met the challenge, and a
permanent scholarship fund was set up through the New
Mexico Conference United Methodist Foundation, Inc.

Tsosie returned from seminary to be ordained as a full elder in
the New Mexico Annual Conference in 1998. Today, his church in

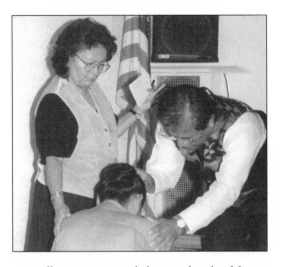

*Reverend and Mrs. Roger Tsosie receive a new member at the Window Rock church.*

Window Rock includes a small sanctuary and three other buildings: one is a conference center used for training Four Corners lay preachers, among other uses; another is a thrift shop; and the third houses the Sunday school. All were built by volunteers.

Though Tsosie became an ordained United Methodist elder, the Presbyterian influence hasn't deserted him. In 2001, the Woodstown Presbyterian Church in New Jersey sent him a surprise mission gift of ten thousand dollars to start a permanent endowment for training Navajo pastors in the Pastor Training Center at the Window Rock United Methodist church. The church made two more gifts in the same amount during the next two years.

The gift was prompted by Rev. Virginia Boardman, who had gone to the Presbyterian Mission at Tselani Valley in the 1950s, fresh out of seminary, when Tsosie was a boy. For fifteen years she worked there, keeping an eye out for the young shepherd who hung out around the little church to hear Bible stories. She insisted he stay in school and that he take Christian training, and she was Tsosie's Christian model.

Boardman heard about the Pastor Training Center as a result of Reverend Tsosie filling the pulpit at the First United Methodist Church in Albuquerque one Sunday. By chance, a short newspaper account of his visit was seen by a friend of Boardman, who sent a clipping to her in New Jersey. She remembered the young Tsosie.[1]

When she visited Tsosie in Window Rock after the first gift was offered, he drove her back to Tselani Valley, where they reminisced about the days when she was young and Tsosie didn't come up to her shoulder, even on tiptoe. He reported part of their conversations in a 2004 interview: "She said she had just finished seminary, and it had been very hard for her. Very hard. She said she didn't think anyone there in Tselani Valley could ever go through anything that hard. So she didn't encourage me to do that. But she did encourage me to stay in school."

Tsosie currently serves as the assistant director of the Four Corners Native American Ministry and as pastor of the church at Window Rock. He's still a man with a dream. Elaborating on that dream, he said:

> Leadership needs to be developed. That was very lacking, as I see it, when we came out here [to Window Rock], seven years ago. The leadership is very much in need. We need training, we need to develop, to raise up the leadership in young people. I'm looking at more seminary-trained pastors.

Tsosie has little doubt that the theology of the Four Corners United Methodist Navajos is right for them as he helps train the lay preachers and Sunday school teachers, and nudges people

*Rev. Roger Tsosie lifts the communion bread at Window Rock United Methodist Church.*

*From* Journal of the New Mexico Annual Conference. *2006 p. 132.*

| 2006 APPOINTMENTS<br>ALBUQUERQUE DISTRICT<br>FOUR CORNERS NATIVE AMERICAN MINISTRIES | |
|---|---|
| Director | Paul N. West (RE) |
| *Aneth | Johnny Ray Billie (lay preacher) |
| Bistahi | Tom Chee (lay preacher) |
| Blue Gap | Billy John (lay preacher) |
| *Burnt Corn | Mary Yazzie (lay preacher) |
| *Cove | Wilma Todacheeny (lay preacher) |
| *Dowozhiibikooh Christian | Norman Mark (lay preacher) |
| *Kitsillie | Sonny Whitehair (lay preacher) |
| *Lakeside | Shirley John (lay preacher) |
| *Many Farms | Joe Tsosie (lay preacher) |
| *Many Farms (West) | Benson Kee (lay preacher) |
| *Naschitti | Sarah Yazzie (lay preacher) |
| Ojo Amarillo | Fred Yazzie (RE) |
| *Oljato | Eugene Chee (lay preacher) |
| *Pinedale | Anita Francisco (lay preacher) |
| *Red Valley | John Benally (lay preacher) |
| *Roughside of the Mountain | Eugene Thomas (lay preacher) |
| *Sawmill | Leonard Harvey (lay preacher) |
| Shiprock | To be supplied |
| *Spider Rock | Mary Alice Wilson (lay preacher) |
| *Spirit Lake | Albert Juan (lay preacher) |

| (continued) | |
|---|---|
| *Thoreau | Bobby Martinez (lay preacher) |
| *Tohatchi | Albert Lee (lay preacher) |
| Tselani Valley | Elmer Yazzie (lay preacher) |
| *White Cone | Guy Nez Jr. (lay preacher) |
| *White Rock Point | Harry Descheene (lay preacher) |
| Window Rock/Assoc. Dir. Four Corners NAM | Roger Tsosie (FE) |
| Gallup, First | Layloni Drake (FE) |

\* *denotes outreach congregation*
*FE - elder in full connection*          *RE - retired full member-elder*

toward seminary training or other Christian vocations:

> The Ministry here is a unique thing. We have those who come along and say, "You have to do it this way." But we want to do it our way. We could go along with other Native Americans who are saying, "You can combine your native beliefs with your Christian religion." But that's just not the way we believe. We developed our Christian way of doing things, and that's what we want to do. We don't want to listen to these people and along the way feel that we've been misled and went down the wrong path . . . The biblical way, that's what we're going after.

So there is little concern among the people of the Four Corners Native American Ministry. With Tsosie in a position of influence, it will be business as usual—more churches, more Christians, more of the Diné who will grow strong in the faith. They know that Jesus will provide. And the shepherd, Reverend Tsosie, knows it, too.

But the hope for the continuation of the work of the Ministry cannot rest in the hands of one person, no matter how dedicated. In the people themselves lies the future for the continuation of the outreach—in the children and the youth.

## CHAPTER FORTY-TWO

# The Power Lies with the People

*. . . my power is made perfect in weakness.*
—2 Corinthians 12:9

A s March 25, 2006, came and went, it was unmarked by any celebration of the twenty-ninth anniversary of the founding of the Ministry, except that Paul and Dorcas West noted it at their breakfast table. Of the five founders of the Ministry, Paul West and Fred Yazzie were still serving their Lord and the Navajo people; Chee Benallie was dropping in to check on the Ministry's operations now and then, though his gait had slowed and his speech called for a careful listening ear; Dr. Ed Hamilton, the former district superintendent, had gone on to his eternal reward; and several years earlier, Dr. Tom Cloyd, who once headed the Methodist Mission School, had left New Mexico for retirement in Tennessee.

The Ministry had just moved into its spick-and-span new building not far from the thrift center on Shiprock's main highway. The metal-sided, metal-roofed structure afforded West his own roomy office and a reception area presided over by Vivian Farley. Behind this area was a large workroom, plus a dormitory complete with showers and room for a dozen to sleep.

Money was tight because contributions were reduced as people across the denomination gave to Hurricane Katrina relief instead of to the Ministry. The number of work teams scheduled for the summer appeared to have dropped also, with some churches sending their volunteers to New Orleans and the surrounding area.

*Andrew Leslie demonstrates a puppet at a training session while
Larry Haskie (left) grins. Arlene Leslie is partially obscured on the right.*

But the work of the Ministry was business as usual, and still there was much to celebrate. West had recently closed a deal to buy an acre of land in Thoreau, New Mexico. It would be the site of a new church at which Bobby Martinez, who had presided over his last meeting as chair of the Ministry's board, would preach. It would be Martinez's first pulpit since his congregation had lost its lease on the converted gas station in which they met.

The people at Burnt Corn, Arizona, wanted to start a church, as did the people at Naschitti, Mitten Rock, and Chinle. With unabated enthusiasm for her Lord, Shirley John stepped up to chair the board, bringing with her a continual flow of ideas.

The Pastor Training Center was churning out lay pastors, and there was hope that a publisher would back Reverend Tsosie's efforts to produce Sunday school material featuring artwork by Ministry artists, including Guy Nez Jr., Larry Haskie, and others, depicting Navajo culture and traditions from a Christian perspective.

So the Ministry moved into its thirtieth year.

In 2006, the Ministry grieved the loss of the Shiprock church's young pastor, Rev. Curtis Minor, a victim of an auto accident. Until a full-time clergy replacement could be appointed, the church was pastored by Frank Hanagarne, the former mission school basketball star, who had earned the title of lay pastor.

As the end of 2006 neared, excitement began to mount in the board meetings. The church at Thoreau had risen despite all the obstacles—when needed, work teams had appeared with building materials and enthusiasm, and with Cecil and Mary Regier overseeing the construction. Bobby Martinez told all who would listen that his church would be the first in the Ministry with a real steeple.

West reported that Bishop Max Whitfield had announced that the 2007 annual meeting of the conference would feature a special recognition program to celebrate the thirtieth anniversary of the founding of the Ministry. He explained in an August 2006 telephone interview that one aim of the celebration would be to "let the rest of the denomination across the country know just what is going on with this Ministry out here in New Mexico." The superintendent of the Albuquerque district, Rev. Jim Hawk, would see that the plans were carried out, and he would raise funds within the district so that the Ministry could be adequately represented at the meeting to be held in Glorieta, New Mexico.

And so it went at the board meetings, where discussions moved on from church matters to spiritual concerns to social issues—such as how to respond to the tribal council's approval of six casinos on the Reservation, which had previously been free of gambling. The spirit was not dampened by occasional reports of setbacks: the little church at Hallelujah Canyon seemed to have fallen out of the Ministry; it had sent no representative to a board meeting for a couple of years, and was seeking a kind of "nursing" that the Ministry did not offer. West explained that the Ministry wanted churches that will grow, bring up their people in the way of the Lord, and not look for hand-outs.

In it all—church sessions, board meetings, training sessions, planning for the future—is hope and joy. The Navajo United Methodists have taken charge—raising issues, addressing them directly, making decisions, and celebrating Jesus. It appears that United Methodism is on the Reservation to stay and that the presence of the Holy Spirit is guaranteed. The future of the Four Corners Ministry lies in the hands of its people, who are not shy about expressing their faith, their connection to United Methodism, or their expectations.

The Diné of the Four Corners Native American Ministry have found that in making disciples, as Chee Benallie experienced when he took his first turn at preaching and as Shirley John said when she explained how a tiny lady could raise a big tent all by herself, and then preach to whoever comes: "When the Holy Spirit is with you, it's easy."

They, and the other Navajos of the Four Corners Native American Ministry, know it's the Holy Spirit that is warming their hearts.

# NOTES

## Chapter 2

1. U.S. Bureau of the Census, *Facts and Figures*. Washington, DC. October 21, 2002.

## Chapter 3

1. Gladys Reichard. *Navaho Religion: A Study of Symbolism*, 2nd ed., Bollingen Series XVIII (Princeton, NJ: Princeton University Press, 1974), 8.

2. David R. Scates. *Why Navajo Churches Are Growing: The Cultural Dynamics of Navajo Religious Change* (Grand Junction, CO: Navajo Christian Churches, n.d.); *Columbia Encyclopedia*, 6th ed., s.v. "Native American Languages." http://www.encyclopedia.com, 2003.

3. The National Division is an arm of the General Board of Global Ministries (GBGM), which is the agency of The United Methodist Church that is devoted to mission outreach. Within GBGM, the National Division addresses mission work in the United States, but not foreign missions.

4. The research for this book disclosed that the reason for the General Board staff's apparent dislike for New Mexico probably had to do with "that hospital out there," referring to the former Bataan Memorial Methodist Hospital in Albuquerque. It was sold with the approval of the annual conference to a nonprofit foundation in 1969. The hospital had been party to several lawsuits, and Bishop Alsie Carleton had sought help defending them from the New York–based GBGM and its Women's Division, who had a hand in the hospital's founding and occasionally in making management decisions. Apparently, their policy was to let local entities handle such legal matters. This led Bishop Carleton to decide that the annual conference should keep the entire two million dollars in cash received from the sale—to the consternation of the New York entities, who had expected a share of the cash. This episode played out eight years before the Four Corners Ministry was created.

## Chapter 4

1. Reichard, *Navajo Religion*, xxxiii–xlviii, 3–144; Clyde Kluckhorn and Dorothea Leighton. *The Navaho*, rev. ed. (Garden City, NY: The Natural History Library, Anchor Books and Doubleday & Company, Inc., n.d.), 178–93; Robert W. Young, "Navajo Religion" in *The Navajo Yearbook* (Window Rock, AZ: Navajo Agency, 1961), 511–35; Paul G. Zolbrod. *Diné bahane`: The Navajo Creation Story* (Albuquerque, NM: University of New Mexico Press, 1984), 4–25.

2. Sheila Moon. *Changing Woman and Her Sisters* (San Francisco, CA: The Guild for Psychological Studies, 1984), 5–6.

3. 42 U.S.C. (1978). 1996.

4. Zolbrod, *Diné bahane`*, 25.

## Chapter 5

1. Oliver La Farge, in foreword to *Navaho Religion* by Reichard, xxi.

2. T. K. Reeves. "The Native American Nations of the Black Mesa Region." http://www.geocities.com/Yosemite/.

3. C. Carson, Colonel, First New Mexico Vols., Comdg., Navajo Expedition, and others reporting. "Operations Against Navajo Indians, N. Mex." in *War of the Rebellion: Official Records of the Union and the*

*Confederate Armies*, Series 1, vol. xxvi (Washington, DC: Government Printing Office, 1902), 232–61, 315–16.

4. H. Baxter Liebler. *Boil My Heart for Me* (New York, NY: Exposition Press, 1969), 10. Liebler tells of an aged Navajo woman who, in the 1940s, gave her birth date and place as 1865, in Alkali Creek, at a time and place from which all Navajos had presumably been removed by Kit Carson's troops.

5. Cormac Antram, OFM. *Laborers of the Harvest* (Gallup, NM: The Indian Trader, Inc., 1998), 47–49.

6. Thomas E. Atcitty. Testimony Before the Subcommittee on Human Resources, House Committee on Ways and Means. 105th Cong., 2nd sess., June 12, 1998.

**Chapter 6**

1. Pauline G. Malehorn. *The Tender Plant: The History of the Navajo Methodist Mission, Farmington, New Mexico, 1892–1948* (Farmington, NM: [1948?], 1–3.

2. C. Carson, 234. Report dated July 24, 1863: "The Navajos have planted a large quantity of grain this year. Their wheat is as good as I have ever seen." Carson seized over 75,000 pounds of wheat as well as "a large amount of corn."

3. Malehorn, 6.

4. Ibid., 10.

5. "Sixteenth Annual Report," presumably of the Women's Home Missionary Society of the Methodist Episcopal Church, North. (1898), 105, quoted in Malehorn, *The Tender Plant*, 12.

6. Malehorn, 11–14.

7. Ibid., 20–23.

8. Ibid., 29–37.

9. Account of Simmons's adventures, *Farmington Enterprise*, October 13, 1911, quoted in Malehorn, *The Tender Plant*, 125–27.

**Chapter 7**

1. Malehorn, 40–44.

2. Lena D. Wilcox (?), "Navajo Indian Field Work." Farmington, NM. [ca. 1921–23]. Mission School Files, New Beginnings.

3. Malehorn, 48–50.

4. Ibid., 66, 72–73.

5. Ibid., 73–76.

**Chapter 8**

1. The word "Bistahi" refers to the location of both the branch school and the church that was later constructed, though maps of New Mexico and of Indian Country label the area "Bisti." When lay pastor Chee Benallie went to Bisti, as it was then called, he decided to change the name to Bistahi, since "Bisti" is an Anglo mispronunciation of the Navajo words "*bis ta hi,*" meaning "clumps of clay." Navajo United Methodists began calling it "Bistahi," since that word more correctly reflects the English phonetic pronunciation of the Navajo phrase. The English designation for the area as the "Bisti Badlands" is a redundancy.

2. Malehorn, 80.

**Chapter 9**

1. Asbury Theological School Web site, http://www.atswilmore.ky.us/; see also Susan Barton's "Asbury Seminary," in *United Methodist Reporter*, August 25, 2003.

**Chapter 10**

1. Robert Prichard. "President Ulysses S. Grant's Peace Policy toward Native Americans and the Ministry of the Episcopal Church." Web site of Virginia Theological Seminary, www.vts.edu/resources/; "Mission and Ministry with Native American Peoples: A Historical Survey of the Last Three Centuries." Racial Ethnic Minorities. Web site of the Presbyterian

Church (USA), http://www.pcusa.org/racialethnic/nativeam/mission.htm.

2. C. Travis Kendall e-mail.

3. Thomas Dolaghan and David Scates. *The Navajos Are Coming to Jesus* (Pasadena, CA: The William Carey Library, 1978), 41.

4. Morris L. Floyd of GBGM to Stella Lee, November 25, 1980.

5. Roger M. Whitman, counsel for the GBGM, to Paul West, March 24, 1980.

## Chapter 11

1. "Window Rock United Methodist Church Chronology," pamphlet, n.d.

2. The State of Arizona was a part of the Southern California–Arizona Annual Conference from 1940–1946; it was a part of the Pacific Southwest Arizona Annual Conference from 1976–1984; and the entire state became the Desert Southwest Annual Conference in 1985. At all these times it has been part of the Western Jurisdiction.

3. *Journal of the New Mexico Annual Conference of The United Methodist Church* (Glorieta, NM: 1979), 114–15.

## Chapter 12

1. C. C. Brooks. Unpublished paper. December 1941.

## Chapter 13

1. Minutes of the Consultation on Ministries with the Navajos. January 8–9, 1975.

## Chapter 15

1. Roland Allen. *Missionary Methods: St. Paul's or Ours?* Grand Rapids, MI: World Dominion Press, 1962.

2. *Good News*, Newsletter of the Forum for Spiritual Renewal. (Wilmore, KY), September 1979.

3. Hector M. Navas to Paul West, 1979.

4. West to Navas, 1979.

## Chapter 17

1. Although an in-depth discussion of syncretism, and its religious and cultural implications, is beyond the scope of this book, readers interested in the subject can find an advocate's analysis in: Richard Twiss. *One Church, Many Tribes: Following Jesus the Way God Made You* (Ventura, CA: Regal Books, 2000), 111–37.

2. Relating to Arminius or his doctrines opposing the absolute predestination of strict Calvinism (1618). *Merriam-Webster's Collegiate Dictionary*, 10th ed. 1999.

## Chapter 18

1. Sharon Mielke. "School's Future Sparks Struggle," *United Methodist Reporter*, May 19, 1978.

2. Ellen Clark. "Among Navajos—A Symbol of Excellence," *New World Outlook*, November 1978.

3. "The Incredible Experiment," *Navajo Mission/Academy Messenger*, June 1984.

## Chapter 20

1. *Journal of the New Mexico Annual Conference of The United Methodist Church*. (Glorieta, NM: 1980), 124–26.

2. Paul West. "Navajo Find Christ Through '4 Corners Native American Ministry.'"Unpublished paper. 1981.

## Chapter 22

1. Douglas W. Johnson. "Research on the Four Corners Area and Churches in the Navajo, Hopi, and Ute Reservation and the Denver Urban Ministry." (New York, NY: Research Office, National Program Division, General Board of Global Ministries, February 1988), 37–38.

2. See, for example: Jerrold E. Levy. *In the Beginning: The Navajo Genesis* (Berkeley and Los Angeles, CA:

University of California Press, 1998), 214–17.

3. Petition adopted by Rocky Mountain Annual Conference on June 12, 1987. Attachment to letter from Earl B. Carter to Richard L. Gilbert, July 13, 1987.

4. Sano, Galvan, and Wheatley were bishops of the Western Jurisdiction of The United Methodist Church, which included Utah, Colorado, and Arizona. Schowengerdt was the bishop responsive to the South Central Jurisdiction, which includes the New Mexico Annual Conference.

**Chapter 23**

1. Sam Wynn to Ira Gallaway, February 9, 1983.

2. "Board of Ministries, Navajos, Develop Lay Pastor Certification Plan for Reservation," *New Mexico United Methodist Reporter.* (Dallas, TX), July 2, 1982.

3. Although the specifics of the requirements for licensing have been modified over the years, in 2006 they remain substantially the same as listed in the original requirements.

4. Lois Jackson, "Missionary Responds to Requirements for Navajo Lay Pastors," *New Mexico United Methodist Reporter.* (Dallas, TX), August 13, 1982.

5. Norton Scrimshire, "Native Americans Set Own Standards for Lay Pastors to Navajo Nation, Minister Explains," *New Mexico United Methodist Reporter.* (Dallas, TX), September 3, 1982.

**Chapter 24**

1. This and the subsequent references on p. 143–44 are from *Newsletter of the Four Corners Native American Ministry.* (Shiprock, NM), September 1988.

2. *Newsletter of the Four Corners Native American Ministry.* (Shiprock, NM), January 2001.

**Chapter 25**

1. "Shiprock Alcoholic Counseling Center—Reporting Period 8–1983." (Shiprock, NM), August 1983.

2. Myong Gul Son to Brodace Elkins, August 7, 1985.

3. Paul West to Elkins, August 22, 1985.

4. Elkins to Son, August 22, 1985.

5. Minutes, Four Corners Ministry Board Meeting, August 31, 1985.

**Chapter 26**

1. "A Report of 1981 Consultations with Ethnic Minority Local Churches." (Nashville, TN: Board of Discipleship, The United Methodist Church, September 1981).

2. A telephone call to the General Board of Discipleship in 2004, to ask why the training had not taken place, produced information that it was at about that time that the work with Native American churches was turned over to the General Board of Global Ministries. No one in the Nashville office in 2004 knew what had happened to the lofty plans they had laid back in 1981.

3. O. A. McBrayer memorandum to Louis Schowengerdt, et al., April 30, 1986.

4. This and the subsequent references on p. 163–64 are from Dick Yeager, Staff Report, November 6, 1985.

**Chapter 27**

1. *Newsletter of the Four Corners Native American Ministry.* (Shiprock, NM), ca. 1985.

2. Elizabeth Bernstein. "You Don't Have to Be Jewish to Want a Bar Mitzvah," *Wall Street Journal,* January 14, 2004.

3. George E. Tinker. *Missionary Conquest: The Gospel and Native American Cultural Genocide*

(Minneapolis, MN: Fortress Press, 1993), 114–15.

4. Homer Noley. *First White Frost: Native Americans and United Methodism* (Nashville, TN: Abingdon Press, 1991).

5. Duane Porter. *Autobiography of Duane Porter* (Minneapolis, MN: Minnesota Annual Conference Archives of The United Methodist Church, 1934), 3, quoted in Noley, *First White Frost*, 192.

6. Linda Green. "Native American Caucus Explores Bringing 'Culture' into Church." Reporter Resources. *The United Methodist Reporter*, December 2, 2005.

**Chapter 28**

1. Paul West to Four Corners Native American Ministry Board Members, August 22, 1980.

2. Lula Garrett to Hector Navas, superintendent, October 18, 1982.

3. Garrett to Richard Lewis, April 25, 1983.

4. Navas to Garrett, May 23, 1983.

**Chapter 29**

1. Lula Garrett to Richard Lewis, October 27, 1983.

2. "The Incredible Experiment," *Navajo Mission/Academy Messenger*, June 1984.

3. Rene O. Bideaux to Louis Schowengerdt, November 8, 1984; Bideaux memorandum to Randolph Nugent, November 6, 1984; Schowengerdt to Paul West, November 9, 1984; H. T. Maclin to Schowengerdt, November 13, 1984.

4. Minutes, Board of Directors Meeting. March 28, 1985; Rene O. Bideaux. "Report on Consultation with Navajo United Methodist Mission School Board of Directors," March 28, 1985.

5. Bideaux to Lewis, June 7, 1985.

6. Minutes, Board of Directors Meeting. Farmington, NM, June 8, 1985.

7. Paul West. "Charge Conference Report." Shiprock, NM, 1985.

8. West to Schowengerdt, October 1, 1986.

9. J. Ann Craig to George Hartzog III, October 26, 1987.

10. News Release, Navajo United Methodist Mission School, March 19, 1988.

11. Lula Garrett and Joyce D. Sohl to Lewis and Hartzog, March 13, 1989.

12. *Newsletter of the Four Corners Native American Ministry*. (Shiprock, NM), November–December 1995.

**Chapter 30**

1. Ely Ades and Roger M. Stressman to Marvin B. Abrams, May 6, 1987.

2. Schowengerdt to Abrams, September 1, 1987.

3. "Proposal Adopted By 4 Corners Native American Ministry." April 9, 1983.

4. Roy I. Sano to Brodace Elkins, September 22, 1987.

5. Elkins to Sano, October 19, 1987.

6. Sano to Elkins, September 22, 1957.

7. West to Abrams, February 1, 1988.

8. Bideaux letter (with two attachments) to Schowengerdt, November 18, 1987.

**Chapter 31**

1. Douglas W. Johnson. "Research on the Four Corners Area and Churches in the Navajo, Hopi, and Ute Reservation and the Denver Urban Ministry." (New York, NY: General Board of Global Ministries, 1988).

2. Cooperative parishes are provided for in ¶¶ 205.2 and 206 of the *Book of Discipline*.

3. Johnson, "Research on the Four Corners Area."

4. Earl B. Carter to C. Leonard Miller, September 13, 1989.

5. Earl B. Carter. "Report to the General Council on Ministries. Native American Ministries in the South Central Jurisdiction." n.d. (attachment to Dr. Carter's letter dated September 13, 1989.)

6. *General Council Ministries Member Experiences with United Methodist Native American Ministries* (Dayton, OH: General Council on Ministries, Fall 1991), 23–26.

**Chapter 32**

1. Montoya note to author, December 22, 2005.

2. *The Book of Discipline of The United Methodist Church* (Nashville, TN: The United Methodist Publishing House, 2000), ¶¶ 301–66.

3. See, for example, "Assemblies of God By-laws," article vii. http://ag.org/top/about/constitution _bylaws.cfm.

4. Paul West to Schowengerdt, February 12, 1992.

5. See note 1, chapter 22.

6. Shirley Montoya and Donna Lee. Untitled paper. [1992?]

7. Minutes, Special Church Conference. First United Methodist Church, Shiprock, NM, December 7, 1992.

8. Montoya note to author.

9. David L. Saucier. Consultation with Shirley Montoya, November 25, 1992.

10. Montoya note to author.

11. Malcolm Brenner, "Navajos Seek Unity," *Farmington Daily Times*, April 8, 1993.

**Chapter 33**

1. Marilyn W. Winters to Four Corners Native American Ministry, November 7, 1991.

2. Paul West to Cynthia Kent, November 21, 1991.

3. Schowengerdt to Winters, November 20, 1991.

4. Lorena Lynch. "Burned but not Destroyed." (Shiprock, NM), Fall 1992. The letters from Lorena Lynch and Vivian Farley to Cynthia Kent were dated February 4, 1992.

5. Paul West. "General Advance Special Cancelled!!!" (Shiprock, NM), Spring 1992.

6. "Report of Meeting between New Mexico Annual Conference Representatives and Ms. Cynthia Kent, General Board of Ministries, Relative to Salary Concerns on the Navajo Nation Reservation." Ojo Amarillo, NM, October 11–12, [1992?].

7. Vivian Farley. A paper. Shiprock, NM: n.p., n.d.

8. Schowengerdt to Anthony Shipley, June 19, 1992.

9. Minutes of Board Meeting. Cove, AZ, August 15, 1992.

10. Navajo Petition to the National Division of GBGM, New York, From the Navajo Members of the Board of The Four Corners Native American Ministry. Cove, AZ, August 15, 1992.

11. Typed telephone message transcription. "August 21, 1992. Friday—8:11 A.M. On Phone Answering Machine."

12. West memorandum to "Dear Pastors and Navajo Leaders," August 24, 1992.

13. "Bishop 'deeply moved' by testimony of Navajo Christian leaders, laity" *New Mexico United Methodist Reporter*, October 9, 1992.

14. Pat Barraza to Fred Yazzie, October 5, 1992.

15. Yazzie to Barraza, October 9, 1992.

**Chapter 34**

1. "November 10th Meeting: An Issue we want to Discuss." A paper. Author unidentified. (Shiprock, NM), Fall 1992.

2. Vivian Farley. "General Advance Special." A paper. (Shiprock, NM), Fall 1992.

3. Minutes, Ojo Amarillo Church. December 12, 1992.

4. Cynthia Kent to Paul West, November 10, 1993.

## Chapter 38

1. Lyle E. Schaller. *It's a Different World* (Nashville, TN: Abingdon Press, 1987), 24–33.

2. Lyle E. Schaller. *The Seven-Day-a-Week Church* (Nashville, TN: Abindgon Press, 1992), 14, 51.

## Chapter 39

1. Fran Marvel. "The Story of Cove Community Church." (Shiprock, NM), May 23, 1994.

2. Minutes of a task force meeting. Gallup, NM. March 9, 1991.

3. "Cove Church 10th Anniversary." *Newsletter of the Four Corners Native American Ministry*. Fall 2001.

4. Paul West e-mail, September 15, 2004.

## Chapter 40

1. Dolaghan and Scates, *The Navajos Are Coming to Jesus*, 54–56.

2. Guy Nez Jr. "Guy Nez, Jr. Has A Heart For His People," *Newsletter of the Four Corners Native American Ministry*. (Shiprock, NM). Winter 2003.

3. Nelson Navarro interoffice memorandum to John Jordan/Jo Bigler, GBGM, New York. June 24, 1985.

4. Paul West to Brodace Elkins, September 6, 1983.

5. West memorandum to "Dear Co-workers," August 16, 1989.

## Chapter 41

1. "Navajo News." *Newsletter of the Four Corners Native American Ministry*. (Shiprock, NM), Spring 2001.

2. *Journal of the New Mexico Annual Conference of The United Methodist Church* (Glorieta, NM: 2006), 132.

# Interviews and Personal Correspondence

*Interviews conducted by the author, unless otherwise noted in text.*

### Personal Interviews

Antram, Cormac. Houck, AZ. September 29, 2003.

Benallie, Chee D., Sr. Shiprock, NM. February 26, 2003.

Clah, Eleanor. Shiprock, NM. March 23, 2003.

Gallaway, Ira. Albuquerque, NM. February 21, 2005.

Gallaway, Ira and Sally. Albuquerque, NM. August 18, 2003

Goodluck-Barnes, Shea. Farmington, NM. February 28, 2003.

Hanagarne, Frank. Shiprock, NM. February 26, 2003.

Haskie, Larry. Window Rock, AZ. August 7, 2004.

John, Shirley. Window Rock, AZ. September 27, 2003.

Lynch, Lorena. Shiprock, NM. June 18, 2004.

Posey, Bonnie, Wes, and William. Ojo Amarillo, NM. June 18, 2003.

Regier, Cecil and Mary. Shiprock, NM. June 18, 2003.

Roberts, Joan. Albuquerque, NM. July 1, 2003.

Scrimshire, Norman. Albuquerque, NM. June 27, 2003.

Tsosie, Anthony. Roughside of the Mountain, NM. February 23, 2003.

Tsosie, Roger. Window Rock, AZ. July 8, 2003; Albuquerque, NM. September 1, 2004.

West, Charley. Shiprock, NM. June 18, 2003.

West, Dorcas and Paul. Albuquerque, NM. January 10, 2003; December 10, 2003.

West, Paul. Navajo Nation Reservation. March 23, 2003.

Westbrook, Ruth. Shiprock, NM. February 26, 2003.

Yazzie, Elmer. Shiprock, NM. September 23, 2003.

Yazzie, Evelyn. Cove, AZ. March 23, 2003.

Yazzie, Fred W. Ojo Amarillo, NM. June 18, 2003.

### Telephone Interviews

Bentley, Terry. November 4, 2003.

Bideaux, Rene O. August 14, 2004.

Brooks, Blanche. January 21, 2003.

Carter, William. December 1, 2003.

Caswell, Bervin. June 3, 2003.

Chester, Milton. June 2, 2003.

Elkins, Brodace. May 13–14, 2003.

Farley, Vivian. June 8, 2004.

Gillingham, Leonard. October 14, 2004.

Ivey-Soto, Daniel. October 14, 2004.

John, Shirley. September 22, 2004.

Montoya, Shirley. November 4, 2003.

Noley, Homer. June 15, 2004.

Posey, Patty. November 5, 2003.

Sillamon, Denny. August 26, 2004.

Sombrero, Evelene. November 6, 2003.

Tutt, David and Goldie. December 2, 2004.

Warden, David. November 4, 2003.

Weyant, David. October 23, 2003.

Whitfield, (Bishop) Max. Telephone interview. August 15, 2006.

### Correspondence

Kendall, C. Travis. E-mail message to author, June 3, 2003.

Montoya, Shirley. Note to author, December 22, 2005.

West, Paul. E-mail message to author, September 15, 2004.

# INDEX

*Numbers in bold indicate captions.*

# ABOUT THE AUTHOR

Stan Sager graduated with a bachelor's degree in zoology from the University of Kansas. He served as a communications and operations officer in the U.S. Navy during the Korean War and later earned a law degree from Washburn University of Topeka, Kansas.

As an attorney in Albuquerque, New Mexico, he founded and grew his own firm to one of New Mexico's largest.

Sager served as a member of the New Mexico Board of Bar Commissioners and cochaired various task forces that addressed the legal needs of New Mexico's poor. His work earned him the New Mexico State Bar's LaFollette Pro Bono Award, the Professionalism Award, and other honors.

He served the New Mexico Annual Conference of The United Methodist Church as chancellor and as treasurer of its foundation. He was a member of the board of the United Methodism's General Council on Finance and Administration. Sager led New Mexico's lay delegation to General Conference three times. He was elected to chair the General Conference Legislative Committee on Financial Administration, chaired the Committee on Audit and Review, and authored or co-authored many fiscal policies of the denomination, as well as a booklet on internal audit and control and revised version of the *Local Church Audit Guide*. He received the Judge Woodrow B. Seals Award from the Perkins School of Theology, Dallas, for his work with the underprivileged and his leadership in restructuring the financial reporting system of the denomination.

Stan Sager lives in Albuquerque with his wife, Shirley.